A GUIDE TO THE ARCHIVES OF LABOR HISTORY AND URBAN AFFAIRS

A GUIDE TO THE ARCHIVES OF LABOR HISTORY AND URBAN AFFAIRS

Wayne State University

compiled and edited by
Warner W. Pflug

Wayne State University Press, Detroit, 1974

Copyright © 1974 by Wayne State University Press,
Detroit, Michigan 48202. All rights are reserved.
No part of this book may be reproduced without formal permission.

Grateful acknowledgment is made to the Wayne State University Archives of Labor History and Urban Affairs for financial assistance in the publication of this volume.

Library of Congress Cataloging in Publication Data

Wayne State University, Detroit. Archives of Labor
    History and Urban Affairs.
    A guide to the Archives of Labor History and Urban Affairs, Wayne State University.

    1. Trade-unions—United States—History—Sources—Bibliography. 2. Wayne State University, Detroit. Archives of Labor History and Urban Affairs. I. Pflug, Warner, ed. II. Title.
Z7164.T7W34 1974   016.33188'0973   73-6004
ISBN 0-8143-1501-1

HD
6508
.W34
1974

CONTENTS

Foreword, *by Philip P. Mason*	7
Preface	9
FUNCTIONS AND SERVICES OF THE ARCHIVES	
Types of Materials Available	10
Accessibility of Materials	10
Queries about Collections	11
Archives Publications	11
The Audio-Visual Collections	12
The Archives Library	13
USE OF THE ARCHIVES	
Hours	15
Who May Use the Collections	15
Rules for Use of Archival Materials	15
Abbreviations	17
Part I: THE COLLECTIONS	21
Personal Papers	21
Air Line Pilots Association	87
Departments	87
Councils	89
American Federation of Teachers	91
Departments	91
State and Local Federations	93
The Newspaper Guild	96
National Office	96
Locals	96
United Auto Workers	98
Departments	98
Regions	103
Locals	105
United Farm Workers	117
National Offices	117
Boycott and State Offices	118

Other Organizations 119
Unprocessed Collections 134

Part II: THE ORAL HISTORY INTERVIEWS 137
Unionization of the Auto Industry 140
Blacks and the Labor Movement 162
New York Times/Columbia University Oral History Program 168

Index 169

FOREWORD

The Archives of Labor History and Urban Affairs was established at Wayne State University in 1960 with the goal of collecting and preserving original source material relating to the American labor movement and related social, political, and economic reform movements. Although special attention was given to the industrial unions, the Archives has attempted to reflect a broad spectrum of the labor movement in its collecting program.

In 1962, at its 18th Constitutional Convention, the United Automobile, Aerospace, and Agricultural Implement Workers (UAW) became the first major international labor union to designate the Archives as the official depository for its inactive records. Since that time about ten million items related to the UAW, including the inactive records of the International's headquarters, regional and sub-regional offices in the United States and Canada, and a carefully selected cross section of the UAW locals, have been preserved. In addition, the personal papers of UAW officers and rank and file members have been given to the Archives. Included in the latter category are the papers of Walter, Victor, and Roy Reuther, R.J. Thomas, Richard Frankensteen, George Burt, Homer Martin, Henry Kraus, Francis Dillon, and George Addes.

In 1962, the Archives was the recipient of over one hundred transcribed oral interviews concerning the development of unionism in the automobile industry. These interviews serve as a valuable supplement to the written records and papers concerning the history of the UAW.

Other international labor unions and organizations have also placed their historical records at Wayne State University. These unions include the American Federation of Teachers, Air Line Pilots Association, Congress of Industrial Organizations, Industrial Workers of the World, The Newspaper Guild, and United Farm Workers.

The records of related organizations and individuals have also been acquired. The files of the Workers Defense League, California Migrant Ministry, Michigan AFL-CIO, Wayne County AFL-CIO, Cesar Chavez, John Edelman, Mary Heaton Vorse, Katherine Pollak Ellickson, Mark

Starr, and Clarence Sayen, provide additional information related to specific labor groups.

As a result of organized labor's involvement in political, social, and economic causes and activities, the scope of the Archives' collecting program was broadened to include the papers and records of politicians, civil rights and community leaders, and organizations concerned with these topics. Some of these collections include the files of the People's Song Library, Detroit Council of Churches, Detroit branches of the American Civil Liberties Union and the National Association for the Advancement of Colored People, Detroit Industrial Mission, Michigan Welfare League, Civil Rights Congress of Michigan, and Detroit Commission on Community Relations. The records of city and state officials, including the papers of Detroit Mayor Jerome Cavanagh, United States Senator Patrick McNamara, Congressman Charles Diggs, and numerous state senators and representatives are included among these collections. Papers of individuals like Aaron Henry, Oscar Ameringer, and Harvey O'Connor also contain items relevant to these areas.

In little over a decade Wayne State University's Archives of Labor History and Urban Affairs has become synonymous with labor history research. The United Automobile, Aerospace, and Agricultural Implement Workers Union has aided the Archives in many ways in the past and has now generously assured the future of the program by financing the construction of the Walter P. Reuther Library to house the Archives' collections.

Philip P. Mason, *Director*
Archives of Labor History and Urban Affairs

PREFACE

This guide is designed to serve as a research aid for patrons of the Archives of Labor History and Urban Affairs at Wayne State University. All collections acquired prior to January 1, 1974, have been either described or listed. The entries give the researcher a general idea of the subject matter, correspondents, type of materials, and size of each collection. More comprehensive individual guides to each collection are available in the Archives.

The *Guide to the Archives of Labor History and Urban Affairs* represents a joint effort on the part of the entire staff of the Archives. However, the contributions of Dennis East, Beverly Fodell, Lawrence Halsted, Margery Long, Roberta McBride, Dione Miles, and many graduate students were great and of especial importance. Special appreciation for the work of Shannon Henry and Jean Spang in editing the entire guide is hereby tendered.

Acknowledgment is also made to the Nicholas Hyshka Memorial Fund and to donors to the Archives Memorial Fund for financial assistance in the publication of this Guide.

FUNCTIONS AND SERVICES OF THE ARCHIVES

Types of Materials Available
In general, the materials in the Archives fall into two categories: 1) the personal papers of individuals, and 2) the official files of labor unions and other organizations. They vary in size from a few to several hundred thousand items.

In addition to written archival and manuscript files, other material of research value is available in the Archives' library and audio-visual collections. Oral history transcripts held by the Archives are another source.

Accessibility of Materials
Some donors place restrictions upon access to their papers, usually closing all, or part of them, for a specified period of time. Because of the sensitive nature of many contemporary records, this practice is understandable and followed by most archives dealing with non-public records. The type of restriction varies according to the wishes of the donor. The United Automobile, Aerospace, and Agricultural Implement Workers, for example, have restricted access to records less than twenty years old, except with special permission. The records of the Air Line Pilots Association are closed for ten years, the American Federation of Teachers, five years. The Archives' staff is presently negotiating with other unions and organizations to work out reasonable access policies.

The personal papers of individuals may also be closed to research for short periods of time. Although the Archives is anxious to make all records available as soon as possible, it is recognized that reasonable restrictions may be necessary if such records are to be preserved.

Since all collections, whether open or closed to research, are described in this guide, researchers should contact the Archives in advance to determine the availability of specific collections.

All published materials in the Archives such as newspapers, books, proceedings, pamphlets, newsletters, broadsides, and leaflets are open to researchers without restriction.

Queries about Collections

The Archives' staff will try to answer all inquiries about materials in the collections, especially for out-of-town researchers who may wish to determine if a visit is justified. Written inquiries which require extensive research by the staff may not be honored. For some collections, a copy of the comprehensive inventory is available upon request.

Archives Publications

The staff of the Archives of Labor History and Urban Affairs not only aids researchers by preparing bibliographies and general descriptions of the holdings, but also attempts to acquaint the public with the work of the Archives through publication of articles and brochures. (Copies of some of these items can be obtained without charge by writing to the Archives.)

A bibliography, *Cesar Chavez and the United Farm Workers,* published in the Spring of 1974, contains listings of articles, books, reports, pamphlets, government documents, bibliographies, and reference works pertaining to the organization of farm labor and Cesar Chavez and the United Farm Workers. Many items refer specifically to Chavez, the grape strike, grape boycotts, the United Farm Workers Organizing Committee, Agricultural Workers Organizing Committee, and the National Farm Workers Association. A number of selected items on general background topics such as Public Law 78 (the importation of foreign farm workers), organizing agricultural workers, living and working conditions of migrant workers, farm labor contractors, and federal and state legislation for workers, are also listed.

For *The Afro-American in Detroit and Michigan* (a bibliography to be completed soon), more than 1,200 entries have already been examined, abstracted, and indexed by subject, geographical area, and personal name. This annotated bibliography will describe all available printed materials concerning the Afro-American in Michigan, with emphasis on the Detroit area and urban problems such as employment, housing, and education.

Three brochures are now available concerning activities of the Archives. *Perspectives on History* discusses non-labor holdings, collections which were gathered by many organizations and individuals concerned with social and economic reform and urban America. *Collections of the Archives of Labor History and Urban Affairs* pertains to collections from groups and individuals in the labor movement, excepting the United Auto Workers. *Preserving the UAW's Heritage* describes the program to preserve the inactive files of the United Auto Workers.

The Archives' work with the UAW led to *The UAW in Pictures* (Detroit: Wayne State University Press, 1971), most of the illustrations for this pictorial history coming from the Archives' collections.

The *Newsletter,* printed three times a year, discusses specific aspects of the Archives such as its collections relating to women, AFT collections, and the IWW. Persons interested in receiving the *Newsletter* may be placed on the mailing list by writing the Archives.

For detailed discussions of the Archives' programs, see "Labor History Archives at Wayne State University" (*Labor History,* Vol. 5, No. 1, Winter 1964), and "The Labor History Archives, Wayne State University" (*Internationale Wissenschaftliche Korrespondenz zur Geschichte der Deutschen Arbeiterbewegung,* Heft 8, June 1969).

The Audio-Visual Collections

The audio-visual collections of the Archives of Labor History and Urban Affairs augment and parallel the written records on deposit. Functioning as a reference and production service for researchers, publishers, and educators, the holdings consist of photographs, motion picture films, filmstrips, color transparency slides, microfilm, audio tapes, phonograph disc records, offset plates, posters, and memorabilia.

The 50,000 black-and-white photographs provide a visual record of the activities of labor unions such as the Industrial Workers of the World, the United Auto Workers, the United Farm Workers, the United Mine Workers, the United Rubber Workers, the Air Line Pilots Association, the American Federation of Teachers, the American Federation of Labor, the Congress of Industrial Organizations, the Knights of Labor, and the Brotherhood of Railway Trainmen. In addition to specific union activities, such topics as political campaigns, social reform movements, civil rights, and twentieth century urban America comprise a significant portion of the photographic holdings. A small number of offset plates from labor union publications is included in the photographic section; proofed plates are treated as graphic images.

A collection of 200 motion picture films records the history of labor movements, strikes, national holidays, and parades, and includes films produced by government agencies, some for technical instruction. Thirty filmstrips designed for educational and training purposes are available to researchers.

The United Farm Workers and the Air Line Pilots Association are major classifications in the collection of 100 color transparency slides.

Microfilm holdings (150 reels), consist of copies of labor publications, grievance records, minutes of union meetings, letters, and documents.

Nearly 5,000 audio tapes record such personalities as Joan Baez, Cesar Chavez, Elizabeth Gurley Flynn, Richard Frankensteen, Barry Goldwater, Hubert Humphrey, Lyndon Johnson, John F. Kennedy, Martin Luther

King, Jr., George Meany, Philip Murray, Guy Nunn, Roy Reuther, Victor Reuther, Walter Reuther, Carl Sandburg, Upton Sinclair, and Roy Wilkins. Also available on tape are proceedings and broadcasts of the AFL-CIO, American Federation of Teachers, Air Line Pilots Association, McClellan Senate Hearings of 1957-58, UAW conventions, and United Farm Workers Organizing Committee. Reports to constituents by both senators and representatives of the United States Congress on legislation affecting labor unions and their members, taped for use of local radio stations and union-sponsored programs, are included in the Archives' collection. Topics such as labor songs, the IWW, and miscellaneous education programs are also covered. Phonograph records (115 discs) of speeches, interviews, and educational topics have been converted to tape but the original recordings may be used if desired. Facilities for monitoring tapes are available at the Archives.

The memorabilia collection is an assemblage of odd articles, buttons, banners, pins, hats, neckties, badges, bumper stickers, emblems, and posters dating from early union days and their conventions reflecting various political contests. The Archives also retained 16 oil wash cartoons depicting the humorous aspects of union summer school life which hung in the dining hall of the FDR-CIO Camp at Lakeport, Michigan.

The Archives Library

The library of the Archives of Labor History and Urban Affairs brings together in one location the reference and background materials most frequently used by staff and patrons in their research projects. It also houses those portions of donors' collections more properly treated as library rather than archival items, that is, books, periodical runs, pamphlets, and other printed materials.

In addition to the book collection, important segments of the library are:

(a) The DiGaetano Newspaper files of some 400 volumes which were collected and bound by UAW Local 7 retiree Nick DiGaetano. The files include many labor newspapers in the Detroit area from 1930 forward, and the house organs of UAW locals throughout the United States and Canada.

(b) A collection of bound labor journals purchased by the University from the John Crerar Library in the early 1950s. The earliest, *Cigar Makers' Official Journal,* begins with volume 12, 1886. Other titles showing the craft emphasis of the labor movement at the beginning of this century are *Bridgeman's Magazine* (1907-48), *Carpenter* (1902-49), *Commercial Telegraphers' Journal* (1904-41), *Inter-*

national Molders' and Foundry Workers' Journal (1896-1945), *Machinists Monthly Journal* (1903-47), and *Painter and Decorator* (1904-51). Two especially valuable items are the publications, *Life and Labor*, of the National Women's Trade Union League for the years 1911-21, and the *Women's Union Journal,* of the Women's Protective and Provident League of Labor, London, 1879-90. Thirty-five titles are included in the collection of 627 bound volumes.

(c) The vertical file, consisting of 35 file drawers of pamphlets, and clippings. Although some of the materials reflect current labor and urban interests, most are of historical value. The file is particularly useful on labor education, black workers, skilled trades, union organizing in the 1930s, and labor's political activities. Several groups of radical pamphlets from the Marxian Education Society, the Trade Union Educational League, the Haldeman-Julius Company, Charles H. Kerr publishers, and similar organizations form an impressive collection.

(d) Files of union and association publications, printed or mimeographed, for those unions and organizations which have designated the Archives as their depository, such as the UAW, AFT, ALPA, United Farm Workers, IWW, Michigan and Wayne County AFL-CIO, The Newspaper Guild, and others. Included are constitutions and by-laws, contracts, journals, proceedings, and departmental and local union publications.

(e) The Brookwood Library of the Brookwood Labor College of Katonah, N.Y., the best known of the many labor schools which opened in the 1920s. When the school closed in 1936, its book collection was purchased by the UAW Westside Local 174, and was later transferred to the UAW Research Library at Solidarity House. Later it was presented to the Archives. Of the nearly 1,000 volumes now in the Brookwood collection, many are of intrinsic value, while others are interesting chiefly as a reflection of labor's interests in the 1920s and early 1930s.

USE OF THE ARCHIVES

Hours
The hours for the Reading Room are 8:30 to 5:00, Monday through Friday, and 9:00 to 12:00 and 1:00 to 5:00 on Saturday. During the academic year, the Reading Room may be open during certain evenings of the week.

Who May Use The Collections
By direction of the Board of Governors of Wayne State University, materials in the Archives are available to persons with a serious scholarly interest. Although this generally includes faculty members of institutions of higher learning and graduate students doing directed research, other persons also qualify. Prospective users should write to the Archives in advance to establish their credentials for using collections. The Director and an advisory committee, made up of members from the academic, labor, and general communities, have final authority in permitting access to collections.

Rules for Use of Archival Materials
1. Positive identification is required of all prospective researchers. This will usually take the form of an I.D. card from your institution and a driver's license.
2. To obtain materials, the Researchers Registration form must be completed.
3. All briefcases and portfolios must be left with the reading room attendant.
4. Please enter your name in the register each day. Note the time you begin and complete your research.
5. All materials are to be used only in the reading room of the Archives.
6. Pencil, ballpoint pen, typewriter, or recording devices may be used for taking notes.

7. No marking of or writing upon archival materials is permitted. Extreme care should be exercised when handling fragile items.
8. Use only one box at a time. Remove only one folder at a time. Do not remove items from the folders.
9. The exact order and arrangement of the papers must be maintained. If any mistake is discovered, please call it to the attention of a staff member.
10. In citing these materials, please cite the full name of the collection and of the Archives. Example: The Joe Brown Collection, Archives of Labor History and Urban Affairs, Wayne State University.
11. It is the responsibility of the researcher to secure permission to publish material in the Archives.
12. No smoking, eating, or beverages are permitted while using archival collections.
13. Policy on photoduplication: The Archives is willing to reproduce selected materials from its manuscript and archival collections for patrons who have done research. Sometimes specific restrictions imposed on a particular collection by the donor may restrict our ability to photoduplicate it. We are not able to reproduce entire collections or large series within such collections, oral history transcripts, or written reminiscences tantamount to an oral history transcript.

ABBREVIATIONS

ACLU	American Civil Liberties Union
ACTU	Association of Catholic Trade Unionists
AFL	American Federation of Labor
AFSCME	American Federation of State, County and Municipal Employees
AFT	American Federation of Teachers
AIWA	Automotive Industrial Workers Association
ALPA	Air Line Pilots Association
AWU	Auto Workers Union of the Trade Union Unity League
CCL	Canadian Congress of Labour
CIO	Congress of Industrial Organizations
COPE	Committee on Political Education
DRUM	Dodge Revolutionary Union Movement
FEPC	Committee on Fair Employment Practices
FLU	Federal Labor Union of AFL
HUAC	House Un-American Activities Committee
IAM	International Association of Machinists and Aerospace Workers
ICFTU	International Confederation of Free Trade Unions
IWW	Industrial Workers of the World
MEA	Michigan Education Association
MESA	Mechanics Educational Society of America
NAACP	National Association for the Advancement of Colored People
NEA	National Education Association
NLRB	National Labor Relations Board
NRA	National Recovery Administration
NWLB	National War Labor Board
OPA	Office of Price Administration
PAC	Political Action Committee
TNG	The Newspaper Guild
UAW	United Automobile, Aerospace and Agricultural Implement Workers of America
UFT	United Federation of Teachers

UFW	United Farm Workers
UMW	United Mine Workers of America
UPW	United Public Workers of America
WPA	Works Progress Administration
WPB	War Production Board

PART I
The Collections

THE COLLECTIONS

The format followed for each entry is the same, whether the papers are those of an individual or of an organization. The first line contains the title and the inclusive dates of the papers in the collection.

The descriptive portion of each entry contains either a brief biographical sketch of the individual, or, in the case of an organization, a brief outline of its activities, location, and other pertinent information. The nature of the material contained in the collection and names of the correspondents, is also contained in the description.

The last line of the entry indicates the size of the collection, usually expressed in linear feet. If the collection comprises less than one-half linear foot, the number of items will be noted. Materials such as bound volumes and scrapbooks are included in the size note where appropriate. If the collection is unprocessed, this information will also be found in the last line. The danger of attempting to describe unprocessed files is recognized, but a belief that researchers could benefit from knowing the location of the material prompted inclusion of these entries.

PERSONAL PAPERS

ABNER, WILLOUGHBY. *Papers, 1961–64.*
Correspondence, reports, newsletters, and miscellaneous publications reflecting Mr. Abner's positions with the UAW and his social concerns. Until 1963 Mr. Abner was with the Education and Citizenship Department of UAW Region 4, located in Chicago. In 1963 he moved to Detroit to become the assistant director of the Leadership Study Center of the UAW. Subjects include the labor movement on local, state, and international levels; urban affairs and social problems.   *4 linear feet.*

ADDES, GEORGE. *Papers, 1936–47.*
Correspondence, reports, UAW International Executive Board minutes, and other office files of Mr. Addes, who served as the UAW's International

Collections

secretary-treasurer from 1936 to 1947. The papers pertain to organizing, factionalism within the UAW, early UAW strikes, UAW Local Union financial statements, and cases appealed by members of the UAW to the union's International Executive Board. An oral history interview with Mr. Addes is available.
65 1/2 linear feet.

AMERINGER, OSCAR. *Papers, 1909–70.*
Correspondence, clippings, photographs, speeches, and pamphlets of Mr. Ameringer, editor of the *Illinois Miner,* the *Oklahoma Leader,* and *American Guardian.* The papers consist of correspondence with friends within the labor and socialist movements and writings on issues affecting the labor movement. Among the correspondents are McAlister Coleman, Eugene Debs, John Dewey, Charles Ervin, Covington Hall, Carl Sandburg, Norman Thomas, Oswald Garrison Villard, and Henry Wallace.
1/2 linear foot.

ANDERSON, JOHN. *Papers, 1962–64.*
Pamphlets and the UAW Public Review Board decision in the case of Anderson vs. UAW Local 15, Fisher Body-Fleetwood in Detroit. Mr. Anderson was on the International Executive Board of the UAW from 1936 to 1937, and was president of Local 15 from 1946 to 1949. The Public Review case grew out of his suspension by Local 15 for charging misuse of union funds by local union officers. An oral history interview with Mr. Anderson is available.
3 items.

AUSTIN, RICHARD H. *Papers, 1964–71.*
Mr. Austin, who in 1941 became Michigan's first black certified public accountant, has been active in Detroit, Wayne County, and Michigan Democratic politics and civic clubs for many years. During the period 1961-63, he was a delegate to the Michigan Constitutional Convention; 1963-65, co-chairman of the Michigan Commission on Legislative Apportionment; 1962, elected to the Wayne County Board of Supervisors; 1964, lost the Congressional race against John Conyers, Jr.; 1966, won a seat on the Wayne County Board of Auditors; 1969, defeated by Roman Gribbs in the Detroit mayoralty race; 1970, elected Michigan's Secretary of State. The material in the collection relates to these topics and to numerous civic and professional organizations to which he belonged. Among the correspondents are Jerome P. Cavanagh, John Conyers, Jr., Charles Diggs, Fred

Harris, Hubert Humphrey, Mildred Jeffrey, James McNeely, Walter Reuther, and G. Mennen Williams. *23 linear feet.*

BAKER, CHARLES. *Papers, 1958–59.*
Correspondence, clippings, press releases, and other files created by Mr. Baker's public relations agency in Toledo, Ohio. The papers pertain to the agency's work for the United Organized Labor of Ohio in their successful campaign to defeat a proposed right-to-work law in Ohio in 1958.
2 linear feet.

BASKIN, ALEX. *Papers, 1964–67.*
Correspondence, reprints, and court orders pertaining to the renewal of a broadcasting license for the Pacifica Foundation; newspaper accounts of the 1967 Detroit riots. *2 linear feet.*

BASSO, JOSEPH. *Papers, 1935–65.*
The bulk of this collection consists of printed pamphlets, brochures, and leaflets on labor and related subjects collected by Mr. Basso during his service with the Wayne County, Michigan AFL-CIO. Also included are Executive Board minutes of the Wayne County AFL-CIO for 1958–63. As secretary to Detroit Recorder's Court Judge George Murphy, he collected campaign materials, speeches, press releases, and clippings concerning the judge and his brother, United States Supreme Court Justice Frank Murphy.
12 linear feet [unprocessed].

BAXTER, WARNER. *Papers, 1885–1901.*
Minutes of Local 3 of Social Democracy of America and printed material on the general topic of socialism and the Socialist Labor Party.
1/2 linear foot.

BEASLEY, OLIVE. *Papers, 1952–65.*
Correspondence, agenda, clippings, and speeches pertaining to Michigan Fair Employment Practices conferences. Mrs. Beasley has served as director of the Flint, Michigan Civil Rights Commission and vice-president of the Michigan State Employees Union, Council 7, AFSCME.
1/2 linear foot; [2 linear feet unprocessed].

BEFFEL, JOHN. *Papers, 1943–54*
Mr. Beffel served as a reporter, writer, editor, and publicist. He edited manuscripts of Slim Brundage, Joseph Cohen, Paul Crouch, Harry Kelly,

Collections

Walter Marshall, Rose Pesotta, Voline, and Vincenzo Vocirca; and did publicity work for the Workers Defense League. In addition to the manuscripts, the collection includes correspondence, drafts, notes, and clippings which deal with the Carlo Tresca Memorial Committee, anarchists, communism, the Joe Hill case, the IWW, and the League for Mutual Aid. Correspondents include, in addition to the authors noted above, Ralph Chaplin, Margaret DeSilver, Max Nettlau, Matilda Robbins, Nicolaas Steelink, Norman Thomas, and Fred Thompson.
13 1/2 linear feet.

BENSON, HERMAN. *Papers, 1944–63.*
Correspondence, clippings, leaflets, and other files of Mr. Benson, a labor journalist who served as trade union editor of *Labor Action* and editor of *Union Democracy in Action.* The papers mainly concern intra-union disputes, particularly fights against corruption within union leadership, including the 1958–61 struggle in Local 88 of the Masters, Mates and Pilots, which led to the ouster and jailing of the International president; the 1949–50 factional dispute within the National Maritime Union; and activities of the Longshoremen, Seafarers' International and Sailors Union of the Pacific. Other topics covered are disputes within the International Association of Machinists; rank and file movements in the unions of the papermaking industry; and the 1960 split between the Air Line Pilots Association and the Air Line Stewards and Stewardesses. The Michigan Commonwealth Federation, a 1944 third party movement, is also covered. Among the correspondents are Barry Goldwater, A.J. Hayes, John Lindsay, George Meany, and Norman Thomas.
4 linear feet.

BISHOP, DOROTHY HUBBARD. *Papers, 1934–40.*
Correspondence, clippings, reports, and educational materials pertaining to Mrs. Bishop's work as supervisor of the WPA Workers Education Division in Michigan.
1/2 linear foot.

BISHOP, MERLIN. *Papers, 1936–37.*
Correspondence, clippings, and other items pertaining to Mr. Bishop's tenure as director of education for the UAW (1936–37), and his work in the sit-downs in the auto industry (1936–37). An oral history interview with Mr. Bishop is available.
1/2 linear foot.

BLACKBURN, SAM. *Papers, 1937–45.*
Correspondence, clippings, transcripts, and resolutions concerned with the relationships between the UAW, the Society of Designing Engineers, and the Federation of Artists, Engineers, Chemists, and Technicians.
1/2 linear foot.

BLAICH, JOHN. *Papers, 1941–47.*
Correspondence, clippings, reports, and other items pertaining to Mr. Blaich's work as chairman of the Tool and Die Division of UAW Local 600, Ford Rouge Plant, Dearborn, Michigan.
25 items.

BLANKENHORN, ANN. *Papers, 1922–68.*
Ann Blankenhorn investigated and publicized the social and economic conditions in the textile, clothing, and coal mining industries in the 1920s and 30s with special emphasis on women and children. Also included are papers relating to the WPA (1934) and the imprisonment of Elizabeth Gurley Flynn in the 1950s. Important correspondents are Peter Blume and Elizabeth Gurley Flynn. The materials consist of correspondence (1931–68), personal notebooks, diaries, and address books.
1 linear foot.

BLANKENHORN, HEBER. *Papers, 1906–67.*
Mr. Blankenhorn was assistant city editor of the New York *Evening Sun;* co-director of the Bureau of Industrial Research; publicity director for the Amalgamated Clothing Workers; foreign correspondent for *Labor;* aide to Senator Robert Wagner in the passage of the NLRA and a staff member for the first two National Labor boards and the LaFollette Committee; director of the UAW investigation into the shootings of Victor and Walter Reuther; and finally returned as a correspondent for *Labor.* Correspondence, memoranda, notes, reports, and other material gathered by Mr. Blankenhorn cover early NLRB activities; the LaFollette Committee; steel and auto unionization; the use of private detectives by the auto industry in the 1930s; the Inter-Church World Movement and the Steel Strike of 1919; the Reuther shootings; and the Spanish Civil War. Correspondents include Robert LaFollette, Jr., John L. Lewis, Walter Reuther, Estes Kefauver, and Peter Blume.
7 1/2 linear feet.

BLUESTONE, IRVING. *Papers, 1938 and 1941.*
Minutes of the UAW International Executive Board (January, 1938);

Collections

signed carbon copy of the first contract between the UAW and Ford Motor Company (1941).   *2 items.*

BORCHARDT, SELMA. *Papers, 1911–67.*
Correspondence, minutes, reports, speeches, press releases, and notes collected by Miss Borchardt, who served as legislative representative and vice-president for the AFT (1924–62), chairman of the AFT International Relations Committee (1927–62), secretary of the AFL Education Committee (1929–55), and director of the World Federation of Education Associations (1927–46). Miss Borchardt also served as a member of many governmental committees and conferences including the National Advisory Board of the National Youth Administration (1934–44); the U.S. Office of Education Wartime Commission (1941–43); the White House Conferences on Children and Youth (1930, 1940, and 1950); and the White House Conference on Education (1955). Subjects include the communist issue within the AFT, exchange teacher programs, federal aid to education, the Institute of World Studies, juvenile delinquency, National Women's Trade Union League, Social Security legislation, vocational education, and workers' education. Correspondents include George Aiken, George Axtelle, Mary Barker, Arthur Capper, John Sherman Cooper, George Counts, Mary Dent, John Eklund, Arthur Elder, Walter George, William Green, Lister Hill, David Starr Jordan, Abraham Lefkowitz, Henry Linville, Jay Lovestone, James Mead, George Meany, Carl Megel, A.J. Muste, Hilda Smith, and Matthew Woll.   *100 linear feet.*

BREWER, GEORGE AND GRACE. *Papers, 1905–21.*
Correspondence, speeches, lectures, newspaper clippings, union membership booklets, newspapers, scrapbooks, and pamphlets collected by Mr. Brewer, chief spokesman for the Socialist Party in the southeastern Kansas region, especially Crawford County (1905–21), and member of the Kansas Legislature (1914–16). Mr. Brewer was also, for a time, traveling secretary to Eugene V. Debs. Subjects include mining strikes and accidents; World War I pacifism and profiteering; Navy League; Socialist Party activities; anti-papism in Detroit and Chicago; Non-Partisan League; southeast Kansas politics; speaking engagements of Eugene V. Debs and George Brewer; and family affairs of George and Grace Brewer. Major correspondents are Eugene and Katherine Debs.   *4 linear feet.*

BROWN, IVAN. *Papers, 1941–67.*
Correspondence, minutes, reports, press releases, grievance records, umpire cases, financial reports, mailing lists, Democratic State Central Committee

reports, and publications collected by Mr. Brown, who served as president of UAW Ford Local 952, Iron Mountain, Michigan (1945–50), and as a UAW International representative for Region 1-D (western Michigan and the Upper Peninsula) (1950–69). Subjects include sale of Ford Motor Company Iron Mountain Plant in 1951, and Kingsford Chemical Company Strike (1953). Among the correspondents are Ken Bannon, G. Mennen Williams, and Leonard Woodcock.
12 1/2 linear feet; [2 linear feet unprocessed].

BROWN, JAMES H. *Papers, 1960–63.*
Correspondence and other documents pertaining to fair employment practices in the Ford Motor Company, and to alleged violations of Executive Order 10925, collected by Mr. Brown, presently serving in the UAW Ford Motor Department. In 1961 Ken Bannon, director of that Department, appointed Mr. Brown to supervise the equal employment opportunity provision of the Ford contract. Subjects include a discrimination complaint filed by the UAW in 1963 against Ford's Atlanta plant. Among the correspondents are Ken Bannon, Philip Hart, William H. Oliver, and Percy H. Williams.
90 items.

BROWN, JOE. *Papers, 1933–42.*
A one-time reporter for the *Federated Press,* Mr. Brown gathered a variety of items for a proposed book on unionism in the auto industry. Clippings, correspondence, handbills, and miscellaneous publications relate to the rise of auto unions during the 1930s and 1940s. Nearly every topic of importance for that time and subject is covered, including sit-downs, drives to organize various plants, and strikes. The scrapbooks contain mostly Detroit newspaper clippings about auto unions.
18 linear feet; 21 scrapbooks.

BROWN, ROY M. *Papers, 1937–70.*
Mr. Brown worked toward the development of the International Association of Machinists (IAM) in California. In 1936 he served as recording secretary of Lodge 1484 and business representative of the newly formed Lodge 1126. He helped organize and became president of the first California Conference of Machinists in 1938, and, by 1942, became a general vice-president of the IAM. Speeches, clippings, and other materials on the aircraft industry; National War Labor Board; UAW-IAM No Raid Agreements; Fry Audit; and Brown's campaign for general secretary-treasurer

are included. Among the correspondents are A.J. Hayes, Asby McGraw, Thomas McNett, H.L. Mitchell, and Leonard Woodcock.
35 1/2 linear feet; 4 oversized folders.

BURKART, ROBERT. *Papers, 1949–65.*
Correspondence, clippings, minutes, reports, and statements relating to the Kohler Strike. Mr. Burkart was one of the UAW International representatives assigned to this strike. Topics covered include the history of unionism at Kohler; contract negotiations; the NLRB and the Kohler Strike; and the Senate Labor Subcommittee's hearings. Among the correspondents are Lyman Conger, Richard Gosser, Emil Mazey, and Donald Rand.
1 linear foot.

BURT, GEORGE. *Papers, 1941–53.*
For nearly thirty years Mr. Burt served as director of the UAW in Canada, retiring in 1968. In this collection are copies of his reports to UAW District Council 26 and minutes and other items of the Council.
1 linear foot [unprocessed].

BURTON, JOHN. *Papers, 1949–59.*
UAW Local 142 Executive Board and membership minutes, financial records, grievance records, and newspaper clippings collected by Mr. Burton, who served as a member of the Bargaining Committee of Local 142, Willow Run, Michigan.
11 items.

CARLSTROM, LAWRENCE. *Papers, 1937.*
Clippings and souvenir programs concerning the 1937 UAW Convention.
5 items.

CAVANAGH, JEROME P. *Papers, 1961–70.*
The papers of Mr. Cavanagh, mayor of Detroit from 1962 to 1970. They include correspondence, reports, studies, speeches, minutes, and other materials of the mayor's office and commissions and departments of the city. Efforts, both local and national, in improving economic and racial conditions in Detroit are recorded in the collection. Subjects of interest include poverty programs; housing; civil disorders and police problems; and all aspects of the urban complex. Smaller groups within the collection are the files of James L. Trainor, Fred Romanoff, Richard Strichartz, Jack Casey, and Sandra McClure, all members of the mayor's staff. Correspondents are government officials on every level: U.S. presidents, vice-

presidents, senators, congressmen, state officials, mayors of other cities, and other prominent public figures.
300 linear feet [unprocessed].

CEDERVALL, TOR. *Papers, mid—1930s.*
Mainly clippings pertaining to Mr. Cedervall's activities on behalf of the IWW in Cleveland, Ohio.
12 items.

CHALMERS, W. ELLISON. *Papers, 1926—38.*
Correspondence, press releases, and reports pertaining to the AFL's efforts to organize the auto industry in the early 1930s; and workers' education, including the Bryn Mawr and the University of Wisconsin summer schools, and the Pittsburgh Labor College. Dr. Chalmers received his Ph.D. from the University of Wisconsin under John R. Commons. The collection contains class notes he took while studying with Professor Commons and other labor economists at Wisconsin. Correspondents include John R. Commons, Francis Dillon, Paul Douglas, William Green, Sidney Hillman, John L. Lewis, Francis Perkins, and Norman Thomas.
3 1/2 linear feet

CHATFIELD, LEROY. *Papers, 1967—68.*
Correspondence, reports, invitations, and election agreements collected by Mr. Chatfield, administrative assistant to Cesar Chavez, director of the United Farm Workers Organizing Committee. Subjects include the negotiations and election at the Christian Brothers' Mont La Salle Vineyards (1967), the development of the Farm Workers Service Center (of which Mr. Chatfield served as director), and fund raising for the United Farm Workers in New York City. Correspondents include A.V. Krebs, Bishop Timothy Manning, Marion Moses, and Pablo O'Higgins.
80 items.

CHIAKULAS, CHARLES. *Papers, 1944—68.*
As a UAW International representative, Mr. Chiakulas worked in many capacities in the labor movement, including assistant director of the Borg-Warner Department, and coordinator of the AFL-CIO Industrial Union Department. In Chicago he set up one of the successful Community Union centers, working in the ghetto with tenant unions. He was a COPE coordinator and was sent abroad three times by the union to work (through the ICFTU) with labor leaders in Cyprus and Greece. His papers reflect his many-faceted career and include material on the following

subjects: AFSCME; Borg-Warner; British colonialism; the J.I. Case Company; the Chicago CUC; Chicago politics; COPE; Community Unions; Cyprus; Cyprus Trade Unions; the 1967 coup in Greece; the Greek Community in Chicago; IUD; ICFTU; UAW Locals 180 and 477; Miss Melina Mercouri; NLRB cases; peace groups; teachers' unions; and the UAW-AFL-AIWU problems. Frequent correspondents include many senators and congressmen, particularly Representative Roman Pucinski. Among the international correspondents are J.M. Aguirre, H.E. Chudleigh, Eiler Jensen, Bill Kemsley, Jay B. Krane, Archbishop Makarios, Fotis Makris, J.H. Oldenbroek, N. Petrides, Michael Pissas, Z. Rossides, and A. Vassilion. Union correspondents are Jack Bollens, Frank Callaghan, Patrick Gorman, Richard Gosser, Pat Greathouse, Joseph Mattson, Victor Reuther, Walter Reuther, Tony Valeo, and Leonard Woodcock.
29 1/2 linear feet.

CICCONE, LOUIS. *Papers, 1945–61.*
Mr. Ciccone served for many years in various offices for UAW-GM Local 216, South Gate, California. Reports, notes, correspondence, and clippings contained in this collection pertain to various activities of Local 216, labor activities in the Los Angeles area, labor and politics, the General Motors Strike of 1945–46, and the noncommunist affidavit provision of the Taft-Hartley Act. Correspondents include Emil Mazey and Wyndham Mortimer.
1 linear foot.

CLANCY, FATHER RAYMOND S. *Papers, 1931–70.*
Correspondence, pamphlets, arbitration awards and opinions, speeches, lectures, radio talks, and invocations collected by Reverend Clancy, who was known in Detroit as the "labor priest." After being ordained on May 25, 1929 and serving as assistant pastor at the Epiphany Church in Detroit, he became interested in the labor movement and was sent to the School of Social Action at Catholic University, Washington, D.C., in 1939. That same year he returned to Detroit and organized workers' schools for the Association of Catholic Trade Unionists and was appointed chaplain for it soon afterwards. In 1941 he was appointed secretary of the Archdiocesan Labor Institute and director of the Archdiocesan Social Action Department. From 1950–53 he was pastor of All Saints; from 1953 until 1969, when he retired, he was pastor of Sacred Heart. Subjects include Detroit Archdiocese and labor; mediation and arbitration (Detroit and Michigan); the Association of Catholic Trade Unionists; his disagreement with Father

Charles Coughlin; Papal encyclicals (*Rerum Novarum* and *Quadragesimo Anno);* and religion.
6 linear feet.

COBB, ALTON. *Papers, 1966–68.*
Mr. Cobb served as president of Local 26, AFSCME. His papers include Executive Board minutes; correspondence; court briefs and exhibits centering on union problems of financial accounting; and disputes over trusteeship of Local 26 and Council 77 of the Detroit AFSCME. National level union changes and elections, and issues of union democracy among the Garbage Workers are involved.
1/2 linear foot.

COHEN, DAVID. *Papers, 1961–67.*
Newspaper clippings, magazine articles, leaflets, newsletters, and correspondence relating to the United Farm Workers Organizing Committee and National Farm Workers Association grape strike and boycott (1965–67); reports, newsletters, clippings, leaflets, minutes, and miscellaneous papers relating to neighborhood community organizations in Detroit and Chicago (1961–67). The materials were collected by Mr. Cohen, who served as a member of the boycott staff and as boycott coordinator in San Diego and Detroit for the United Farm Workers (1966); founder and director of the Canfield Tutorial Project in Detroit (1965); and member and chairman of the Library Committee of the West Central Organization in Detroit (1965–66). Saul Alinsky, community organizations in Detroit, the Delano grape strike and grape boycotts, University City II, urban renewal, and the Woodlawn Organization are discussed. The major correspondent is Cesar Chavez.
1 1/2 linear feet.

COLLIER, JOHN (William Armistead Collier, Jr.) AND
COLLIER, PHYLLIS. *Papers, 1881–1967.*
Correspondence, notes, literary manuscripts, clippings, photographs, pamphlets, and memorabilia relating to Mr. Collier's activities as a writer and social critic. Also correspondence, clippings, notes, and miscellaneous printed materials concerning Mrs. Collier's activities as secretary of the American Labor Party in New York (1919–20) and social worker in Los Angeles (1932–58). John Collier (1874–1947) was interested in various socialist, radical, liberal, and anarchist causes, and was a life-long student of philosophy, theology, mysticism, and psychic phenomena. Subjects include American Labor Party, Garland Farm and Garland Fund (1920–

26), Helicon Home Colony (1906–07), IWW, Tom Mooney defense, Sacco and Vanzetti Case, Upton Sinclair's gubernatorial campaigns (1934, 1936), Single-Tax and co-operative colonies, the Workers Defense League, and psychic phenomena. Correspondents include Roger Baldwin, V.F. Calverton, Malcolm Cowley, Floyd Dell, Theodore Dreiser, Max Eastman, Elizabeth Gurley Flynn, Emma Goldman, Sidney Hook, Frieda Lawrence, Sinclair Lewis, Mabel Dodge Luhan, Scott Nearing, Margaret Sanger, Max Schactman, Upton Sinclair, Norman Thomas, and Louis Untermeyer.
11 1/2 linear feet; 1 oversize folder.

COLLINS, VIRGIL. *Papers, 1948–72.*
Mr. Collins has served in several offices with UAW Local 216, which services the General Motors Assembly Division plant in South Gate, California. Proceedings, correspondence, and other items cover such areas as intra-local disputes and the 1972 election of the director for UAW Region 6.
1/2 linear foot.

CONNOR, EDWARD. *Papers, 1935–66.*
Correspondence, reports, press releases, notes, drafts of articles, minutes, resolutions, newspaper clippings, election campaign publicity, scrapbooks, photographs, and memorabilia collected by Mr. Connor, who served with the Public Works Administration in Gary, Indiana, and Chicago, Illinois (1935–43). He was executive director of the Detroit Citizens Housing and Planning Council (1943–48), a member of the Detroit Common Council (1948–66), chairman of the Wayne County Board of Supervisors (1954–58), and a Detroit Recorder's Court judge (1966–1967). Mr. Connor also served as secretary of the Southeastern Michigan Community Research Corporation (1958–63), director of the National Association of County Officials (1959), and as a member of the National Advisory Committee on Urban Health Affairs (1963–64). Subjects include Works Progress Administration; Adult and Workers Education (1935–43); civic, housing, health, transportation, and industrial problems of the Detroit metropolitan area (1943–66); urban health problems in Russia (1964); election campaigns for Detroit Council (1948–65); primary election for governor of Michigan (1960); Recorder's Court election (1966). Correspondents include Al Barbour, Edward Carey, Jerome P. Cavanagh, Eleanor Coit, John Dingell, Philip Hart, Nicholas Hood, Frank Kelly, John F. Kennedy, Robert Kennedy, Frank Martel, Mel Ravitz, Roy Reuther, Dorothy K. Roosevelt, and G. Mennen Williams.
33 linear feet.

CONYERS, JOHN, SR. *Papers, 1937–45.*
Organizing leaflets, articles, invitations, newspaper clippings, and pamphlets collected by Mr. Conyers, who served as chief steward of UAW Chrysler Local 7 and as a UAW International representative for the Chicago area and for Region 1, Michigan.
13 items.

COPELAND, WILLIAM. *Papers, 1965–70.*
Mr. Copeland has represented the Twenty-seventh District (the Downriver area of Wayne County) in the Michigan House of Representatives since 1952. He serves as chairman of the House Appropriations Committee and is also a member of the Capital Outlay, Administrative Rules, Air Pollution, and Water Pollution committees. His papers cover tuition grants, Michigan Osteopathic College, pollution problems, water resources planning, mental health, state budgets, and Democratic politics. Correspondents include William Broomfield, Jerome Cavanagh, John Dingell, Philip Hart, and Walter Reuther.
17 linear feet.

COTE, EDWARD. *Papers, 1937–48.*
Clippings, memoranda, and UAW Education Department booklets collected by Mr. Cote. Subjects include job classification and wage rates at Ternstedt Division of General Motors (1937).
3 items.

COUSENS, LEON. *Papers, 1932–37.*
Correspondence, course outlines, notes, and bibliographies relating to Brookwood Labor College (1934–35); reports, clippings, pamphlets, and miscellaneous materials dealing with labor and social reform in the 1930s; speeches, reports, writings, notes, and travel itineraries of Mr. Cousens, who was a member of the Detroit Local of the Socialist Party and state organizer for the Socialist Party of New Mexico. Subjects include labor education, New Deal labor boards, New Mexico Farm Holiday Association, Socialist parties of America, New Mexico, and Detroit, and the thirty-hour week.
1 linear foot.

COUSER, JAMES G. *Papers, 1946–49.*
Minutes of the Executive Board of UAW Ford Local 600 for 1948; pamphlets and circulars on the United Electrical Workers; circulars and lists of the Wayne County CIO; copies of *In Fact* for 1948 and 1949. Of

Collections

particular interest is the "Report to the UAW International Executive Board by the Convention Investigating Committee" of March 1947, which deals with racketeer influence within unions. Mr. Couser was a member of that committee. An oral history interview with Mr. Couser is available.
1/2 linear foot.

CRAIG, ROGER. *Papers 1965–70.*
Papers and correspondence of State Senator Roger Craig, who represented Michigan's Tenth District from 1964 to 1970. Abortion, civil liberties, open housing, Democratic Party and politics, higher education, firearms control, implied consent, pollution, welfare, the grape boycott, migrant labor, the Viet Nam war, and various other matters of legislative concern are discussed. Correspondents include Jerome Cavanagh, Cesar Chavez, John Conyers, Zoltan Ferency, James Hare, Philip Hart, Delores Huerta, Hubert Humphrey, Sander Levin, Emil Mazey, Eugene McCarthy, William Milliken, Walter Reuther, George Romney, Neil Staebler, and John Swainson. *24 linear feet.*

CRANEFIELD, HAROLD. *Papers, 1932–66*
A labor attorney, Mr. Cranefield served with the NLRB in Chicago and Detroit, as an investigator for the La Follette Committee, and as an associate counsel with the UAW. Correspondence, briefs, clippings, and speeches cover such topics as unionizing the J.I. Case Company in Racine, Wisconsin (1934–35); work of the NLRB in the auto industry; industrial espionage; and the shootings of Victor and Walter Reuther. Correspondents are Heber Blankenhorn, J. Edgar Hoover, Wayne Morse, Joseph Rauh, Walter Reuther, Helen Sobell, and Robert Wohlforth.
2 linear feet.

CROCKETT, GEORGE. *Papers, 1944–46.*
Correspondence, clippings, and notes collected by Judge Crockett, a former general counsel of the UAW and director of its Fair Employment Practices Committee (1944–46). He was elected to Recorder's Court of Detroit in 1966. Subjects include fair employment practices, discrimination, and the United Negro College Fund. Among the correspondents are Victor Reuther and Walter Reuther. An oral history interview with Judge Crockett is available.
1/2 linear foot.

CROSBY, JACK. *Papers, 1899–1932.*
Correspondence (1932) and a souvenir Labor Day program published by the Central Trades and Labor Assembly of Syracuse, New York, and

vicinity (1899), collected by Mr. Crosby. The history and officers of labor organizations affiliated with the Syracuse Central Trades and Labor Assembly in 1899 are discussed.
3 items.

CURRENT, GLOSTER. *Papers, 1942–44.*
Minutes, reports, and financial statements of the Executive Board of the Detroit Branch of the NAACP. The bulk of the material is concerned with events in 1943.
35 items.

CUSHMAN, EDWARD. *Papers, 1943–69.*
Presently executive vice-president at Wayne State University, Mr. Cushman has had a long career in labor relations. He held positions with the Michigan Unemployment Compensation Commission, the War Manpower Commission, the Retraining and Reemployment Administration, the Department of Labor, and the International Labor Organization. During the late 1940s and early 1950s, he served as arbitrator in disputes involving fifty-three major companies and fifteen international unions. From 1954 to 1966, he was director of Industrial Relations and vice-president of American Motors. In 1966, Mr. Cushman returned to Wayne State University as executive vice-president; he had earlier been a professor of Public Administration and an organizer and director of the Institute of Industrial Relations. He has also been active in many community organizations including Citizens for Michigan, the Detroit and Michigan Council of Churches, the Detroit Commission on Community Relations, and the Citizens' Committee for Equal Opportunity. Correspondence, reports, and minutes cover Mr. Cushman's work in the above areas. Among the correspondents are Richard Austin, John Cardinal Dearden, Arthur Goldberg, John Hannah, Hubert Humphrey, William Milliken, Walter Reuther, George Romney, and Brendan Sexton.
24 1/2 linear feet; [4 linear feet unprocessed].

CUTTLE, RAYMOND. *Papers, 1942–67.*
Minutes of UAW Local 137, Greenville, Michigan, collected by Mr. Cuttle, who served as president of this local, which represented employees of the Gibson Refrigerator Company.
1/2 linear foot [unprocessed].

D'AGOSTINO, JOHN J. *Papers, 1950–63.*
In his work as an International representative of the UAW, Mr. D'Agostino was instrumental in launching the Kent-Montcalm-Ottawa Regional Rec-

reation Program in the early 1950s. In 1954 he assisted Detroit recreation employees in their fight for higher wages. The papers in this collection reflect these facets of his work and the union's recreation program as a whole. Correspondents are Edward Connor, Kenneth House, Karl Lindgren, Olga Madar, Louis Miriani, Del A. Smith, and Eugene J. Van Antwerp.
1/2 linear foot.

DANN, SOL A. *Papers, 1933–70.*
Correspondence, legal documents, clippings, articles, literary manuscripts, briefs and position papers, notes and memoranda, and miscellaneous documents relating primarily to stockholders' suits, including appeals and related collateral suits against the Chrysler Corporation and several of its officers and directors (1960–66). Other general subject areas in the collection relate to the stockholders' suit against Studebaker-Packard Corporation (1950–58); the Jack Ruby trial and appeal (1964–68); the Middle East, Israel, and Zionism (1946–70); general information files on subjects such as anti-communism, socialized law, Freud and psychiatry, the Detroit Public Bank failure; and general correspondence (1933–70). The materials were collected by Mr. Dann, a prominent attorney and activist for civil rights, freedom movements, and the protection of stockholders' rights. A native Detroiter, Mr. Dann practiced law in Detroit from 1924 until his retirement in 1970. Correspondents include Melvin Belli, John Conyers, Jr., Moshe Dayan, Harry Golden, Martha Griffiths, Hubert Humphrey, William Kunstler, Ernest Mazey, and Louis Wolfson.
28 linear feet [unprocessed].

DAY, WALTER. *Papers, 1933–62.*
In 1950, Walter Day was elected president of UMW Local 12229, District 50. The union dispute with Berry Brothers, jurisdiction disputes at Acme Paint Company, chemical workers' unions, and some union reports and minutes are discussed. One of Mr. Day's correspondents was Homer Ferguson.
1 1/2 linear feet.

DESHETLER, IRWIN L. *Papers, 1933–68.*
Correspondence, minutes, reports, financial statements, press releases, news bulletins, testimony, agreements, rate classifications, petitions, legal briefs, membership lists, notes, newspaper clippings, leaflets, published material, photographs, and memorabilia collected by Mr. DeShetler as secretary-treasurer of the AFL Flat Glass Workers Union (1935–37),

Personal Papers

president of the CIO Federation of Glass, Ceramic and Sand Workers (1939-42), CIO regional director of southern California (1946-52), CIO assistant regional director of Region 13 (1952–55), AFL-CIO assistant regional director of Region 22 (1955–68) and National AFL-CIO coordinator for Farm Workers (1968–71). Various activities of the Glass Workers Union, such as Executive Board meetings (1935–39), factional disputes and organizing, political campaigns in California (1953–68), jurisdictional raiding, AFL-CIO merger, the United Farm Workers Organizing Committee, and welfare programs in Los Angeles (1947–56) are covered. Correspondents include John Brophy, Edmund G. Brown, Helen Gahagan Douglas, Clair Engle, Daniel Flanagan, Paul Fuller, Adolph Germer, Arthur Goldberg, Allan Haywood, Sidney Hillman, William Kircher, William Knowland, Thomas Kuchel, John L. Lewis, John Livingston, George Meany, James P. Mitchell, Philip Murray, Jacob Potofsky, Walter Reuther, Victor Riesel, John Riffe, James Roosevelt, William Schnitzler, August Scholle, and Benjamin Spock.
52 linear feet; [8 linear feet unprocessed].

DiGAETANO, NICK. *Papers, 1929–52.*
Reports, UAW materials, posters, and memorabilia form the bulk of Mr. DiGaetano's papers. There are copies of *Economic Outlook* (1943–50); *Ammunition* (political supplements from the 1940s); *Labor's Monthly Survey* (1947–52); and *Striking Workers Local 7 Bulletins* and circulars from the Chrysler plants (1948–50). Mr. DiGaetano, a long-time union man, has also donated chief stewards' grievance books; various agreements and constitutions; a collection of union pins, neckties, and hats; and a few IWW leaflets and programs. An oral history interview with Mr. DiGaetano is available.
2 1/2 linear feet.

DIGGS, CHARLES C. *Papers, 1951–64 (predominantly 1954–64).*
Correspondence, reports, press releases, notes, newspaper clippings, campaign publicity, and published material collected by Mr. Diggs, who was a Michigan state senator (1951–54), and has served as a U.S. congressman from Detroit since 1954. Subjects include civil rights and discrimination cases, veterans' legislation, and political campaigns. Correspondents include Ralph Abernathy, Everett Dirksen, Paul Douglas, Philip Hart, Estes Kefauver, Herbert Lehman, George McGovern, Wayne Morse, Adam Clayton Powell, Sam Rayburn, Victor Reuther, Walter Reuther, Thomas Dodd, Hubert Humphrey, Lyndon B. Johnson, Kenneth Keating, John F. Kennedy, and G. Mennen Williams.
34 1/2 linear feet.

Collections

DILLON, FRANCIS J. *Papers, 1934–43.*
This collection consists of correspondence and official communications of the United Automobile Workers of America and AFL Federal Labor Unions in the auto industry (1934–36); minutes and proceedings of the National Council of the Federal Labor Unions (1934–35); press releases (1934–41); newsletters (1934); and six scrapbooks of newspaper clippings and memorabilia (1934–43). The materials were collected by Mr. Dillon, who was assigned in 1933 as an AFL organizer in the automobile industry in the Detroit, Flint, and Pontiac, Michigan, area. From 1935 to 1936, he served as the first president of the United Automobile Workers of America, appointed to the post by AFL President William Green. Subjects include AFL and CIO organizing and jurisdictional disputes; Automobile Labor Board; communism within unions; company unions; labor legislation; origins of the UAW; and UAW internal conflicts. Major correspondents are William Collins, William Green, Ed Hall, Otto Kleinert, Michael Manning, Homer Martin, John Pickering, Fred Pieper, Thomas Ramsay, Herbert Richardson, Franklin D. Roosevelt, Robert F. Wagner, and Forrest Woods.
1 linear foot; 6 scrapbooks.

DINGWELL, ROBERT. *Papers, 1950–68 (predominantly, 1964–66).*
Correspondence, notes, reports, press releases, minutes, publicity material, lists, and newspaper clippings, from Mr. Dingwell, who served with the Michigan AFL-CIO Council and as a member of the Michigan House of Representatives (1964–66). Subjects include campaigns for state representative (1954–68); industrial safety legislation (1964–65); labor problems (1964–65); and workmen's compensation legislation (1964–65). Correspondents include Basil W. Brown, Frank Kelley, August Scholle, Donald Stevens, Robert Vander Laan, Nat Weinberg, G. Mennen Williams, and Myra Wolfgang.
3 linear feet.

DITZEL, JOSEPH. *Papers, 1937.*
Newspaper clippings from Detroit and Toledo papers concerning labor activities and the Flint Sit-Down Strike, collected by Mr. Ditzel, a participant in that strike and an organizer in the Toledo area. An oral history interview with Mr. Ditzel is available.
106 items.

DOOLEY, ROY E. *Papers, 1951–67.*
Mr. Dooley was active in the Air Line Pilots Association and served as chairman of the Organizational Structure Study Committee (1956), and of

the Military Affairs Committee (1958). The collection consists of correspondence, listings, reports, resolutions, and statements covering air safety; air crash investigations; the fourteenth, fifteenth and eighteenth biennial conventions; elections; negotiations; hearings; national defense; the Organizational Structure Study Committee (1955–60); pilots' pensions; training and retirement programs; and strikes. David L. Behncke, Leverett Edwards, George Meany, and Clarence N. Sayen are among the correspondents.
1 1/2 linear feet.

DORY, EDWARD. *Papers, 1902–15.*
This collection contains the constitution and rules of order of the Iron Molders Union (July 24, 1902), and two dues books of the International Molders Union No. 31 (1905; 1915).
3 items.

DUFTY, WILLIAM. *Papers, 1941–43.*
During the late 1930s and early 1940s, Mr. Dufty served in various public relations positions with the UAW. He was public relations director for the UAW's drive to organize the aircraft industry; most of the correspondence and clippings in the collection concern this phase of his career.
30 items.

DUKES, OFIELD. *Papers, 1964–69.*
These files pertain to Mr. Dukes's service as assistant director of information for the President's Commission on Equal Employment Opportunity, and as a member of Vice-President Hubert Humphrey's staff (1964-68). The collection is particularly interesting on the role of blacks in the 1968 presidential campaign. Other subjects covered are the Youth Opportunity Program, Black Cabinet, and the black press and media. Correspondents include Edward Brooke, Ramsey Clark, Louis Martin, Jackie Robinson, Strom Thurmond, and Jesse Unruh.
1 linear foot.

DUNAYEVSKAYA, RAYA. *Papers, 1941–69.*
Correspondence, drafts of articles, clippings, published items, and other materials pertaining to "Marxist-Humanism." Included are files on the State-Capitalist Theory, the Johnson-Forest Tendency, Correspondence committees, and News and Letters committees. In addition to numerous pamphlets and articles, Miss Dunayevskaya is the author of *Marxism and Freedom,* which first posited the American and humanist roots of Marx-

Collections

ism. It also contained the first English translation of Marx's humanist essays and of Lenin's discussion of Hegel's *Science and Logic*.
2 1/2 linear feet.

DUNN, ROBERT W. *Papers, 1920-38.*
Research notes and other material gathered for Dunn's *Labor and Automobiles* (New York: 1929). The collection also includes a few clippings pertaining to subsequent events in the labor movement in the auto industry, such as the Battle of the Overpass, sit-down strikes of 1937, and earlier 1930s auto strikes.
1 linear foot.

EDELMAN, JOHN. *Papers, 1926-63 (predominantly 1943-63).*
Minutes of Textile Workers Union of America Executive Board (1953 – 57), memoranda and reports on activities of TWUA Washington Office (1947-59), correspondence, congressional and legal testimony, newspaper clippings, press releases, speeches, monographs, pamphlets, and congressional hearings collected by Mr. Edelman, who served as director of the TWUA Washington Office from 1943 to 1963. Subjects include anti-union activity of southern textile companies; agricultural labor; civil rights and civil liberties; cost of living; cooperatives; credit unions; equal pay and equal rights for women; health insurance; housing; labor education; minimum wage; public power and conservation; Social Security; Taft-Hartley Act; textile industry legislation; unemployment and workers compensation. Correspondents include Chester Bowles, James Carey, Joseph Clark, Thomas Dodd, Arthur Goldberg, Lyndon Johnson, Estes Kefauver, John F. Kennedy, John McCormack, Patrick McNamara, George Meany, Wayne Morse, Philip Murray, Robert Oliver, Drew Pearson, Mrs. Gifford Pinchot, William Pollock, William Proxmire, Leverett Saltonstall, Paul Sifton, John Sparkman, Stuart Udall, and George L. P. Weaver.
44 1/2 linear feet; [6 linear feet unprocessed].

EDWARDS, GEORGE. *Papers, 1865-1958.*
Family papers and correspondence, notes, clippings, financial papers, journals, diaries, legal papers, memorabilia, and miscellaneous printed materials collected by Mr. Edwards, a Dallas attorney and former teacher. Mr. Edwards established the first free night school in Dallas (1901), helped pass the first child labor law in Texas, campaigned for many social reforms, and was twice a candidate for governor of Texas on the Socialist Party ticket (1906 and 1932). Subjects include Detroit and Dallas politics, Yale-Towne Strike, Fort Smith arrest and trial, and Socialist Party conven-

tions (1936 and 1938). Major correspondents are George C. Edwards, Jr., Maury Maverick, Sam Rayburn, and Norman Thomas.
16 1/2 linear feet.

EDWARDS, GEORGE Jr. *Papers, 1921–63.*
Correspondence, notes, reports, speeches, memoranda, miscellaneous family papers, clippings, campaign materials, court opinions and case notes, and memorabilia. The materials were collected by Judge Edwards, who served as director of the UAW Welfare Department (1938–39); secretary, Detroit Housing Commission (1940–41); member of Detroit Common Council (1941–49); probate judge, Wayne County Juvenile Court (1951–54); Circuit Court judge, Wayne County (1954–56); Michigan Supreme Court justice (1956–61); Detroit Police commissioner (1962–63); and judge, U.S. 6th Circuit Court of Appeals (1963 to the present). Subjects include Yale-Towne Strike (1937); UAW Convention (1937); Committee on Militarism in Education; criminal law and penal codes; urban housing; League for Industrial Democracy; juvenile delinquency; Detroit and Michigan politics; Child Welfare League; and Michigan Welfare League. Correspondents include Eugene F. Black, James B. Carey, John R. Dethmers, John Dingell, Felix Frankfurter, Philip Hart, Hubert Humphrey, Thomas M. Kavanagh, Harry F. Kelly, Blair Moody, Walter Reuther, Murray D. Van Wagoner, John Voelker, and G. Mennen Williams.
49 linear feet.

EDWARDS, NEAL. *Papers, 1941–59.*
Correspondence, minutes, speeches, reports, radio scripts, agreements, rate classification records, demands, election publicity, memo books, newspaper clippings, convention proceedings, minutes of Bargaining Committee meetings of UAW Local 662, and published material collected by Mr. Edwards, who served as president of UAW-GM Local 662, Anderson, Indiana (1944–47), president of the Indiana CIO Council (1947–54), and as a UAW International representative for the Indiana region. Subjects include Local 662 (1941–47) and Indiana CIO conventions (1941–54). Among correspondents are John Brophy, Allan S. Haywood, Leon Henderson, Roy Reuther, Walter Reuther, and Harry S. Truman.
5 1/2 linear feet.

ELDER, ARTHUR. *Papers, 1921–53.*
Correspondence, reports, and a scrapbook relating to the AFL and education (1941–49); correspondence, reports, resolutions, studies, hearings, and clippings pertaining to the American Federation of Teachers (1934–

Collections

50), the Michigan Federation of Teachers (1937—49), and the Detroit Federation of Teachers (1921—51); correspondence relating to the organizing efforts of the MFT (1939—53), and to the dismissal of teachers in the Flint area (1937—49); correspondence, clippings, and documents pertaining to the Workers Education Service (1936—48); and miscellaneous office files. The materials were collected by Mr. Elder, who served as vice-president of the AFT, president and secretary of the Michigan and Detroit federations, and director of the University of Michigan Workers Education Service. Subjects include AFT and the communist issue, history of the AFT, federal aid to education, New York City teachers' dispute, tenure for teachers, and the termination of the U of M Workers Education Service. Among the correspondents are Frank Martel, Frank Murphy, Mark Starr, Norman Thomas, and Arthur Vandenberg.
10 linear feet.

ELDON, JOHN. *Papers, 1883—1959 (predominantly 1938—40).*
Knights of Labor traveling card (1883) and scrapbooks of newspaper clippings (1938—40 and 1947—59) collected by Mr. Eldon, who was a member of Briggs Local 212 of Detroit and was on the staff of the Education Department of the UAW International (1937—40), and International representative to the Canadian Region of the UAW (1940—59). Subjects include UAW organizing and negotiations; NLRB and labor legislation; Briggs and Chrysler strikes (1939), Father Coughlin; Homer Martin and UAW factionalism; Canadian labor (1947—49); and Nikita Khrushchev's visit to the U.S. (1959). An oral history interview with Mr. Eldon is available.
1 linear foot.

ELLICKSON, KATHERINE POLLAK. *Papers, 1929—69.*
Labor economist Katherine Ellickson, formerly assistant director of Social Security and associate director of research for the AFL-CIO, deposited a wide variety of papers in the Archives, reflecting the range of her long career in the labor movement. She donated the earliest original records of the CIO; her handwritten minutes and notes, and material on Brookwood Labor College (Katonah, New York); West Virginia miners and Southern textile workers in the Depression years; company unions; and early credit unions. There is much material on the Guaranteed Annual Wage, unemployment insurance, Social Security, Medicare legislation, Equal Employment Opportunity Commission records, and women's rights. Correspondents include John Brophy, James B. Carey, Wibur Cohen, Philip Murray,

A. J. Muste, Esther Peterson, David Saposs, and many other prominent labor personalities.
51 1/2 linear feet.

ELLIS, E.K. *Papers, 1921.*
Stock certificate from the Federation of Labor Temple Company preserved by Mr. Ellis. Money raised by the sale of this stock was to be used in the construction of a labor temple in Detroit.
1 item.

ELLMANN, ERWIN. *Papers, 1969–71.*
Mr. Ellmann, an attorney and general counsel for the Michigan Chapter of the American Civil Liberties Union, has long been active in the work of the ACLU. Correspondence, minutes, and reports cover such topics as women's rights, Viet Nam, abolition of the draft law, and amnesty for draft resisters.
4 linear feet.

FLESCH, FRITZ. *Papers, 1949–52.*
Press releases, newsletters, constitution, and publicity material collected by Mr. Flesch, who was active in UAW Kaiser-Frazer Local 142 and Detroit West Side Local 174. The collection is concerned with labor education and principally Jewish reactions to racial policies in South African elections.
26 items.

FRANCIS, EVERETT. *Papers, 1933–43.*
Correspondence, minutes, resolutions, grievance records, and newspaper clippings collected by Mr. Francis, who served as recording secretary of Federal Labor Union 18331 (1933–35), and as president of UAW Fisher Body Local 581, Flint, Michigan. Major topics are National Recovery Act, settlement of 1934 GM Strike, Automobile Labor Board, FLU 18331, Local 581, and American Federation of Labor. Correspondents include James Couzens, William Green, Hugh Johnson, Frank Martel, and Arthur Vandenberg. An oral history interview with Mr. Francis is available.
1/2 linear foot.

FRANKENSTEEN, RICHARD T. *Papers, 1930–64.*
Mr. Frankensteen served as president of the Automotive Industrial Workers Association, one of the independent attempts to organize the auto industry in the early 1930s. He later served as president of UAW Dodge

Local 3. In 1937 he was elected a vice-president of the UAW-CIO. Correspondence, speeches, clippings, and other materials on the Ryan Aeronautical Company Strike (1944); the National War Labor Board; North American Strike (1941); factionalism within the UAW-CIO; activities of the UAW during the late 1930s and early 1940s, and Mr. Frankensteen's unsuccessful campaign for mayor of Detroit in 1945 are included. Among the correspondents are George Addes, Adolph Germer, Homer Martin, and Philip Murray. An oral history interview with Mr. Frankensteen is available.
5 1/2 linear feet; 3 scrapbooks.

FULLER, ALEX. *Papers, 1949–55.*
Correspondence collected by Mr. Fuller during his tenure as vice-president of the Wayne County CIO Council. Among subjects treated are FEPC legislation and the Michigan Coordinating Council for Fair Employment Practices. Principal correspondent is William Oliver.
15 items.

GALLAGHER, DANIEL M. *Papers, 1937–47.*
The papers of Mr. Gallagher, former UAW International representative and member of the National War Labor Board, include correspondence and papers dealing with NWLB disputes and cases; Homer Martin; workman's compensation; copper and logging cases in northern Michigan and Minnesota; wage stabilization; Detroit West Side Local 174 and labor organizing in the 1930s. Among the correspondents are George Addes, Melvin Bishop, Michael Manning, Louis Miriani, and R. J. Thomas. An oral history interview with Mr. Gallagher is available.
4 linear feet.

GANLEY, NAT. *Papers, 1934–69.*
Mr. Ganley was active in the early days of the UAW and served in several capacities with Local 155, the tool and die local for the east side of Detroit. He was also active in the Communist Party of Michigan, serving for a time as editor of the *Michigan Worker.* In 1954 he was convicted of violation of the Smith Act, but his conviction was later overruled by higher courts. Transcripts, clippings, briefs, notes, and other items cover these phases of Mr. Ganley's life. Other topics include the no strike pledge, postwar reconversion, political action, civil rights, automation, and the guaranteed annual wage. The collection also has about 60 books and over

600 pamphlets on socialism and communism. An oral history interview with Mr. Ganley is available.
18 1/2 linear feet.

GANLEY—WELLMAN. *Papers, 1945–53.*
Nat Ganley and Saul Wellman both served in several capacities with the Communist Party, particularly in Michigan. These files, consisting of notes, leaflets, speeches, and other material, relate to party conventions, committee meetings, the Smith Act and other anti-left legislation, the House Un-American Activities Committee, the Taft-Hartley Act, and political activities.
4 linear feet.

GARMAN, PHILLIPS. *Papers, 1907–47.*
Correspondence, newspaper clippings, newsletters, pamphlets, statements, speeches, and press releases collected by Mr. Garman, who worked with the AFL in 1934 and with the Department of Economics at the University of Chicago in 1936. From 1938–41 he served as director of research for the International Printing Pressmens and Assistants Union; in 1941 he became the chief of the War Production Board's industrial relations section; in June, 1945 he was appointed co-chairman of the Wage Stabilization Board. Presently, Mr. Garman is teaching at the University of Illinois. Subjects include AFL's organizing of unskilled industrial workers (1934–36), especially auto workers; auto strikes; Auto Labor Board (1934–35); company unions (1934–36); CIO formation (1934–35); union factionalism, (1934–35); GM Strike (1945–46); government administration of coal mines (1946); Labor-Management Conference called by President Truman (November, 1945); and unionization of newspaper and publishing industries (1907–42). Major correspondents are William Collins, Francis Dillon, and Leo Wolman.
3 linear feet.

GARST, DELMOND. *Papers, 1934–71 (predominantly 1938–60).*
An early officer of UAW Local 25, General Motors (St. Louis), Mr. Garst later served on the UAW International Executive Board (1936–42). In 1942 he was named regional director for the CIO for Eastern Missouri and Southern Illinois. Mr. Garst is now a regional director for AFL-CIO Region 15, with offices in St. Louis. Correspondence, photographs, scrapbooks, and minutes of the UAW General Executive Board (1936–42); War Labor Board; Missouri plan for vocational education (1940); and Metropolitan Committee on Preparedness for National Defense are included in the

Collections

collection. Topics include community involvement of a labor leader, organizing campaigns, and wage stabilization. Among the correspondents is Wayne Morse.
6 linear feet.

GENSKE, WILLIAM. *Papers, 1940—60.*
Correspondence, minutes, reports, pamphlets, and miscellaneous printed materials collected by Mr. Genske, who served as financial secretary and chairman of the Shop Committee, UAW Local 581 at the Fisher Body plant, Flint, Michigan. He was also a participant in the 1937 Flint sit-downs. Material covers UAW factionalism (1940—60). Correspondents are David Dubinsky, Richard Gosser, John L. Lewis, Ralph Marlatt, Blair Moody, Philip Murray, Jacob Potofsky, Victor Reuther, and G. Mennen Williams. An oral history interview with Mr. Genske is available.
1 linear foot.

GILMORE, HORACE W. *Papers, 1957—69.*
Correspondence, pamphlets, booklets, newsletters, clippings, reports, and notes collected by Mr. Gilmore, who has been active politically in Detroit and Michigan. In 1952 he was special assistant U.S. attorney for the Office of Price Stabilization under Philip A. Hart; from 1955-56 he served as deputy attorney general of Michigan; from 1956 to the present he has been a Wayne County Circuit Court judge; from 1965-68 he helped to organize the Detroit Citizens Committee for Equal Opportunity and led its Police-Community Subcommittee; since 1965, he has chaired the Michigan Committee for Revision of the Criminal Code; he has been a member of the Michigan Commission on Law Enforcement and Criminal Justice since 1967, leading the commission's Task Force on Administration of Justice. In 1969 he was elected a member of the Judicial Tenure Commission; from 1970—71 he headed the Round Table of Jews and Christians Institute of Police-Community Relations; and from 1971—72 he was president of NARCO (Narcotics Addiction Rehabilitation Coordinating Organization). Subjects include police training, criminal code revision, community relations, the 1967 Detroit riot and civil rights, and Detroit community projects. Major correspondents are Richard Emrich, Mildred Jeffrey, and G. Mennen Williams.
8 linear feet.

GOLDMANN, WILLIAM. *Papers, 1937—59.*
Clippings, correspondence, briefs, affidavits, notes, contracts, minutes, and leaflets collected by Mr. Goldmann, who was president (1940—46) and

member of the Shop Bargaining Committee of UAW Local 230 (Chrysler-Los Angeles), and International representative to UAW Region 6 (Western U.S.). Subjects include the conspiracy trial of Local 230 members (1939); LaFollette Senate Committee Hearings; and Local 230 Strike (1957). George Addes is a principal correspondent.
1/2 linear foot.

GOSSER, RICHARD T. *Papers, 1953–57.*
Correspondence and other official files of Mr. Gosser during most of his years as vice-president of the UAW (1947–64). UAW Executive Board meetings, union regional business, competitive shops problems, apprenticeships, skilled trades, and the various large industrial departments are discussed. Correspondents include most well-known union leaders.
24 linear feet.

GOULD, JEAN. *Papers, 1907–22.*
The collection, consisting of twelve letters and part of another from Eugene Debs to C.W. Ervin, publisher and editor of the New York *Daily Call,* covers the period 1907–19 (one letter is from 1922), and deals with Debs's reaction to events in Philadelphia, his comments on the socialist factional struggles of the time, and various other problems of the socialist movement.
13 items.

GROVES, PHYLLIS. *Papers, 1968–69.*
Letters to Mrs. Groves from her mother, Bertha Cannon McNeill, concerning coal miners in southern Illinois from about 1918 through the Depression.
10 items.

HAESSLER, CARL. *Papers, 1916–61.*
Pamphlets, leaflets, handbills, clippings, articles, radio scripts, and union newspapers collected by Mr. Haessler, who was managing editor of the Federated Press (1922–56); editor of the *United Auto Worker* and many local union papers; a member of the public relations staff of the United Rubber Workers; and was responsible for public relations and publicity for various groups and organizations. Subjects include civil rights, social reform, socialism in Britain, labor legislation, the NLRB, and federal court hearings on the Ford Motor Company (1930–41). An oral history interview with Mr. Haessler is available.
2 linear feet; [8 linear feet unprocessed].

Collections

HALBEISEN, ROBERT. *Papers, 1937–56.*
Correspondence, reports, newsletters, lists, union handbills, expense statements, proposed agreements, songs, anti-union propaganda, minutes, and newspaper clippings collected by Mr. Halbeisen, who served as a representative of the Textile Workers Organizing Committee in Eaton Rapids, Michigan, during 1937. He was also vice-president of Local 191, United Public Workers (1946–48), and president of Local 52, Government Workers Organizing Committee (1950–56). Organization of textile workers in Michigan (1937); Horner Woolen Mills Strike (1937); United Public Workers factionalism (1947–48); Schoolcraft Gardens Cooperative Housing Project (1949–50); reorganization of Michigan government (1951); collective bargaining demands to Michigan Civil Service Commission (1952–53); and welfare reform (1953) are covered. Correspondents include Irwin DeShetler, George Edwards, John Hannah, Barney Hopkins, Milton Murray, Jacob Potofsky, Frank Rosenblum, and H. Schneid.
3 1/2 linear feet.

HALL, COVINGTON. [Undated.]
A xerox copy of a draft of Hall's 238-page manuscript, *Labor Struggles in the Deep South.* The original of this draft is held by the Tulane University Library. In his work, Mr. Hall discusses the labor movement in New Orleans and the Louisiana-Texas area from the pre-Civil War period to the outbreak of World War I. The role of the IWW is particularly well covered.
1 volume.

HAMILTON, HENRY. *Papers, 1966–68.*
Mr. Hamilton served as a vice-president of the Michigan Federation of Teachers and was active in the Warren, Michigan, local. Most of the collection deals with the conflict between the Detroit Federation of Teachers and locals representing surrounding communities.
57 items.

HAUGHTON, RONALD W. *Papers, 1946–69.*
Clippings, briefs, transcripts, correspondence, notes, and other materials gathered by Mr. Haughton, who served with the U.S. Social Security Board (1941–42); the Detroit and National War Labor boards (1942–45); the U.S. Conciliation Service (1946–47); the Institute of Industrial Relations at the University of California at Berkeley (1947–50); as impartial arbitrator for the UAW and Ford Motor Company (1950–55); and, with Wayne State University, first as director of the Institute of Labor and Industrial Relations and later as vice-president for Urban Affairs. Mr. Haughton also

Personal Papers

served as co-arbitrator for the dispute involving the DiGiorgio Corporation, the National Farm Workers Association, the Agricultural Workers Organizing Committee, and the Teamsters Union. He was appointed president of the Board of Mediation for Community Disputes in New York City in 1970, and also mediated teachers' strikes in Detroit. Subjects discussed include campus disputes, collective bargaining for farm workers, and strikes by public employees. Among the correspondents are Edmund Brown, Cesar Chavez, Robert DeGiorgio, William Kirchner, and George Murphy.
2 1/2 linear feet.

HENRICKSON, MERLE. *Papers, 1945–50.*
Correspondence, constitutions, newsletters, reports, and financial statements collected by Mr. Henrickson, who served as president of United Public Workers Local 275 of Detroit in the late 1940s. His papers include material on the United Public Workers, United Office and Professional Workers, Michigan CIO Council, CIO Political Action Committee, and the Greater Detroit and Wayne County Industrial Union councils. Subjects include merger of the State, County and Municipal Workers and the Federal Workers of America into the United Public Workers of America (April 23, 1946). Important correspondents are Barney Hopkins, Emil Mazey, and August Scholle.
2 linear feet.

HENRY, AARON. *Papers, 1965–69.*
Mr. Henry, a native of Mississippi, has been a leader in the struggle for civil rights in that state for many years. He has been president of the Clarksdale NAACP, state president of the Mississippi NAACP, chairman of the Mississippi Voter Registration and Education Project, president of the Mississippi Freedom Democratic Party and also its delegate to the 1964 Democratic National Convention. The collection deals with nearly every phase of the civil rights battle, Democratic politics, and various government poverty programs in Mississippi. Letters of Ramsey Clark, John Doar, Everett Dirksen, Charles Evers, Orville Freeman, Hubert Humphrey, Edward Kennedy, Robert Kennedy, Martin Luther King, James Meredith, Sargent Shriver, and nearly every leader in the field of civil rights appear in this collection.
6 1/2 linear feet.

HENSON, FRANK. *Papers, 1950–63.*
Correspondence regarding a joint labor-management library project, in-

Collections

cluding items on Henson's work in establishing a labor library in Marion, Ohio.
22 items.

HERRICK, MARY J. *Papers, 1932–66.*
Long active with the AFT, Miss Herrick was its director of research and vice-president, and served in other positions with that union. During the 1930s, she was particularly concerned with organizing teachers in the Chicago area. The communist controversy in the AFT, federal aid to education, Workers Defense League, and teacher salaries and problems are covered. Correspondents include Irvin Kuenzli, Jerome Davis, Selma Borchardt, Charles Cogen, Estes Kefauver, and Paul Douglas.
2 linear feet.

HILL, CHARLES A. *Papers, 1942–51.*
Reverend Charles A. Hill served as a Baptist minister in Detroit for many years. Interested in labor unions, he encouraged his parishioners (men employed by the Ford Motor Company) to unionize and, in 1941, to strike. He was active in the Sojourner Truth Housing Project in 1942, and was a member of the committee investigating the 1943 race riot in Detroit. These activities are covered in the papers, as is the Lantz Hill interrogation. Correspondents include Prentiss Brown, John Dingell, William R. Hood, Thurgood Marshall, and C. F. Palmer. An oral history interview with Mr. Hill is available.
1/2 linear foot.

HOFFMAN, BERNARD G. *Papers, 1940–60.*
Mr. Hoffman served as union steward at the Briggs Manufacturing Company and Chrysler Corporation in the 1940s and 1950s. He also served as secretary of the Briggs Joint Apprenticeship Committee and secretary-treasurer of the National Skilled Trades Council, UAW-CIO. The bulk of the collection comprises minutes, pamphlets, newsletters, agreements, and personal notes relating to his union activities. Of particular value are Mr. Hoffman's daily notes on plant activities written during his years at Briggs and Chrysler.
3 linear feet [unprocessed].

HOFFMAN, CLAUDE. *Papers, 1934–52.*
Correspondence, clippings, minutes, briefs, and other items from the files of Mr. Hoffman who participated in the sit-down strike in Anderson, Indiana, and served as director of education for UAW Local 663 at the Guide Lamp plant in Anderson. Subjects include factionalism in UAW

Personal Papers

Local 146 in Anderson, the Employees Association at Guide Lamp, the LaFollette Committee, and efforts by the Metal Polishers International Union Local 52 to represent workers in the Guide Lamp plant. Among the correspondents are William Green and Victor Reuther.
16 items.

HUGHES, ARTHUR. *Papers, 1943–60.*
Mr. Hughes has served as the assistant director of the UAW Chrysler Department since 1948. He was previously president of Amalgamated Local 140 in Warren, Michigan. The collection of correspondence, minutes, reports, and clippings cover principally the Chrysler negotiations from 1945 to 1960. An oral history interview with Mr. Hughes is available.
3 linear feet; [3 linear feet unprocessed].

HUMPHREYS, WILLIAM. *Papers, 1944–53.*
Correspondence, minutes, briefs, agreements, clippings, and miscellaneous materials collected by Mr. Humphreys, who served as president of UAW Local 539 at the Campbell Wyant and Cannon Foundry, Muskegon, Michigan; vice-president of Michigan CIO Council; UAW International representative; and assistant director of the UAW Foundry Wage and Hour Council. Subjects include NLRB election at Albion Malleable Iron Company (1952–53), and National War Labor Board (1945). An oral history interview with Mr. Humphreys is available.
1/2 linear foot.

HUTTON, CARROLL. *Papers, 1948–63.*
After holding several offices in UAW Local 662, Delco-Remy in Anderson, Indiana, Mr. Hutton became director of education for UAW Region 3 from 1949–57. In 1957 he became assistant director of education for the International Union of the UAW. From 1960–69 he was director of the Education Department. After a short period as administrative assistant to UAW Vice-president Pat Greathouse, Mr. Hutton was again named director of education. The summer schools of Region 3 are covered by these papers. Correspondence, reports, notes, and other items illustrate the establishment and operation of summer schools in one region of the UAW. Other files of Mr. Hutton may be found in the UAW Education Department collection.
4 linear feet.

HYSHKA, NICHOLAS. *Papers, 1944–66.*
Correspondence, reports, minutes, speeches, notes, press releases, outlines of conferences, union cards, awards, memorabilia, and photographs col-

Collections

lected by Mr. Hyshka, who served as director of education for UAW locals 80 and 544 in Detroit. Labor education is the major subject of the collection. Correspondents include Mildred Jeffrey, Olga Madar, Norman Matthews, and Brendan Sexton.
1 linear foot.

IGNASIAK, ANDREW J. *Papers, 1946–66.*
Correspondence, clippings, leaflets, and flyers collected by Mr. Ignasiak, who served as president of the Gear and Axle Division of UAW Ford Local 600 (1943–47), and International representative with the Auditing Department of the UAW (1949–66). The Local 600 election of 1946 is discussed.
34 items; [1 linear foot unprocessed].

JABLONOWER, JOSEPH. *Papers, 1936–68.*
The trial of three New York teachers (1917–18) led Mr. Jablonower to join other teachers founding the New York City Teachers Union, associated with the New York Teachers Guild and the American Federation of Teachers. Correspondence, speeches, clippings, and other materials on his appointment to the Board of Examiners (1938); the Brooklyn Society for Ethical Culture; his aid to European refugees, and his receiving the Linville Award (1959) are included. Among the correspondents are Charles Cogen, Jacob Greenberg, and Arthur Levitt.
2 linear feet [unprocessed].

JACOBS, SAMUEL, *Papers 1939–57.*
Correspondence, reports, press releases, newspaper clippings, pamphlets, and monographs collected by Mr. Jacobs, who served as a research consultant with the UAW Washington Office (1951–55), and as instructor for the University of Michigan's labor education program. Subjects treated are agriculture (1939–57); automation (1954–58); labor education (1956); offshore oil legislation (1953); and wage and price increases (1946–50). Correspondents include S. I. Hayakawa and Roy Reuther.
2 1/2 linear feet.

JEFFREY, NEWMAN. *Papers, 1944–72.*
Correspondence, reports, minutes, and clippings collected by Mr. Jeffrey, who served as a labor representative to various government agencies during World War II; chief of Labor Relations Section, U.S. Military Government in Berlin (1945); UAW International representative (1946–59); and director, U.S. AID Mission to Uganda (1960s). Labor's role in the occupation of Germany (1944–45); Michigan Governor's Advisory Committee on

executive reorganization (1958–59); and U.S. AID Mission to Uganda (1963) are covered in the collection.
1/2 linear foot.

JOHNSON, EDGAR G. *Papers, 1943–66.*
Correspondence, minutes, news clippings, and printed materials concerning Mr. Johnson's service as co-chairman of the Michigan Study Commission on Migratory Labor, 1951–55. The main focus of the collection is the problem of migratory labor, particularly in Michigan.
2 1/2 linear feet.

KADISH, JACK. *Papers, 1942–65.*
Mr. Kadish served in various capacities for the Amalgamated Clothing Workers of America and was national representative in the Detroit area. Correspondence, clippings, transcripts, and speeches document the attempts to organize clothing workers in Detroit.
1/2 linear foot.

KANTER, ROBERT. *Papers, 1939–41.*
Newspaper articles collected by Mr. Kanter, who served as Strike Committee chairman during the Cadillac sit-downs (1937), worked for Detroit West Side Local 174 (1937–39), and fought in the Battle of the Overpass. The Homer Martin split (1939) and the Ford Strike (1941) are covered. An oral history interview with Mr. Kanter is available.
6 items.

KENNY, CASPER P. *Papers, 1944–48.*
Casper P. Kenny was a member of the Michigan House of Representatives from 1943 to 1948 and was active in CIO affairs. The items donated concern the Gabriel Retirement plan, the no-strike pledge, and interrogations by the House Un-American Activities Committee.
3 items.

KINGERY, BRUCE. *Papers, 1956–65.*
Correspondence and clippings collected by Mr. Kingery, who served in several offices for UAW Local 292 of the Kokomo, Indiana, Delco-Remy plant. In the late 1950s, he was also a member of the Kokomo city council. These papers pertain mainly to his political activities. Correspondents include senators Vance Hartke and Birch Bayh.
1/2 linear foot; 1 scrapbook [2 linear feet unprocessed].

Collections

KIRCHER, WILLIAM. *Papers, 1966–73.*
Mr. Kircher went to work in a defense plant in Cincinnati in 1941 and helped organize UAW Local 647. Subsequently, he held a number of staff positions with the UAW until 1955, when he became assistant director of organization of the AFL-CIO. From 1956 to 1964, Mr. Kircher served as assistant director of Region IX of the AFL-CIO. After returning to his former position as assistant director of organization (1964–65), Kircher was appointed to succeed John W. Livingston as director of organization of the AFL-CIO, a position he held until his resignation in 1973. The collection relates to Kircher's activities with and on behalf of the United Farm Workers Organizing Committee. Included is information on the Agricultural Workers Organizing Committee; contract negotiations; grape and lettuce boycotts; national and state legislation regarding farm labor organizing and the importation of foreign farm workers; organizations supporting and opposing UFWOC; Teamsters organizing farm workers; UFWOC finances; and representational elections.
18 linear feet [unprocessed].

KIRK, L. K. *Papers, 1933.*
The Year 1933 at Standard Accident is a diary by L. K. Kirk, an agent with that insurance company. He recalls the Depression Bank Holiday, the Michigan bank situation, and the value of securities at that time.
1 volume.

KITZMAN, HARVEY. *Papers, 1937–60.*
Three scrapbooks containing clippings, correspondence, union rally and meeting notices, strike bulletins, flyers, newspaper ads and photographs, and pamphlets concerning the activities of UAW Local 180 (J. I. Case Company in Racine, Wisconsin). Mr. Kitzman began work at the J. I. Case Company in 1929, and in 1937 was elected president of the newly created local, a position he held until 1947. In that year, he set up the Agricultural Implement Department of the UAW, serving as director of the department until July, 1949 when he was elected director of UAW Region 10. Mr. Kitzman was also elected for two terms, the first in 1939, as president of the Wisconsin CIO. The scrapbooks deal with Local 180's contract negotiation activities, particularly the strikes of 1938, 1945–47, and 1960. An oral history interview with Mr. Kitzman is available.
1 reel of microfilm.

KLASEY, THOMAS. *Memorabilia, 1937.*
Memorabilia of the Flint sit-down strikes of 1937 collected by Mr.

Klasey, a worker in Chevrolet Plant 9 who participated in the strike. An oral history interview with Mr. Klasey is available.
1/2 linear foot.

KOBE, MATT. *Papers, 1914–21.*
Miscellaneous labor material including a 1914 copy of the *Miners Bulletin,* concerned with the copper strike in Calumet, Michigan. Also in the collection is a 1921 letter from Frank X. Martel, head of the Detroit Federation of Labor, discussing a proposal to move Labor Day from September to May.
8 items.

KOCH, LUCIEN. *Papers, 1938–65 (predominantly 1948–52)*
Mr. Koch, after serving as director of Commonwealth College from 1923 to 1935, held several positions in the labor movement and in government agencies concerned with labor. Among these were the NRA, the Department of Labor, the Industrial Union of Marine and Shipbuilding Workers of America, the NWLB, and the Air Line Pilots Association. Transcripts, affidavits, correspondence, and clippings cover such topics as Commonwealth College, activities of the Marine and Shipbuilders Union, Koch's federal security hearing, and ALPA negotiations. Correspondents include Roger Baldwin, James Carey, Edith Christenson, John Edelman, and Hilda Smith.
4 linear feet.

KOWALSKI, JOSEPH J. *Papers, 1958–67.*
As speaker of the Michigan House of Representatives, Mr. Kowalski was responsible for the introduction of many liberal reforms in the state. Formerly a lawyer and union organizer, he directed UAW educational programs before his election as a representative of the Nineteenth district, Wayne County, in 1948. Papers and correspondence of 1965 and 1966 are most comprehensive on caucus and committee meetings, minutes and proposals, court reorganization, Democratic Party affairs, civil rights, civil service, liquor control, insurance problems, prisons and jails, reapportionment, aid to parochial schools, and many other state problems. Correspondents include Richard Austin, John D. Dingell, Gerald R. Ford, Zoltan Ferency, Martha Griffiths, James Hare, Philip Hart, Clarence Hilberry, William R. Keast, James H. Lincoln, Walter Reuther, George Romney, August Scholle, Neil Staebler, Robert E. Waldron, and G. Mennen Williams.
14 linear feet; [8 linear feet unprocessed].

Collections

KRAUS, HENRY. *Papers, 1926—40.*
Mr. Kraus was the first editor of the UAW's newspaper *The United Auto Worker* (later changed to *Solidarity*). He was active in the early attempts by the UAW (first under the AFL and later under the CIO) to organize the auto industry. Files for the late 1920s and early 1930s cover the attempts by groups, including the Auto Workers Union of the Trade Union Unity League, to organize auto workers, and discuss such events as the Murray Body Strike (1929); the Ford Hunger March (1932); and the Briggs Strike (1933). There are many items pertaining to the AFL's work in the auto industry, such as material on the threatened auto strike of March 1934, the Toledo Auto-Lite and Chevrolet strikes of 1934 and 1935, and conferences and conventions of the UAW-AFL. The collection also has many files of the AFL's Detroit office for the early 1930s. Particularly well covered are the activities of the UAW-CIO from 1936 to 1940, including the South Bend Convention, the sit-downs, early attempts to organize Ford, and the Homer Martin controversy (resulting in the split of 1939). Correspondents include nearly every major AFL, CIO, and UAW leader of the period. Among them are John Brophy, F. J. Dillon, Adolph Germer, William Green, John L. Lewis, Homer Martin, Rose Pesotta, Walter Reuther, and R. J. Thomas. Public figures include Charles Coughlin and Frank Murphy.
8 linear feet.

LaBITA, FRANK. *Papers, 1953—55.*
Correspondence, reports, and publicity material collected by Mr. LaBita while serving as UAW International representative for Region 1 in the Detroit area. Subjects include Allegheny-Ludlum Steel Corporation organizing activity (1953); dues reports of unions serviced by Mr. LaBita; organizing publicity; and political activity. Walter Reuther is the principal correspondent.
1/2 linear foot.

LANE, GARLAND. *Papers, 1964—67.*
Correspondence, clippings, appointment books, Michigan Senate and House Bills, reports, and miscellaneous printed materials collected by Mr. Lane, who has been a member of the Appropriations Committee of the Michigan State Senate since his election from Genessee County in 1948, serving as chairman from 1964 to 1967. Correspondents include Richard H. Austin, Zoltan Ferency, James Hare, Philip Hart, Hubert Humphrey, Frank J. Kelly, Edward Kennedy, T. John Lesinski, and George Romney.
2 linear feet.

LATCHEM, E. W. *Papers, 1915—59.*
Mr. Latchem, a member of the IWW since 1912, helped to organize the Agricultural Workers Organization, chartered in 1915. His papers include minutes of the Harvest Workers Conference (1915); leaflets; and material on the IWW General Administration controversy (1924).
12 items.

LAUCK, W. JETT. *Papers, 1937—38 and 1946.*
The collection consists of correspondence between W. Jett Lauck, an advisor to John L. Lewis during the 1930s, and Jay Lovestone. Among the topics discussed are United Auto Workers' factionalism; developments in the labor movement, especially the CIO and John L. Lewis; the CIO and the Communist Party; the late 1930s UAW Strikes at GM; the International Ladies Garment Workers Union under David Dubinsky.
65 items.

LEVIN, SANDER. *Papers, 1962—70.*
Correspondence, clippings, reports, press releases, campaign literature, lists, and speeches collected by Mr. Levin, an attorney who has been an important figure in Michigan Democratic politics. He served on the Oakland County Board of Supervisors for three terms; in 1961, he was chairman of the Berkley Democratic Club; from 1962—64, he was the Democratic chairman of Oakland County. From 1965—70, Mr. Levin was a State senator, serving from 1965—66 as chairman of the Senate Labor Committee, vice-chairman of the Senate Education Committee; and chairman of the Special Subcommittee to study Special Education Programs for Handicapped Children. From 1969—70, he was the senate minority leader. Outside the Senate, he was elected Democratic state chairman (1967—68), and in 1969, was associate chairman of the Political Reform Commission. In 1970, Mr. Levin won the Democratic nomination for governor but lost the November election to William Milliken. Subjects include Oakland County, Michigan, and U.S. Democratic politics; his elections to the Michigan Senate; the 1968 Presidential election; the 1970 Michigan gubernatorial race; education; labor; and taxation. Major correspondents are John Bruff, Paul Donahue, William Haber, Philip A. Hart, Mildred Jeffrey, James McNeely, and Neil Staebler.
105 linear feet [unprocessed].

LEVINSON, EDWARD. *Papers, 1910—45.*
Correspondence, clippings, research notes, and other materials collected by Mr. Levinson, author of *I Break Strikes,* and *Labor on the March,* and direc-

Collections

tor of publicity for the UAW. Subjects include strikebreaking in the National Maritime Union, early unions in the auto industry, the Black Legion, the Socialist Party, war production, and wage and price ceilings. Among the correspondents are Victor Reuther, Franklin Roosevelt, and R. J. Thomas.
4 linear feet.

LEWIS, JOHN L. *Papers, 1879–1969.*
This microfilm edition of the John L. Lewis papers contains his more personal files. Materials included are: correspondence (1907–69), with letters from Amelia Earhart, Dwight D. Eisenhower, J. W. Harriman, and Lyndon B. Johnson; speech drafts and printed copies of speeches and reports (1912–57); UMWA financial and travel notebooks (1911–26), which show Lewis's rise from AFL representative to UMWA president; photos of Lewis's public and private life (1901–06, 1960–69); genealogical information (1879, 1906–43); household records (1913–61); and magazine and newspaper clippings. *4 reels.*

LINVILLE, HENRY RICHARDSON. *Papers, 1912–41.*
Mr. Linville was elected president of the Teachers Union of New York City, and served as president and executive director until 1935. From 1931–34, he served as president of the American Federation of Teachers. The following year he was elected president of the New York Teachers Guild. Mr. Linville was also editor of the *American Teacher.* Correspondence, radio addresses, speeches, clippings, and printed material pertaining to the AFT, the Teachers Union of New York City, and the period of 1921–41 are covered. The collection also contains drafts of chapters for his book, *Communists at Work.*
1 linear foot.

LIVINGSTON, JOHN W. *Papers, 1947–55.*
The papers and correspondence of Mr. Livingston cover his earlier years as vice-president of the UAW until he was named director of organization for the AFL-CIO in 1955. The UAW Aircraft and Agricultural Implement departments, CIO organization drives, wage contract data in the aircraft industry, and the IAM and its relations with the UAW-CIO are discussed. Correspondents include Ben Blackwood, A.B. Connole, Roy L. Reuther, Walter Reuther, and Stuart Symington.
7 1/2 linear feet.

LOHR, FRANK. *Papers, 1939–61.*
Correspondence, hearings, trial examiner's reports, dues assessment cards, leaflets, and newspaper clippings collected by Mr. Lohr, who served as a

member of UAW Local 325 at the Ford plant in St. Louis, Missouri. The collection has information on an NLRB hearing (1938); NLRB case: Ford Motor Company vs. Local 325 (1940); and the drive to unionize Ford.
12 items.

LUTZAI, GEORGE. *Papers, 1919-65.*
An early member of the IWW and of UAW Local 314 in Detroit, Mr. Lutzai has long been interested in various radical movements. This collection contains materials on communism and anti-religious movements, as well as humanist, rationalist, and free-thought pamphlets from the 1950s and 1960s. Other periodicals and newspapers have items on the American Civil Liberties Union, Father Charles Coughlin's Social Justice Movement, and problems of senior citizens.
7 linear feet.

LYONS, GEORGE. *Papers, 1940-64.*
Correspondence, minutes, clippings, and educational material collected by Mr. Lyons during his work in Detroit West Side UAW Local 174, including his tenure as chairman of the local's Education Committee. Among the subjects covered are the General Motors Strike of 1946, labor education, and UAW factionalism. Correspondents include Walter Reuther, R. J. Thomas, and G. Mennen Williams.
1 linear foot.

McCLENDON, JAMES J. *Papers, 1932-69.*
An active member of the Detroit Branch, NAACP, Dr. McClendon was president of that group from 1938 to 1945. These papers include material on the fight against racial discrimination in Detroit and the armed services, and on fund-raising problems. The collection also has papers relating to Dr. and Mrs. William A. Thompson of Detroit, who were active supporters of the NAACP. Correspondents include Edward J. Jeffries, Jr., Henry L. Stimson, and Arthur H. Vandenberg.
1/2 linear foot.

McGHEE, ROSA. *Papers, 1966-67.*
Correspondence, reports, and other items collected by Miss McGhee, a vice-president of the AFT.
1/2 linear foot [unprocessed].

McGRAW, ASHBY C. *Papers, 1935-65.*
Mr. McGraw was active in the unionization of the California aircraft industry from the early 1930s to the 1960s. Correspondence, press re-

Collections

leases, handbills, notes, proceedings, and other materials document his career as an International Association of Machinists Local Lodge president, district secretary-treasurer, business representative, and Grand Lodge representative. He also served on advisory committees to the Institutes of Industrial Relations at the University of California and UCLA. Among the topics considered are UAW-IAM jurisdictional disputes, IAM elections, organizing and factionalism, and the Harvard Trade Union Program. Correspondents include Roy M. Brown, Eric Peterson, A. J. Hayes, and Wyndham Mortimer.
12 1/2 linear feet.

MACMILLAN, HUGH. *Papers, 1917–21.*
Correspondence of Samuel Gompers and Duncan McLeod on the Buffalo Hotel Owners and Waiters controversy, and description of a Canadian tour.
5 items.

McNAMARA, PATRICK VINCENT. *Papers, 1942–66.*
Patrick V. McNamara was Detroit Area rent director for the OPA (1942–45), member of the Detroit Common Council (1946–47), member of the Detroit Board of Education (1949–55), and a U.S. senator (1954–66). With the exception of scrapbooks dating from 1942, the collection covers his term of office in the Senate while serving on the Public Works Committee (chairman, 1963–66), Labor and Public Welfare Committee, Select Committee on Improper Activities in the Labor or Management Field, Select Subcommittee on Poverty, and the Special Committee on Aging. The collection is arranged into the following series: Subject Files, Legislative, Campaign, Public Information, Post Office, Detroit Office, Case Files, Memorabilia, and Library. Subjects covered include problems of the aged, civil rights, atomic energy, education, taxes, public works, federal highway acts, and labor. Correspondents include all major political figures of the period and many labor leaders.
427 1/2 linear feet, 500 volumes.

McNETT, THOMAS. *Papers, 1936–70.*
Diaries, job descriptions, grievances, minutes, correspondence, and clippings collected by Mr. McNett, who served in many capacities for the International Association of Machinists in the aerospace industry. The offices held by Mr. McNett included recording secretary of Lodge 751 at Boeing (early 1930s), Grand Lodge representative to organize the southern California aircraft industry (1938), president of Lodge 727 at Lockheed (1944–46), business representative for Lodge 727 (1947–57), Grand Lodge representative (1957–61), and president, Lodge 727 (1961–69).

Organizing of the southern California aircraft industry, wage stabilization in World War II, relations between the IAM and the UAW in the aerospace industry, and negotiations at Boeing and Lockheed are covered. Major correspondents are Roy Brown, A. J. Hayes, Roy Reuther, A. O. Wharton.
12 linear feet.

MADAR, OLGA. *Papers, 1966.*
In 1966 Miss Madar became the first woman to be elected to the UAW's International Executive Board, and in 1970 was elected a vice-president of the union. These papers are concerned with her election to the Executive Board and the activities of the UAW Recreation Department.
64 items.

MANNING, MICHAEL. *Papers, 1934–42.*
Correspondence, minutes, reports, and leaflets collected by Mr. Manning, who served in many offices during the 1930s period of auto unionization. He was a member of the AFL's National Council of Automotive Federal Labor Unions (1934–35), president of AFL Federal Labor Union 18677 at the Kelsey-Hayes plant in Detroit (1934–35), member of the General Executive Board of the UAW (1935), and president of UAW West Side Local 174 in Detroit. The Automobile Labor Board, National Industrial Conference Board (1934), and NLRB elections at Kelsey-Hayes are covered. Correspondents include Francis Dillon, William Green, Frank Morrison, Louis Rabaut, and Arthur Vandenberg. An oral history interview with Mr. Manning is available.
1/2 linear foot.

MARQUART, FRANK. *Papers, 1936–50.*
Reports, leaflets, articles, minutes, press releases, transcripts of radio addresses, pamphlets, and clippings collected by Mr. Marquart, who was education director for UAW Dodge Local 3 (1937–41), UAW Ford Local 600 (1941–44), UAW Briggs Local 212 (1944–58), and also served on the University of Michigan Workers' Education Service (1948). Subjects include the Briggs Strike (1933), and UAW factionalism (1939). An oral history interview with Mr. Marquart is available.
2 linear feet.

MARRIN, BLAINE. *Papers, 1947–55.*
Correspondence, reports, and other items collected by Mr. Marrin, former president of UAW Local 157 (the UAW's tool and die local for western Detroit), and a trustee of the International Union.
24 items.

MARSH, DONALD C. *Papers, 1940s–1960s.*
Correspondence, reports, minutes, and other items covering a wide variety of interests, such as the AFT at Wayne State University, the International Institute of Detroit, Detroit's Coordinating Council on Human Relations, fair employment practices, and fair housing. As a professor of sociology at Wayne State University, Mr. Marsh was active in the AFT and in various organizations concerned with urban problems.
6 1/2 linear feet [unprocessed].

MARTIN, HOMER. *Papers, 1934–41.*
Homer Martin was the first elected president of the UAW-CIO (1936–39), and in 1939 became the leader of the UAW-AFL, later retiring from the auto union to do other organizing work. The collection includes correspondence, clippings, speeches, and articles which indicate the power struggle in the union; union dissension over the AFL and CIO; politics (internal and external); left-wing factions; and the AIWA. Correspondents include George Addes, John Brophy, William Collins, Father Charles Coughlin, Richard Frankensteen, Ed Hall, and Wyndham Mortimer.
2 linear feet; 1 volume.

MASTERS, FRED. *Papers, 1942–45.*
Mr. Masters served in several offices for UAW Local 50, which represented the workers at the Willow Run Bomber Plant during World War II. The collection contains mostly materials from Local 50 elections.
33 items.

MATTHEWS, NORMAN. *Papers, 1942–55.*
Correspondence, reports, memoranda, minutes, agreements, and pamphlets from various UAW departments, primarily Social Security, Skilled Trades, Ford, and General Motors (1942–55); UAW International officers (1942–47); Regional Directors (1942–50); Local Unions (1945–53); and miscellaneous files on labor mediation, wage rates, pensions, NLRB, FEPC, and the Wage Stabilization Board (1942–55). The materials were collected by Mr. Matthews, who was UAW vice-president (1955–62), director of the UAW's Chrysler, American Motors, Budd, Eaton, Bendix, and Office and Professional departments; member of the Executive Board's Education Committee (chairman), and Policy and Skilled Trades committees. Correspondents include George Addes, Ken Bannon, George W. Crockett, Jr., Richard Frankensteen, Richard Gosser, John Livingston, Emil Mazey, Walter Reuther, R. J. Thomas, Leonard Woodcock, and A. L. Zwerdling.
9 1/2 linear feet.

MATTSON, JOSEPH. *Papers, 1947–50.*
In the UAW, Mr. Mattson was local union president, regional director, and director of the union's Agricultural Implement Department. This collection covers mainly the 1947 UAW Agricultural Implement Conference, and the 1950 organizing drives. George Addes, Victor Reuther, Walter Reuther are the principal correspondents. An oral history interview with Mr. Mattson is available.
45 items.

MEZERIK, A. G. AND MARIE HEMPEL. *Scrapbook, 1937–38.*
A. G. Mezerik and his wife Marie Hempel Mezerik worked for the protection of civil rights. Mr. Mezerik was active in the early days of the UAW and also headed the Aid the Spanish Republic and China Aid committees. The scrapbook contains leaflets, newsletters, bulletins, and clippings on the Black Legion Citizens Committee; Aid the Spanish Republic and China Aid committees; and the Conference for the Protection of Civil Rights (1937–38).
1 scrapbook.

MILES, ISADORE. *Papers, 1958–61.*
Correspondence, notes, and bulletins gathered by Mrs. Miles, a past president of AFT Local 6 in Washington, D.C.
15 items.

MILLER, RICHARD. *Papers, 1956–65.*
The collection consists of correspondence, press releases, memoranda, bill summaries, campaign material, legislative newsletters and reports, and fact sheets concerning areas related to Mr. Miller's activities in Michigan government. During the period 1958–59, Miller was secretary to Michigan Attorney General Paul L. Adams, and was involved in the Criminal Division of the Attorney General's office. In 1958, he also worked on the Michigan election campaign. During 1959–60, Miller served as administrative assistant to the late Joseph J. Kowalski, Democratic Floor Leader of the Michigan House of Representatives. In 1961, he worked in the Executive Office of the State of Michigan, serving as a legislative assistant to former Governor John B. Swainson. Subjects include the Civil War Centennial Commission (1959–61); Kierdorf Case (1958); Midwest Democratic State Legislators for Kennedy (1960); Michigan State Elections (1958–60); the 1964 presidential election, including Rural Americans for Johnson-Humphrey. Correspondents include John M. Bailey, Zoltan A. Ferency, Joseph J. Kowalski, Neil Staebler, and G. Mennen Williams.
3 1/2 linear feet.

MILLS, JEWEL. *Papers, 1962–68.*
Reports, minutes, resolutions, correspondence, convention reports and proceedings, and miscellaneous printed materials relating to the American Federation of Teachers, Michigan Federation of Teachers, and various local federations. Mr. Mills was an organizer of the Utica (Michigan) Federation of Teachers (1948), vice-president of the MFT and delegate to the state conventions (1964–67), and delegate to the AFT National Convention in Cleveland, Ohio (1968). Subjects include teacher bargaining and AFT vs. NEA. Mary Ellen Riordan is the major correspondent.
1 linear foot.

MILLS, ROBERT. *Papers, 1953–65.*
Miscellaneous materials gathered by Mr. Mills, who served as president of UAW Local 155 which represents workers in small, independent automotive supply plants on the east side of Detroit. Reports, resolutions, minutes, and clippings cover UAW conventions, UAW Skilled Trades conferences, and Local 155.
1 1/2 linear feet [unprocessed].

MONTGOMERY, DONALD. *Papers, 1943–55.*
Mr. Montgomery was the consumer counsel of the UAW from 1943–52, and director of the UAW Washington office, 1952–57. He was the author of a number of articles on consumer problems and developed the NBC radio program, *Consumer Time.* The collection has many articles and scripts with material on union institutes and educational conferences, subsidies, price controls, rationing and food shortages, consumer advice, and cooperatives. Correspondents include Milton Eisenhower and Walter Reuther.
4 1/2 linear feet.

MORRIS, KEN. *Papers, 1955–59.*
Mr. Morris was elected director for UAW Region 1-B, Southeast Michigan, in 1955 after a career of union activity including the presidency of UAW Briggs Local 212. The papers concern agreements, collective bargaining, and hourly classifications. An oral history interview with Mr. Morris is available.   *1/2 linear foot.*

NORRIS, HAROLD. *Papers, 1940–62.*
Briefs, transcripts, and notes of legal cases; American Civil Liberties Union and personal correspondence; speech drafts, pamphlets, clippings, articles, and books reflecting Mr. Norris's positions as chairman of the ACLU of Metropolitan Detroit, secretary of the National Lawyers Guild, and dele-

gate to the Michigan Constitutional Convention. His papers reveal his interest in civil rights and liberties in Michigan and, specifically, in Detroit.
17 linear feet [unprocessed].

NOWAK, STANLEY. *Papers, 1941–52.*
Mr. Nowak, a former CIO organizer, served as a Michigan state senator from the Twenty-first District (Dearborn–West Detroit) in the middle 1940s. The collection includes papers on political campaigns from 1942 to 1952; correspondence; speeches; a diary; scrapbooks, and other items. Loyalty investigations, the American Slav Congress, and city and state politics are reviewed. An oral history interview with Mr. Nowak is available.
2 1/2 linear feet.

O'CONNOR, HARVEY. *Papers, 1927–67.*
Mr. O'Connor is the author of numerous books, articles, and pamphlets of social and economic interest. He was bureau manager for Federated Press from 1927 to 1930, and from 1935 to 1937 was managing editor of *Peoples Press.* He edited *Ken* from 1937 to 1938, and from 1957 to 1960 was on the editorial advisory board of the *Nation.* Active in several civil liberties organizations, Mr. O'Connor became a controversial figure during the McCarthy investigations. His books include *Mellon's Millions* (1933); *Steel-Dictator* (1935); *The Guggenheims* (1937); *The Astors* (1941); *World Crisis in Oil* (1961); and *Revolution in Seattle* (1963). Subjects of interest in this collection are the steel strikes of the 1930s; coal miners' conditions; Pittsburgh politics of the 1930s; Hull House, Chicago; peace groups of various years; the 1948 Progressive Party; and the world oil industry. Correspondents include Anne and Carl Braden, Clark Foreman, Harold Golden, M. Guggenheim, O. A. Knight, Thomas W. Lamont, E. M. Livingston, Dorothy Marshall, Ernest Mazey, J. P. Morgan, James Roosevelt, and Frank Wilkinson.
48 1/2 linear feet.

OGDEN, WILLIAM. *Papers, 1937.*
Copy of the original Studebaker-UAW contract of May 21, 1937, and a pen used to sign it, preserved by Mr. Ogden, who was president of Local 5, South Bend, Indiana, and one of the signers.
2 items.

OLIVER, WILLIAM. *Papers, 1946–51.*
The first black to serve on the executive board of UAW Ford Local 400 in Highland Park, Michigan, Mr. Oliver joined the staff of the international

union in 1945. Since 1946, he has served as co-director of the union's Fair Practices and Anti-Discrimination Department. Among the topics are activities of the NAACP and the UAW's fight to end discrimination by the American Bowling Congress. Correspondents include Hubert Humphrey, Emil Mazey, and Walter Reuther. An oral history interview with Mr. Oliver is available.
2 linear feet.

ONEKA, JOHN. *Papers, 1937-64.*
John Oneka, a former member of the IWW, was a member of UAW Local 235 at the Chevrolet Gear and Axle Plant. At various times he served as its president, trustee, and Shop Committee chairman. The papers include some of the Shop Committee minutes for 1937-46 and materials on political matters, the IWW, Medicare, and other union concerns. Among the correspondents are John Dingell and Philip Hart.
1 1/2 linear feet; [5 linear feet unprocessed].

O'ROURKE, FRANCIS. *Diary, 1936-37.*
Mr. O'Rourke participated in the sit-down at the Fisher Body Plant 2 in Flint, Michigan. His diary notes cover the entire period of the strike from December 30, 1936 to February 11, 1937. The seventeen pages consist of short entries for each day of that strike.
1 volume.

ORR, CHARLES. *Papers, 1950-67.*
Executive Board minutes, press releases, information bulletins, circulars, documents, and reports relating to the International Confederation of Free Trade Unions (1950-54), correspondence (1967), and miscellaneous articles, pamphlets, and magazines. The materials were collected by Mr. Orr, who was resident officer of the ICFTU (1950-54), acting head of the Adult Education Section of UNESCO (1952), involved in the Workers Education Mission to India and Malay for the International Labor Organization (1960), and professor of economics at the University of Wales and at various universities in the United States. Subjects include Africa; comparative labor movements and economic growth in Africa and other newly developed areas; workers' education; and world and regional education conferences of the ICFTU.
2 1/2 linear feet; [12 linear feet unprocessed].

OVERTON, CARRIE BURTON. *Papers, 1856-1969.*
Mrs. Overton served as a stenographer for the NAACP from 1924-28; executive secretary to Julian Rainey, head of the "Colored Division" of

the National Democratic Committee for 1932, 1936 and 1940; and in secretarial positions with Howard University, Vanguard Press, and the Community Church of New York City. Her papers comprise correspondence, leaflets, reports, notes, and clippings, and cover black voters, employment in the federal government for blacks, activities of the NAACP, Democratic politics, and Mrs. Overton's early years in Wyoming. Correspondents include Mary Bethune, Gloster Current, James Farley, Harold Ickes, Mary White Ovington, Julian Rainey, Algernon Tassin, Lyman Ward, and Walter White.
5 1/2 linear feet.

PAGANO, JOSEPH F. *Papers, 1938—46.*
UAW and Non-Partisan League material; union badges and emblems; 1940 UAW constitution and by-laws; 1940 radio broadcasts of station WJBK; clippings of the early 1940s; and correspondence on the PAC and the WPA. An oral history interview with Mr. Pagano is available.
1/2 linear foot.

PANZNER, JOHN. *Papers, 1922—38.*
Mr. Panzner began his labor career with the IWW in the far west, organizing mine and agricultural workers. For his work with the IWW, he was sentenced to Leavenworth Federal Prison. After his release, he returned to Detroit and was active in the early development of the UAW. Among his papers are materials on labor relations at Chrysler Corporation and Ford Motor Company and some pamphlets on social reform, including a description of the case which resulted in his imprisonment. An oral history interview with Mr. Panzner is available.
1 linear foot.

PARKER, FRANK A. *Papers, 1943—49.*
This collection consists of some letters of Mr. Parker's (of Riverdale on Hudson, New York) and a newsletter he wrote, entitled the *Green Mountaineer.* Various right-wing pamphlets, leaflets, and articles are included.
1 linear foot.

PASKAL, OSCAR. *Papers, 1955—64.*
Minutes, grievance records, Chrysler Corporation notices, agreements, and by-laws collected by Mr. Paskal, who served on the editorial board of the UAW Local 227 newspaper. The papers of this collection pertain to Local 227, which services the Chrysler-Imperial Plant in Detroit. Subjects include House Un-American Activities Committee vs. Lodge 113, International Association of Machinists; production standards complaints; violation of

contract complaints; pension plans; UAW-Chrysler agreement (1961); and ideas for planning education programs on civil rights (1963).
1 1/2 linear feet.

PECK, RAYMOND. *Papers, 1937–68.*
Correspondence, minutes, financial statements, and bulletins collected by Mr. Peck, who served the Ohio Federation of Teachers as president, executive secretary-treasurer, and legislative lobbyist. He was also a vice-president of the American Federation of Teachers. The collection reflects concern with such problems as teacher education and certification, school financing, labor, and politics.   *1 1/2 linear feet.*

PERSON, CARL. *Papers, 1910–20.*
Affidavits, correspondence, notes, proceedings, membership lists, and miscellaneous materials relating to the strike against the Illinois Central and Harriman Lines (1911–15); testimony, notes, proceedings, correspondence, and clippings pertaining to Mr. Person's trial for killing a strikebreaker (1914); correspondence, credentials, and other items pertaining to Mr. Person's expulsion from the International Association of Machinists (1916–20); strike bulletins; photographs; and memorabilia. The materials were collected by Mr. Person, who served as strike secretary during the 1911–15 Illinois Central Strike and as writer, editor, and distributor of the weekly strike bulletins. The U.S. Commission on Industrial Relations and strike-breaking are discussed. Among the correspondents are Elizabeth Gurley Flynn, Carlo Tresca, and Woodrow Wilson.
4 1/2 linear feet; 1 oversize box.

PETITPREN, VINCENT. *Papers, 1964–67.*
Mr. Petitpren served in the Michigan House of Representatives from 1964 to 1970 for the Thirty-seventh District, representing Westland, Wayne, and the surrounding areas. He was chairman of the Colleges and Universities Committee, vice-chairman of the State Affairs Committee, and member of the House Policy and Youth committees. Correspondence, clippings, and reports cover the Michigan Osteopathic College, the Community Health Authority, out-of-state fees at universities, and state financial support for colleges and universities. Correspondents include Jerome Cavanagh, Philip Hart, Patrick McNamara, George Romney, Neil Staebler, and Willard Wirtz.   *8 linear feet.*

PICONKE, JOSEPH. *Papers, 1942–63.*
Correspondence, reports, and newspaper clippings collected by Mr. Piconke, who served as a staff member of the UAW Skilled Trades

Department (1943–55), and as a commissioner with the Federal Mediation and Conciliation Service. Subjects include biographical information and labor-management relations (1963). An oral history interview with Mr. Piconke is available.
1/2 linear foot.

PIEPER, FRED. *Papers, 1936–40.*
Minutes of and reports to the UAW Executive Board collected by Mr. Pieper, who was elected to the first Executive Board of the UAW in 1936, and was a member of the UAW General Motors Local 34, Atlanta, Georgia. He was also a CIO representative in the New Orleans area in 1939. Subjects include shift of the UAW from the AFL to the CIO; early organizing in the automobile industry; the suspension from the UAW of George Addes and Richard Frankensteen; and the Homer Martin dispute.
1/2 linear foot.

POKEMPNER, IRVING. *Papers, 1931–59 (predominantly 1931–46).*
Various socialist, radical, left-wing, and miscellaneous periodicals, newspapers, pamphlets, and leaflets collected by Mr. Pokempner, a Detroit businessman with a life-long interest in movements of social and economic reform. Periodicals include *New Masses* (1931–41), *International Press Correspondence* (1932–37), *American Socialist Monthly* (1936), and *International Review* (1936–38).
5 linear feet.

POLAND, JAMES. *Papers, 1934–56.*
A long-time employee of Bendix Corporation in South Bend, Indiana, Mr. Poland was an early member and officer of Federal Labor Union 18347, which later became UAW Local 9. He was also active in establishing an international union of auto workers. In the late 1930s and early 1940s, he served as an International representative for the UAW in the Indiana-Illinois area. Subjects covered are formation of the UAW, the Homer Martin factional struggle, and early years of Local 9. Correspondents include George Addes, Richard Frankensteen, John L. Lewis, Homer Martin, and Walter Reuther.
1 linear foot; 2 scrapbooks.

POLLOCK, SAM. *Papers, 1958.*
Leaflets, newsletters, press releases, campaign material, radio and television scripts, speeches, and newspapers collected by Mr. Pollock, who served as president of Meat Cutters Local 427, Cleveland, Ohio, and was an active member of the United Organized Labor of Ohio, a committee established

Collections

to oppose the "Right-to-Work" amendment to the Ohio Constitution. This collection pertains to the 1958 right-to-work campaign.
2 linear feet.

RAHOI, PHILIP. *Papers, 1934–68.*
Correspondence, speeches, and clippings relating to Mr. Rahoi's career as a Michigan state representative from Iron Mountain, Michigan (1934–36) and as a state senator (1954–66). Subjects include aid to dependent children and unemployment bills. Major correspondents are George Romney and G. Mennen Williams.
1/2 linear foot.

REUTHER, ROY. *Papers, 1934–70 (predominantly 1951–68).*
Correspondence, newspaper clippings, newspapers, reports, notes, and pamphlets collected by Roy Reuther, who served as national director of the UAW's Citizenship and Legislative Department and administrative assistant to Walter P. Reuther. In addition, he was co-director of the National Voters' Registration Committee in John Kennedy's presidential campaign (1960), director of AFL-CIO's voter registration campaign (1962 and 1964), and appointed member of a President's commission to study state and local laws concerning voter registration and elections (1963). Subjects include UAW's PAC registration drives; AFL-CIO's COPE registration drive and financial affairs; Democratic politics and elections (national, Michigan, and Detroit); congressional debate on civil rights (1958-59); Brookwood Labor College (1936); Wayne County CIO Council; and the Third World Congress of the International Confederation of Free Trade Unions (1953). Major correspondents are Victor Reuther, Walter Reuther, and Paul Sifton. An oral history interview with Mr. Reuther concerning the Flint sit-downs is available.
19 linear feet [unprocessed].

REUTHER, VICTOR. *Papers, 1936–38.*
Correspondence, speeches, and clippings related to organizing auto workers in Indiana and to personnel changes in the UAW, preserved by Mr. Reuther, who was active in organizing auto workers in Detroit and Flint (1936–37). He was UAW director of organization for Indiana (1937); organizer and officer of Detroit West Side Local 174; assistant director of the UAW's War Policy Division; member of the War Manpower Commission and the War Production Board; UAW director of education (1946–51); and currently is director of the UAW Department for International Affairs. Mob violence and vigilantes during the Anderson Strike of 1937; the LaFollette Committee; and UAW factionalism are discussed. Cor-

Personal Papers

respondents include George Addes, Homer Martin, Roy Reuther, Walter Reuther, Maurice Sugar, and Mary Heaton Vorse. Additional files of Mr. Reuther may be found under the appropriate UAW department collections listed in this guide. An oral history interview with Mr. Reuther is also available. *41 items.*

REUTHER, WALTER P. *Papers, 1936–70.*
Mr. Reuther's official files reflect all phases of his career as president, UAW West Side Local 174 (1936); UAW Executive Board member (1936); director, UAW General Motors Department (1939–48); UAW vice-president (1942–46); UAW president (1946–70); president, CIO (1952–55); vice-president, AFL-CIO (1955–67); and president, AFL-CIO Industrial Union Department (1955–67). The records also document Mr. Reuther's work on numerous governmental boards and agencies and many public institutions. The collection contains material on his work in civil rights, politics, poverty programs, medical care, and other social concerns. Other topics include collective bargaining, political action by labor, defense production, government and labor, workers' education, and most other areas of interest to labor. The papers are tentatively arranged into the following series: UAW Local 174; UAW; CIO; AFL-CIO; Industrial Union Department; Other U.S. Labor Unions and Groups; Government--U.S., State, and Local; Political; Calendar; Non-Government Groups; Speeches and Statements; Correspondence; Social Issues; and World War II. The collection contains correspondence with major political leaders in the U.S. and abroad, leaders in the U.S. and foreign labor movements, and with many other public figures.
58 linear feet processed; [500 linear feet unprocessed].

REUTHER, WALTER P.: THE CITIZEN'S CRUSADE AGAINST POVERTY FILES. *Papers, 1964–68.*
The UAW provided the most continuing support for the CCAP, a coalition of persons and organizations concerned with poverty problems. Walter Reuther was chairman. (In 1969, CCAP merged with the Center for Community Change.) The CCAP established a national training program, a Citizens Advocate Center, published poverty information, and was involved in other activities focused on poverty.
3 1/2 linear feet.

RINEHART, BLANCHE. *Papers, 1949–66.*
Correspondence, drafts, and manuscripts relating to Ms. Rinehart's biography of Samuel Gompers. Also included are interviews with Mary Anderson, Elizabeth Christman, and Mary Erb. *1 linear foot.*

ROBBINS, MATILDA. *Papers, 1900–63.*
Manuscripts (articles and stories), clippings, correspondence, personal papers, and photographs collected by Mrs. Robbins, who was a labor organizer and writer for the IWW from 1912 until her death in 1963. Subjects include textile organizing, Lawrence Strike, Paterson Strike, Bill Haywood, and the IWW.
1 linear foot.

ROBERTS, GEORGE. *Papers, 1933–60.*
Mr. Roberts served as an International representative for the United Rubber Workers, mainly in Alabama, Ohio, and California. News releases, bulletins, clippings, and correspondence document the unionization of rubber workers in Gadsden, Alabama, and at Goodyear Tire and Rubber in Akron, Ohio. The beating Roberts suffered in Gadsden because of union activities is discussed. Other subjects covered are the Los Angeles CIO Council, the National Defense Mediation Board, the National War Labor Board, and the War Production Board. Major correspondents are William Collins, William Green, and Homer Martin.
2 linear feet.

ROBINSON, REMUS. *Papers, 1945–66.*
Dr. Robinson was the second black physician to receive advanced residency training in Detroit, and the first elected to the Detroit Board of Education (1955). He was prominent in the struggle for social justice in Detroit's public schools and hospitals. The bulk of the collection comprises correspondence, minutes, and a variety of printed material relating to his years on the Detroit Board of Education. Also included are correspondence and some campaign literature on his unsuccessful bid for a seat on the Board of Education in 1953 and the successful attempt in 1955. Major correspondents are Charles Diggs, Jr., Clarence Hilberry, Frank J. Kelly, and Roy Reuther.
18 linear feet; 1 scrapbook [unprocessed].

ROCKWELL, ROBERT N. *Papers, 1956–66.*
A captain with Northwest Airlines, Mr. Rockwell has held many important positions in the Air Line Pilots Association (ALPA): central safety chairman of NWA; area safety chairman, Region III; alternate of the Accident Investigation Committee; chairman of the Master Executive Council; member of the Local Executive Council I; and chairman of the Pilot Negotiating Committee. Official notices, newsletters, handwritten notes, legal dockets, correspondence, charts, and maps reflect his work on these committees. A large portion of the collection deals with contract negotia-

tions, safety, and accident reports. Major correspondents are J.C. Christie, Robert A. Ebert, A.S. Monroney, Donald W. Nyrop, Charles H. Ruby, Clarence N. Sayen, and Henry Weiss.
12 1/2 linear feet.

ROEDER, CECIL. *Papers, 1937–48.*
Correspondence, agreements, rate classification, grievance records, constitutions, resolutions, minutes, speeches, and published material collected by Cecil Roeder, who served as a committeeman of UAW Delco-Remy Local 662, Anderson, Indiana (late 1930s and early 1940s). Subjects include General Motors Sit-Down Strike at Anderson (1937); UAW factionalism including the Homer Martin controversy; elections and factionalism of Local 662; union shop drives of Local 662; civil rights campaigns; and the General Motors Strike (1945–46). Correspondents include John L. Lewis, Sherman Minton, Philip Murray, Victor Reuther, and Walter Reuther.
2 linear feet.

ROSS, HARRY. *Papers, 1912–62 (predominantly 1928–62).*
Correspondence, minutes, election materials, financial records, press releases and newsletters, songs and poems, newspaper clippings, pamphlets, and published material collected by Mr. Ross, who served as a UAW International representative and staff member of the UAW Fair Practices and Anti-Discrimination Department. Subjects include UAW factionalism (1937–39 and 1946–47); UAW Dodge Local 3; and UAW Ford Local 600. Among the correspondents are George Addes, Charles Coughlin, William Green, Barney Hopkins, John L. Lewis, Frank Martel, Francis Perkins, August Scholle, and R.J. Thomas. An oral history interview with Mr. Ross is available.
5 1/2 linear feet.

ROTH, HERRICK S. *Papers, 1948–70 (predominantly, 1961–70).*
Mr. Roth has served as a vice-president of the American Federation of Teachers and president of the Colorado Labor Council. He has also been president and executive secretary of the Denver Federation of Teachers and executive secretary of the Colorado Federation of Teachers. Other offices included terms as a member of the Colorado House of Representatives and State Senate. Correspondence, minutes, reports, and other items include such topics as the Committee on Political Education, AFT elections and conventions, and anti-teacher union activities. Correspondents include Charles Cogen, Carl Megel, Dave Selden, and Al Shanker.
14 linear feet.

Collections

SANDS, FRANK. *Papers, 1930s–1950s.*
Correspondence, clippings, reports, and similar materials reflecting Mr. Sands's work in several capacities with UAW Local 378, which represents workers of the J.I. Case Plant in Rockford, Illinois.
3 1/2 linear feet [unprocessed].

SAYEN, CLARENCE N. *Papers, 1930–65.*
The papers of Clarence N. "Clancy" Sayen, who was president of the Air Line Pilots Association (1951–62) and of the International Federation of Air Line Pilots (1952–64), include materials such as correspondence, research studies, tape recordings, photos, books, and files on subjects including pension plans; insurance problems of pilots and stewardesses; airline strikes in the U.S. and other countries; flight engineer and "third man" problems; loyalty investigations; David Behncke (former Air Line Pilots Association president); employment agreements; national defense and the executive reserve; national emergency transportation planning; legal problems and arbitration; international aviation meetings; supersonic transport; safety studies; the Air Navigation Committee of ICAO; and other aviation subjects. Correspondents include Leverett Edwards, Nathan Feinsinger, Arthur Goldberg, Edgar F. Kaiser, John F. Kennedy, James Landis, George Meany, Newton Minow, Vassily Mishinkin, A.S. "Mike" Monroney, E.R. Quesada, W.J. Rodgers, Karl Ruppenthal, Sargent Shriver, Eugene C. Thompson, George Weaver, and W. Willard Wirtz.
25 1/2 linear feet; 21 volumes.

SAYER, ALBERT. *Papers, 1936–65.*
Mr. Sayer, a New York teacher, served as vice-president of the New York Teachers Guild in 1950. He left the Guild to help form Local 378 of the CIO, a N.Y. teachers' union which disbanded in 1954. Later Sayer aided in obtaining an AFL-CIO charter for the United Federation of Teachers and served this organization in several capacities. Mr. Sayer also served as member and chairman of the New York State chapter of Americans for Democratic Action. In the summer of 1964, he and his wife Florence went to Mississippi to assist black children in their fight for civil rights. The material appears in the form of correspondence, notes, booklets, proceedings, clippings, press releases, party platforms, reports, and papers. Subjects include the Constitution of the State of New York; growth of unions; formation of the United Federation of Teachers; the educational budget of New York City; civil liberties; and human rights. Correspondents include Robert M. Haig, William Jansen, Arthur Levitt, Frederick C. McLaughlin, Joyce Martin, Milton Murray, George S. Reuther, Jr., Walter Reuther, and Leo Weitz.   *6 linear feet.*

SCHNEIDER, PETER B. *Papers, 1949–55.*
Daily report for January 1955, and a dues book of the International Photo-Engravers Union of North America covering January 1, 1949 to December 31, 1951. The daily report deals with miscellaneous matters, such as pension and insurance problems.
2 items.

SCHOLLE, AUGUST. *Papers, 1937–45 (predominantly 1940–45).*
Correspondence, reports, memoranda, financial and legal papers, speeches and miscellaneous materials relating to various CIO-affiliated unions and their locals in Michigan; and to Michigan CIO conventions; county and local industrial union councils; activities of CIO field representatives; and the general office operation of the Michigan Regional Office of the CIO. The materials were collected by Mr. Scholle, who served as CIO regional director for Michigan (1937–54); and president, Michigan CIO Council (later the Michigan AFL-CIO) from 1940 to 1943, and 1946 to 1971. Correspondents include George Addes, John Brophy, James B. Carey, Adolph Germer, John Gibson, Allan S. Haywood, Philip Murray, Lee Pressman, Walter Reuther, and Murray D. Van Wagoner.
4 1/2 linear feet; [2 linear feet unprocessed].

SCHROEDER, ALLEN. *Papers, 1941–70.*
Allen Schroeder was international representative for the UAW in Ottawa, Ontario, from 1951–60; in 1960, he was sent to St. Catharines, Ontario, to serve in the same capacity. In 1961, he was appointed education director for the Canadian Region, UAW. The collection consists of various publications and printed material; correspondence; Canadian Labour Congress policy statements (1968); and two notebooks on the "Course Outline and Material on International Affairs," Canadian Labour Congress. Various pamphlets deal with topics such as the Canadian UAW, Canadian arbitration (1970), the Canadian UAW Economic conferences (1967, 1970), the Federal Task Force on Housing and Urban Development, and U.S.-Canadian Auto Products Trade Agreement (1969, 1970). Among the correspondents are George Burt, Hugh Peacock, Gloria Ramesbottom, and Dilis Sheehan.   *3 linear feet.*

SEABRON, WILLIAM M. *Papers, 1935–71.*
Correspondence, reports, clippings, resolutions, financial reports, minutes, notes, and speeches collected by Mr. Seabron. He served as the Industrial Relations Secretary for the Minneapolis Urban League from 1944–50; from 1950–56, he was the assistant to the director of the Michigan Fair Employment Practices Commission; from 1962–65, assistant to the direc-

tor of personnel in the Department of Agriculture. Since 1965 he has been a special assistant to the Secretary of Agriculture. Additional activities involve civil rights and the Pioneers Club of Detroit. Subjects include fair employment, civil rights, the Pioneers Club of Detroit, and Detroit politics. Major correspondents are John C. Dancy, Orville L. Freeman, Hubert Humphrey, and G. Mennen Williams.
2 1/2 linear feet.

SHAFFER, LEO D. *Papers, 1941—54.*
Correspondence, clippings, and leaflets collected by Mr. Shaffer, who has served as committeeman, editor, convention delegates, and president of UAW Local 163 (Detroit Diesel Division of General Motors Corporation), and as chairman of the Wayne County Retired Workers Council of the UAW. Subjects include General Motors/Ford contract comparisons, H.L. Hunt, McCarthyism, and the Rosenberg case. An oral history interview with Mr. Shaffer is available.
15 items.

SHEAR, WARREN. *Papers, 1934.*
Letters of recommendation concerning Mr. Shear's activities on various relief programs during the Depression. He also served as an NRA Compliance Board investigator.
14 items.

SHERWOOD, LILLIAN. *Papers, 1943—55.*
Convention proceedings, clippings, and photographs concerning Mrs. Sherwood's service with the Kent County, Michigan, and National Congress of Women's Auxiliaries of the CIO.
2 linear feet.

SHIER, CARL. *Papers 1949—66.*
Correspondence, reports, newspaper clippings, press releases, leaflets, and published material collected by Mr. Shier, who served as a member of the Shop Committee of UAW Local 6, Melrose Park, Illinois (1950); as financial secretary of UAW International Harvester Council; and as a UAW International representative for the Competitive Shop Department (1958). In 1960 he joined the organizing staff of the UAW and was especially active in organizing and servicing local unions in Illinois. Subjects include the agricultural implement industry; the Aurora-Caterpillar organizing campaign (1958); the Barber-Colman organizing campaigns (1955—61); the Paper Converting and Finishing Company; and John W. Hobbs Corporation organizing campaigns (1962—63); the Monroe Auto Equipment Com-

pany (Cuzard, Nebraska) organizing campaign (1961–1963); union relations with the International Harvester Corporation; factional fights of the American Federation of State, County, and Municipal Employees, and of the International Association of Machinists, Lodge 113. Correspondents include Paul H. Douglas, Pat Greathouse, Carroll Hutton, John Livingston, Guy Nunn, Brendan Sexton, and Leonard Woodcock.
2 1/2 linear feet.

SHULTZ, A.G. *Papers, 1937–67.*
Correspondence, articles, election handbills, resolutions, proceedings, and newspaper clippings collected by Mr. Shultz, who served as financial secretary of GM Local 222, Oshawa, Ontario, and participated in the General Motors Strike of 1937. From his position as financial secretary of Local 222, he became one of the original organizers of the credit union movement in Canada. In the 1940s, he was a member of the Reuther Caucus, and president of the Canadian Labour Congress. He is presently a member of the board of directors of the Canadian Credit Union Society. Subjects include the 1937 GM Strike in Oshawa, credit unions, and the UAW Political Action Convention (1943).
1/2 linear foot.

SIFTON, Paul. *Papers, 1943–58.*
Correspondence, clippings, pamphlets, and miscellaneous materials collected by Mr. Sifton, who served as a labor columnist, reporter, and legislative and public relations director for the National Farmers Union (1942–47), and national legislative representative for the UAW (1947–63). Subjects include FEPC, OPA, the Taft-Hartley Act, and the UAW-General Motors dispute (1945).
1/2 linear foot.

SILBER, IRWIN. *Papers, 1886–1968.*
Mr. Silber was an early organizer and worker in Peoples' Songs, Inc. (The activities of the group are described in the Guide's entry, *People's Songs, Inc.*) Mr. Silber's collection consists of a representative portion of the group's files, mostly early labor and social reform songs.
1 1/2 linear feet.

SILVER, PAUL. *Papers, 1946–63.*
Resolutions of UAW conventions of 1946, 1953, 1957, 1959, and 1961; Detroit Community Services Budget Committee recommendations (1958–63). Mr. Silver was a member of the UAW Resolutions Committee, a member of the Budget Committee of the United Community Services

Collections

(1958–63), and was president of UAW Local 351 in Detroit (1946–64). He is currently serving on the Wayne County Board of Supervisors.
2 linear feet; [5 linear feet unprocessed].

SIMONS, BUD. *Papers, 1937–62.*
Correspondence, notebooks, picket cards, songs, newspaper clippings, photographs, and memorabilia collected by Mr. Simons, who was strike chairman of Fisher Body Plant 1 during the Flint sit-down strikes of 1937. The collection deals solely with the strike and contains correspondence with John L. Lewis. An oral history interview with Mr. Simons is available.
1/2 linear foot.

SLINKARD, LUTHER. *Papers, 1930s–1960s.*
Mr. Slinkard was a charter member of UAW Local 25 at the General Motors plant in St. Louis, Missouri. He later joined the staff of UAW Region 5, and, at retirement had worked for ten years for the Wage-Contract section of the UAW's Research Department. Correspondence, reports, clippings, and other documents cover nearly every phase of Mr. Slinkard's career, with emphasis on the latter years.
35 linear feet [unprocessed].

SNYDER, JOSEPH M. *Papers, 1958–72.*
Correspondence, reports, and clippings of Michigan State Representative Joseph Snyder, reflecting various facets of his career as a UAW International representative, as a city official of St. Clair Shores, Michigan, and as a state legislator. Subjects include the Michigan Constitutional Convention, local election campaigns, conservation, union issues, DRUM, mental health, St. Clair Shores politics and government, and other matters of legislative concern. Correspondents include James Hare, Philip Hart, William Milliken, George Romney, John Swainson, Harry S. Truman, G. Mennen Williams, and various legislators.
29 1/2 linear feet.

SPARKS, NEMMY. *Papers, 1942–73.*
Mr. Sparks worked in a Russian chemical factory for two and a half years after World War I. He joined the Communist Party of the United States in 1924, organized seamen in New York, founded the *Marine Workers Voice,* headed the Communist Party in New England, directed the party's work in Pittsburgh during the drive to unionize the steel industry, led the Communist Party in Wisconsin, and served as chairman of the Southern California organization of the party. Upon his retirement, Mr. Sparks assumed the duties of the party's education director in Southern California. Correspon-

dence, manuscripts, speech notes, and course outlines deal mainly with education within the Communist Party but discuss a wide range of topics.
6 linear feet [unprocessed].

SPETH, ROY. *Papers, 1934–36.*
"Report of the Committee on Credentials and Rules of Order" for the UAW Convention of April 27, 1936; the 1936 speech of Homer Martin to executive officers of Region 9; and a copy of the *American Federationist* of July 1934. An oral history interview with Mr. Speth is available.
3 items.

STARR, MARK AND HELEN. *Papers, 1920–56.*
Correspondence, minutes of meetings, pamphlets, course outlines, clippings, and photographs from Mark Starr, education director of the International Ladies Garment Workers Union, instructor and extension director at Brookwood Labor College, and vice-president of the American Federation of Teachers, and his wife, Helen Norton Starr, instructor in labor journalism at Brookwood Labor College. The collection contains the office files of Brookwood Labor College, 1923–37, as well as information on workers' education in the United States, Europe, Africa, and Asia; labor politics; labor songs; communism; and the Liberal Party in the Borough of Queens and New York City.
40 linear feet [unprocessed].

STEELINK, NICOLAAS. *Papers, 1912–53.*
Mr. Steelink was an IWW member convicted of criminal syndicalism in the California trials of 1920. He was a contributor for many years to the IWW paper, *Industrial Worker,* under the pseudonym, Ennaes Ellae. The collection is comprised of personal correspondence, including letters written during his imprisonment in San Quentin, and deals with the IWW, the trials and imprisonment, San Quentin, William Haywood's departure for Russia, civil rights, and economic questions. Correspondents include William T. Brown, Alice Chase, Lily R. Iverson, Fanny Bixby Spencer, Mrs. Fannia Steelink, and Harold H. Story, as well as a number of fellow IWW members, F.A. Blossom, Joseph Ettor, Scott Nearing, Fred Thompson, and others.   *2 linear feet.*

STEPHAN, LIONEL. *Papers, 1931–32.*
The files of one of the early "Key Men" or organizers for the ALPA. Correspondence, notes, and bulletins document Mr. Stephan's activities in the Cincinnati, Ohio, area. Among the correspondents is David Behncke.
1/2 linear foot.

Collections

STODDARD, LYNN P. *Union Cards, 1905 and 1908.*
Collection contains quarterly working card, Journeyman Plasterers Local 246 (1905), and union card for the P.M. and P. Union No. 17 of Michigan (February 1908).
2 items.

STUART, YALE. *Papers, 1945–49.*
Mr. Stuart served as president of the Detroit Joint Board of the United Public Works. His papers document the activities of the United Public Workers-CIO, and the work of Mr. Stuart with City of Detroit employees. Wage increases, collective bargaining for municipal employees, union elections, and loyalty oaths are covered.
1 linear foot.

SUGAR, MAURICE. *Papers, 1960.*
Chief counsel for the UAW from 1937 to 1946, Mr. Sugar's career as a labor lawyer began in 1916. The items in this collection pertain to his song, *Sit Down*, a favorite of the sit-downers of the mid-1930s.
6 items.

TAPPES, SHELTON. *Papers, 1949–68.*
Miscellaneous materials collected by the first chairman of the Foundry Unit of UAW Ford Local 600, of the Rouge plant in Dearborn, Michigan. Mr. Tappes was active in the drive to organize the Ford Motor Company from the campaign's beginnings in 1937 and served Local 600 as recording secretary from 1942–44. The Ford organizing drive and strike of 1949 are discussed. An oral history interview with Mr. Tappes is available.
28 items.

THOMAS, R.J. *Papers, 1936–64.*
Minutes of the UAW Executive Board (1940–47), correspondence, clippings, reports, and memorabilia collected by Mr. Thomas during his tenure as president of the UAW (1939–46), and vice-president (1937–39 and 1946–47). He was assistant to Philip Murray from 1947 to 1956, and to George Meany from 1956 to 1964. Subjects of interest in the collection are UAW factionalism, General Motors Strike (1945–46), Allis Chalmers Strike (1947), the UAW war effort, and the organization of the West Coast aircraft industry. Correspondents include George Addes, John Brophy, Richard Frankensteen, Homer Martin, George Meany, Wyndham Mortimer, Frank Murphy, Victor Reuther, Walter Reuther, August Scholle, Maurice Sugar. An oral history interview with Mr. Thomas is available.
15 linear feet.

Personal Papers

THOMPSON, HUGH. *Papers, 1936-50.*
Mr. Thompson was an organizer for the AFL, the Steel Workers Organizing Committee, and was one of the first paid organizers for the UAW. He was active for the UAW in the Anderson, Indiana, area in early 1937, and directed the strike against General Motors in Oshawa, Ontario, in the spring of 1937. These events are particularly well documented in the collection. Correspondents include George Addes, Francis Dillon, Richard Frankensteen, John L. Lewis, Homer Martin, Philip Murray, David McDonald, Walter Reuther, and R.J. Thomas. An oral history interview with Mr. Thompson is available.
1/2 linear foot; 1 scrapbook.

VAN CAMP, LAWRENCE AND DOROTHY. *Papers, 1925-45.*
Mr. Van Camp was active in the Socialist Party during the 1920s–1940s. The collection contains pamphlets and magazines dealing with a variety of topics such as the Socialist Party, World War II, the New Deal, Moscow trials, Spanish Civil War, Marxist theory, Norman Thomas, and Leon Trotsky.
2 1/2 linear feet [unprocessed].

VANDERPLOEG, JAN B. *Papers, 1906-66.*
A landscape architect in Muskegon, Michigan, Mr. Vanderploeg served on the Board of Trustees of Michigan State University, and the Michigan State Senate, and held many local offices. Correspondence, reports, minutes, and other items cover election campaigns, university participation in education abroad, and political activities. Correspondents include Birch Bayh, Jerome Cavanagh, Mark Clark, Gerald Ford, Robert Griffin, Albert Gore, Philip Hart, Hubert Humphrey, Lyndon Johnson, John F. Kennedy, Clark Kerr, Mike Mansfield, Gaylord Nelson, Dean Rusk, Adlai Stevenson, Stuart Symington, and Harry S. Truman.
36 linear feet.

VAN KLEECK, MARY. *Papers, 1900-1940s.*
Correspondence, reports, minutes of meetings, clippings, and published material of Mary Van Kleeck, director of the Commission on Women's Work and Industrial Studies, and associate director of International Industrial Relations Institute of the Russell Sage Foundation. In addition to Miss Van Kleeck's files concerning her work with the Sage Foundation and the Inter-Professional Association are the papers of Knickerbocker Boyd, an architect interested in the relationship of architects with the building trades unions, and Edward Wieck, a colleague of Miss Van Kleeck's at the Sage Foundation. Activities of the United Mine Workers Union, 1900–

Collections

1940s; organizing and unionizing in the automobile and steel industries in the 1930s and 1940s; and the operations and reports of the Sage Foundation are among the subjects included in the collection.
20 linear feet [unprocessed].

VORSE, MARY HEATON. *Papers, 1841–1966.*
Literary manuscripts and related papers, correspondence, daily notes and journals, reference and research material, notes, clippings, pamphlets, personal and family papers, and memorabilia, collected by Mrs. Vorse, writer, labor journalist, and social critic of the U.S. She also covered strikes, civil and labor disturbances, wars, revolutions, and political upheavals in other parts of the world. From the textile strike in Lawrence, Massachusetts (1912) to the textile strike in Henderson, North Carolina (1959), her writings and activities include the International Women Suffrage Convention (1913); the IWW; child labor; Consumers League; the organization of the Provincetown Players (1915); mining strikes in Michigan and Minnesota (1916); the rise of Hitler; invasion of Poland; postwar conditions in Europe after both world wars; the Scottsboro case; the steel strikes of 1919 and 1936–37; organizational drive of the Amalgamated Clothing Workers (1920–21); the Sacco-Vanzetti case (1920); Palmer raids and criminal syndicalist cases (1921–23); textile strikes in Passaic (1926) and Gastonia (1929); Farmers Holiday Association (1932); migrant workers; automobile sit-down strikes (1936–37); UNRRA (1945–47); the Sinarquistas in Mexico (1949); crime on the New York-New Jersey waterfronts (1950–54). Correspondents include John Dewey, John DosPassos, Dave Dubinsky, John Edelman, Elizabeth Gurley Flynn, William Z. Foster, John F. Kennedy, John L. Lewis, Sinclair Lewis, Robert E. Peary, Walter Reuther, Theodore Roosevelt, Lincoln Steffens, and many other prominent persons in the labor, literary, and political fields.
77 linear feet.

WALES, GILBERT. *Papers, 1949–65.*
Correspondence, reports, newspaper clippings, press releases, and scrapbooks collected by Mr. Wales, who served in the Michigan House of Representatives as a delegate from the Upper Peninsula from 1949 until 1965. Agriculture, conservation, hunting and fishing legislation, education, tourism in the Upper Peninsula, taxes, unemployment, and the minimum wage are discussed. Correspondents include Jerome P. Cavanagh, Philip Hart, Patrick McNamara, Neil Staebler, and G. Mennen Williams.
4 linear feet.

WHEELER, MARY R. *Papers, 1938-67.*
These papers reflect Miss Wheeler's career as a vice-president of the AFT, and as an officer of the West Suburban Teachers Union (Chicago area) and the Illinois Federation of Teachers. Correspondence, minutes, reports, and other documents are included. Among the topics are professional standards for teachers, retirement plans, and negotiations and strikes by teachers.
1 1/2 linear feet.

WIECK, EDWARD A. *Papers, 1886-1953.*
Papers of a one-time coal miner and miners' union officer. In his later years, Mr. Wieck was a research associate in the Department of Industrial Studies of the Russell Sage Foundation. The author of several articles and books mainly concerned with coal mining, Mr. Wieck also wrote reports on the automobile, rubber, and steel industries under the NRA. His research materials form part of this collection. Handbills, correspondence, proceedings, and clippings document the attempt to organize coal miners from the time of the Knights of Labor to the days of John L. Lewis. There are many items pertaining to the American Miners' Association. Among the correspondents are Louis Brandeis, James Carey, Samuel Gompers, Max Lerner, John L. Lewis, T.L. Lewis, Robert M. Lovett, H.L. Mencken, Theodore Roosevelt, and Oswald Garrison Villard.
9 linear feet.

WILLIAMS, M.A. (BILL). *Papers, 1937-64.*
Correspondence, minutes, clippings, and other materials relating to the organization of the Ford plant in Richmond, California. Mr. Williams served in several capacities with UAW Local 560 at this plant. Topics include the NLRB case involving Ford (1938-41); the California labor movement (1937-42); and the Ford Strike (1958). Major correspondents are Richard Leonard, Emil Mazey, and Lew Michener.
2 linear feet.

WILSE, JACK. *Papers, 1945.*
During World War II, Mr. Wilse served as labor representative to the Region 5 War Labor Board. Correspondence, briefs, and reports reflect this activity. An oral history interview with Mr. Wilse is available. *100 items.*

WINN, FRANK. *Papers, 1940-62.*
Clippings of articles, news stories and editorials (1940-62), political cartoons (1958-61), and miscellaneous speeches and press releases (1948-

Collections

61), collected by Mr. Winn, former director of the UAW Public Relations Department, and editor of *Solidarity* (1946–63). Subjects include UAW conventions (1947–53); Kohler Strike (1957–59); war production; wage and price controls; United Nations (1950–54); collective bargaining and contract negotiations; U.S. Government departments and agencies (1946–55); Ford Strike (1949); United Steel Workers (1943–54); United Rubber Workers (1940–55); car price cuts (1957–59); white-collar workers; and various organizations, individuals, and labor unions.
7 1/2 linear feet; 37 scrapbooks [9 linear feet unprocessed].

WOLF, HERMAN. *Papers, 1924–58.*
Drafts of articles, correspondence, reports, press releases, minutes, publicity material, and newspaper clippings collected by Mr. Wolf, who was a labor editor from 1934 to 1940 for the Textile Workers Union, the International Ladies Garment Workers, the Amalgamated Clothing Workers, and the American Labor Party. He was radio director for the Greater New York Fund and operated his own public relations firm. In 1941, he served on the British-Management Labor Commission, and wrote *Labor Defends America,* a war handbook discussing the role of labor in production, morale, war controls, and training. From 1941 to 1944, he served with the Treasury Department and the War Production Board; was president of Fuller Homes, Inc. (1944–61), and was an editor for the Bridgeport *Herald* (1947–50). From 1947 to 1953 he was active in Connecticut politics, helping with publicity for A.D.A. sponsored candidates, running as a Democratic candidate for the State House of Representatives in 1949, and was elected as chairman of the Stratford Democratic Town Committee in 1950. Included are drafts, notes, correspondence, and research for articles (1932–52), and newspaper and magazine articles. The Socialist Party (1932–36); ILGWU (1936–41); Treasury Department, War Bond campaigns (1941–43); War Production Board, labor-management cooperation (1943–44); Fuller Homes (1944–46); and Connecticut politics (1949–53) are covered. Correspondents include William Benton, Chester Bowles, James B. Carey, Sidney Hillman, John W. Livingston, Edward Levinson, Clair Booth Luce, George Meany, Henry Morgenthau, A. Philip Randolph, Victor Reuther, A.A. Ribicoff, and Norman Thomas.
16 linear feet.

YOUNG, COLEMAN A. *Papers, 1964–68.*
After serving in the Army Air Corps during World War II, Mr. Young became a national representative of the United Public Workers Union, and later became director of organization for the Wayne County, Michigan,

CIO. During 1951—55, he headed the National Negro Labor Council, and in 1961 was elected to the Michigan Constitutional Convention Committee. In 1964, he became a member of the Michigan Senate from the Fourth District of Wayne County. Correspondence, reports, minutes, press releases, mailing lists, and clippings deal with automobile insurance legislation; aid to the disadvantaged; fiscal reform; open housing and urban renewal legislation; civil rights; the 1966 election campaign; police-community relations; and the Mayor's Committee for Human Resources Development. Correspondents include James H. Brickley, Jerome P. Cavanagh, Charles C. Diggs, Hubert Humphrey, Emil Mazey, and George Romney.
4 linear feet.

YOUNG, HOLGATE. *Papers, 1948—57.*
Caucus leaflets for local union elections, newsletters, financial reports, company letters to all employees, minutes and clippings from UAW Local 6 (International Harvester Co., Melrose Park, Illinois) from 1948—55. From the State, County, Municipal Employees of Kenosha, Wisconsin, there are newsletters, notes on bargaining, contracts, and grievances from twenty-five locals, and educational and miscellaneous material (1956—57).
6 linear feet [unprocessed].

YOUNG, OPEL. *Papers, 1936—37.*
Clippings, leaflets, and newspapers pertaining to the UAW's drive to organize the Delco-Remy plant of General Motors in Anderson, Indiana. Included are items on the General Motors sit-downs and the formation of UAW Local 146 in Anderson.
1/2 linear foot.

ZAREMBA, JOHN. *Papers, 1935—61.*
Mr. Zaremba was an early leader of the Automotive Industrial Workers' Association and took an active part in the formation of Dodge Local 3 of the UAW. Minutes, correspondence, clippings, and other files document early union activities at the Chrysler Corporation, especially the Dodge Main Plant. Topics covered include the Chrysler 1937 Sit-Down and the 1939 Strike; the Wayne County Industrial Union Council; the Civil Rights Federation; and union education programs. Among the correspondents are George Addes, George Edwards, Richard Frankensteen, John L. Lewis, Homer Martin, Philip Murray, and R.J. Thomas. An oral history interview with Mr. Zaremba is available.
4 1/2 linear feet.

ZWEIBACK, RICHARD. *Papers, 1964–66.*
Papers of a former International representative for the American Federation of State, County, and Municipal Employees Union in the Michigan area. Correspondence, clippings, and handbills cover negotiations with local governments of suburban Detroit.
35 items.

AIR LINE PILOTS ASSOCIATION

Departments
ALPA BOARD OF DIRECTORS. *Papers, 1932—73.*
The meetings of the Board of Directors are comparable to conventions held by other trade unions. In some years, the Association's meetings have been referred to as conventions. The Board of Directors is the supreme governing body of the Association. Membership is comprised of a captain representative, a co-pilot representative, and, where applicable, a flight engineer representative of each local council. Affiliation with the AFL, air mail legislation, political endorsements, professional standards, and other matters of concern to flight personnel are discussed. Included are transcripts of all meetings, compilations of actions, correspondence, ballots, roll calls, officer and committee reports, and related files.
25 linear feet; 52 volumes.

ALPA COMMITTEES. *Papers, 1952—62.*
General files created by the committees of Physical Standards, Professional Standards, Organizational Structures Study, and Insurance Study. Additional material relating to these and other ALPA committees may be found in the various departmental files.
1 linear foot.

ALPA EMPLOYMENT AGREEMENTS DEPARTMENT. *Papers, 1939—67.*
Correspondence, reports, briefs, and other materials regarding agreements between ALPA and all airlines whose pilots are represented by the Union. Included are the agreements covering not only basic working relationships but also those pertaining to particular areas, such as mergers, pensions, crew complements, and interchanges between airlines. The newly formed Contracts Administration Department has replaced this department.
304 linear feet.

ALPA ENGINEERING AND AIR SAFETY DEPARTMENT. *Papers, 1935—70.*
Concerned primarily with air safety, the files include material pertaining to studies of airports; air traffic control; lighting; accidents; new aircraft evaluations; crew training and related areas; noise abatement; the SST; and all-weather flying. There is much documentation of the work done in these fields by the International Federation of Air Line Pilots Associations and the International Civil Aviation Organization.
276 linear feet.

Collections

ALPA EXECUTIVE BOARD. *Papers, 1947–73.*
The Executive Board, made up of the chairman and vice-chairman of each Master Executive Council, is responsible for the general management of the Association, subject to review by the Board of Directors. Included are minutes and a compilation of actions and correspondence. Topics covered are strikes, working conditions, federal regulations of airlines, and organizing of pilots and other flight crew personnel.
5 linear feet; 23 volumes.

ALPA EXECUTIVE COMMITTEE. *Papers, 1953–73.*
Correspondence, files, and proceedings for the Association's Executive Committee, composed of the president, first vice-president, five regional vice-presidents and the vice-president of the Steward and Stewardess Division. Topics include flight time duty study, FAA and CAA Enforcement Committee, and collective bargaining.
1 linear foot; 19 volumes.

ALPA LEGAL DEPARTMENT. *Papers, 1932–70.*
The Legal Department represents not only the Association in matters of concern to the union, but also deals with grievances of individual members. Problems handled by the Department include proposed mergers of airlines, route changes, alleged violations by pilots, and seniority disputes. Also included in these files is the initial legal documentation which led to the formation of ALPA. This includes various governmental decisions regulating the airline industry. Individual grievances comprise the bulk of the files. These cases are now handled by the new Contracts Administration Department.
456 linear feet.

ALPA PRESIDENT'S DEPARTMENT. *Papers, 1931–73.*
The office files for the chief executive officer of the Association, including those of presidents David Behncke (1931–51), Clarence Sayen (1951–62), Charles Ruby (1962–70), and James O'Donnell (1970 – present). Correspondence, minutes, briefs, reports, and agreements cover subjects such as the third crew member controversy, strikes, air safety, the factional dispute with American Air Line pilots, and the founding of ALPA. Major correspondents are Hugo Black, Dwight D. Eisenhower, William Green, Lyndon Johnson, John F. Kennedy, Fiorello LaGuardia, Melvin Maas, James Mead, George Meany, Mike Monroney, E. R. Quesada, and Walter Reuther.
109 linear feet.

Air Line Pilots' Association

ALPA PUBLIC RELATIONS DEPARTMENT. *Papers, 1932–69.*
Clippings, bulletins, news releases, correspondence, and tape recordings pertaining to such topics as strikes, accidents, air safety, mergers, hijackings, noise abatement, and similar subjects of interest to airline pilots.
52 linear feet.

ALPA STEWARD AND STEWARDESS DIVISION. *Papers, 1959–73.*
In the late 1940s, ALPA aided flight attendants in forming an organization to improve wages and working conditions. Air Line Stewards and Stewardesses Association became an affiliate of ALPA. In 1960, the Stewards and Stewardesses Division was established as an integral part of ALPA. These files, consisting of correspondence, newsletters, seniority lists, agreements, and other items, cover such topics as elections, schedules, and mergers.
14 1/2 linear feet; 5 volumes.

Councils

ALPA DELTA COUNCIL 43. *Papers, 1959–66.*
Files relating to the representation of flight crews for Delta Air Lines in the Chicago area. Correspondence, reports, and minutes discuss such subjects as air safety, professional standards, and negotiations.
1 linear foot.

ALPA DENVER JOINT COUNCIL. *Papers, 1948–70.*
Files of the office representing the interests of ALPA in the Denver, Colorado, area. Many of the records pertain to relations between ALPA and Southern, Western, Continental, United and (predominantly) Frontier airlines. Correspondence, minutes, negotiating notes and other items discuss air safety, organizing, professional standards, mergers, and retirement and other benefits for pilots. *15 linear feet.*

ALPA LOS ANGELES JOINT COUNCIL. *Papers, 1953–71.*
The activities of ALPA in the Los Angeles area, particularly with Continental, Flying Tiger, Los Angeles, Pan American, Trans World, United, and Western airlines, are documented. Correspondence, minutes, reports, and other items discuss such topics as negotiations, professional standards, mergers, air safety, and the needs of the military for civilian aircraft and crews. *14 linear feet.*

ALPA MIAMI JOINT COUNCIL. *Papers, 1936–67.*
Office files pertaining to the work of ALPA in the Miami, Florida, and the Caribbean areas. Among the airlines covered are Riddle, Eastern, National,

Collections

Delta, and Pan American. Correspondence, minutes, clippings, and other items discuss such topics as air safety, training of flight crews, flight engineer disputes, negotiations, and retirement plans.
43 linear feet.

ALPA MINNEAPOLIS JOINT COUNCIL. *Papers, 1949–69.*
Correspondence, reports, and financial records pertaining to the activities of ALPA in the Minneapolis, Minnesota, area. The main topics covered are air safety (including accident reports) and finances.
6 1/2 linear feet.

ALPA NEW YORK JOINT COUNCIL. *Papers, 1954–70.*
Correspondence, minutes, reports, and other records documenting the activities of ALPA in the New York area. Topics covered include air safety, mergers, noise abatement, and the supersonic controversy.
19 linear feet.

ALPA O'HARE JOINT COUNCIL. *Papers, 1958–65.*
Nearly all of the files consist of grievances brought by stewards and stewardesses against United Air Lines. Subjects of the grievances include working conditions, physical standards, and mergers.
7 linear feet.

ALPA PAN AMERICAN COUNCIL 56. *Papers, 1957–67.*
These files pertain to Pan American Council 56, representing Pan Am crews operating out of San Francisco, California. Minutes, correspondence, reports, and financial files cover such topics as retirement, safety, and disputes over flight engineers.   *1 linear foot.*

ALPA SEATTLE JOINT COUNCIL. *Papers, 1953–69.*
Files documenting the activities of ALPA in the Pacific northwest, particularly with Alaska, Northwest, and United airlines. Correspondence, minutes, reports, and other records cover such areas as negotiations, strikes, mergers, and jurisdictional disputes between ALPA and the Flight Engineers Union and between the Airline Stewards & Stewardesses Association and the Transport Workers Union.   *12 linear feet.*

ALPA SOUTHERN COUNCIL 112. *Papers, 1949–68.*
Files of the office representing the interests of the pilots for Southern Airways in the Atlanta, Georgia, area. Correspondence, reports, press releases, and other material discuss such topics as strikes against Southern Airways, negotiations, and air safety.   *2 linear feet.*

AMERICAN FEDERATION OF TEACHERS

Departments

AFT COMMUNICATIONS. *Papers, 1934-57.*
Form letters, reports, newsletters, and bulletins from the national office to members of the Executive Council and AFT locals. Topics covered include AFT budgets; AFT elections; AFT factionalism; proposal to change the AFT affiliation from the AFL to the CIO in 1938; vocational education; federal and state aid to education; and establishment of an International Education Association.
8 linear feet.

AFT CONVENTIONS. *Papers, 1916-72.*
Proceedings, resolutions, reports, and other materials pertaining to the annual conventions of the AFT. A selected list of topics covered includes academic freedom, federal aid to education, federal works programs, integration, loyalty investigations, anti-war movements, price controls, and vocational education.
20 linear feet.

AFT DEFENSE CASES. *Papers, 1930s-1960s.*
Correspondence between the AFT national office, state federations, locals and individual members concerning legal action by or against members of the union. Also included are applications for grants from the AFT defense fund. Topics covered include academic freedom and the National Educational Policies Committee.
9 linear feet.

AFT DEFUNCT LOCALS. *Papers, 1921-65.*
Correspondence, reports, charter applications, and per capita reports from inactive locals of the AFT. Subjects include adult education, college and university teachers, federal aid to education, the communist issue, civil rights, tenure, and teachers under the W.P.A. Among the correspondents are most officers of the AFT.
23 linear feet.

AFT EXECUTIVE COUNCIL. *Papers, 1930-70.*
Proceedings, ballots, correspondence, and miscellaneous material pertaining to the American Federation of Teachers Executive Council. Topics covered include contracts, conventions, and public relations. Among the

correspondents are Charles Cogen, Jerome Davis, Arthur Elder, George Guernsey, Irwin Kuenzli, and Carl Megel.
15 linear feet.

AFT LOCALS. *Papers, 1916–68 (predominantly 1930s–1960s).*
Correspondence, charter applications, per capita reports, and other items pertaining to relations between the AFT national office and member locals of the union. Topics discussed include charter revocations, conventions, finances, and tenure. Among the correspondents are William Green, Hubert Humphrey, Nelson Rockefeller, and Robert Wagner.
61 linear feet.

AFT MEMOS AND MIMEOGRAPHED MATERIAL. *Papers, 1921–67.*
Memos, form letters, and financial statements sent from the AFT national office to the executive council, state federations, and locals. Topics covered include the communist issue, early AFT history, grievances, organizing, political action by teachers, teacher ratings, segregated locals, and tenure.   *7 linear feet.*

AFT MISCELLANEOUS OFFICE FILES. *Papers, 1916–61.*
Reports, correspondence, and other files pertaining to academic freedom, amendments to the American Federation of Teachers Constitution, federal aid to education, international teachers organizations, universal military training, strikes, workers' education, and AFT conventions. Also included are thirty-four financial ledgers for the years 1916–61. Among the correspondents are Hubert Humphrey, Blair Moody, and Maurice Tobin.
10 linear feet; 34 ledgers.

AFT PRESIDENT'S DEPARTMENT. *Papers, 1914–67.*
The files of the chief executive officer of the American Federation of Teachers cover nearly every phase of the union's activities from its earliest days. Correspondence, minutes, reports, clippings, and other items discuss such topics as civil rights, collective bargaining, political action, federal aid to education, organizing, international labor bodies, problems of the aged, and strikes by teachers. Correspondence may be found from nearly all prominent labor leaders including Cesar Chavez, George Meany, and Walter Reuther. Among leading political figures whose letters may be found in these files are Paul Douglas, Hubert Humphrey, Lyndon Johnson, John F. Kennedy, George McGovern, and Adlai Stevenson. Civil rights leaders corresponding with AFT presidents have included Martin Luther King, A. Philip Randolph, Bayard Rustin, Roy Wilkins, and Whitney Young.
37 linear feet.

American Federation of Teachers

AFT STATE FEDERATIONS. *Papers, 1922–67.*
Charter applications, clippings, correspondence, per capita reports, and notes from the various state federations of teachers to the national office. Topics covered include collective bargaining, membership drives, organizing of American teachers abroad, and school financing. Among the correspondents are Arthur Elder, William Green, and Hubert Humphrey.
6 linear feet.

State and Local Federations

AFT (MICHIGAN FEDERATION). *Papers, 1951–63.*
Correspondence, minutes, and reports. Subjects include Administrative Board meetings; American Federation of Teachers; conventions; Detroit Federation of Teachers; Executive Council meetings; Haven Hill conferences; legislative lobbying activities; membership campaigns; metropolitan teachers' institutes; Michigan AFL-CIO Council; Michigan Constitutional Convention (1961); teachers' salary and fringe benefits surveys; treasurer reports; White House Conference on Children and Youth (1960). Correspondents include Detroit city officials, Michigan congressmen and state officials, and national congressmen and officials including John F. Kennedy and Lyndon Johnson. Most of the letters are answers to invitations for speaking engagements.
14 1/2 linear feet; [23 linear feet unprocessed].

AFT LOCAL 28 (ST. PAUL). *Papers, 1898–1970.*
The St. Paul (Minnesota) Federation of Teachers, Local 28, is the fifth oldest American Federation of Teachers local in continued existence in the U.S. and the first teacher's union in Minnesota. It evolved from the Grade Teachers Federation (1898) and received its AFT charter June 18, 1918 under the St. Paul Federation of Women Teachers, Local 28. The St. Paul Federation of Men Teachers was chartered February 19 of the following year as Local 43. The two locals worked together closely through the Joint Council of Teachers and in 1957 merged into the present federation. Correspondence, minutes, bulletins, and other materials on formation of these unions and their merger are included, as is material concerning the merit pay system, tenure cases, strike efforts, and membership recruitment.
4 linear feet.

AFT LOCAL 61 (SAN FRANCISCO). *Papers, 1951–71.*
Minutes of the Executive Boards (1951–52, 1956–68) and general membership meeting minutes (1956–68); clippings, bulletins, memos, and photos concerning the 1968 strike and negotiations; clippings from the

Collections

1971 strike; reports and correspondence of the Bargaining Committee and various other committees; and newsletters.
6 linear feet [unprocessed].

AFT LOCAL 250 (TOLEDO). *Papers, 1933–68.*
Office files of the Toledo (Ohio) Federation of Teachers, Local 250 of the American Federation of Teachers. Included are the files of the Salary and Professional Standards committees; minutes of general meetings; Board of Directors meetings; and meetings of building representatives. Subjects include AFT conventions, legislation pertaining to education, teacher salaries, and school taxation. Among the correspondents are Arthur Elder, Carl Megel, and Stephen Young.
35 linear feet; 2 volumes.

AFT LOCAL 400 (PITTSBURGH). *Papers, 1968–69.*
Reports and agreements of AFT Local 400, which serves teachers in the Pittsburgh, Pennsylvania, school system.
8 items.

AFT LOCAL 420 (ST. LOUIS). *Papers, 1961–70 (predominantly 1962–67).*
Office files of the AFT local representing the teachers of St. Louis, Missouri. Correspondence, clippings, minutes, press releases, and other materials dealing with such topics as tenure, membership drives, and collective bargaining by teachers. Several of the files consist of the records of Betty Finneran as a vice-president of the AFT.
6 linear feet.

AFT LOCAL 698 (EAST DETROIT). *Papers, 1953–64.*
Teachers of East Detroit, Michigan, were first organized into the American Federation of Teachers in 1942, as members of the Macomb County Federation of Teachers, Local 698. The papers of the EDFT, beginning in 1953, include correspondence, minutes, constitutions, school board policy papers, and material on collective bargaining, co-ops, financial statements, conferences, grievances, merit rating, millage campaigns, strikes, mediation, insurance, retirement, and other matters of interest to teachers. Correspondents include Henry Linne, Carl Megel, Mary Ellen Riordan, Harold Ryan, and August Scholle.
4 linear feet.

American Federation of Teachers

AFT LOCAL 1052 (HAMTRAMCK). *Papers, 1957–63.*
This collection consists of correspondence, notes, bulletins, and reports of the Federation's activities in Hamtramck, Michigan. There are also copies of *Hamtramck Teachers* and of UFT newsletters.
1 linear foot.

AFT LOCAL 1295 (WAYNE STATE UNIVERSITY). *Papers, 1940s–1960s.*
Serving employees of Wayne State University, this local was originally established as a branch of the Detroit Federation of Teachers. The collection contains minutes, reports, and some correspondence.
2 linear feet [unprocessed].

AFT LOCAL 1425 (ECORSE). *Papers, 1960–68 (predominantly 1960–65).*
Correspondence, reports, press releases, publicity, membership records, and newspaper clippings of the Ecorse (Michigan) Federation of Teachers. Subjects include membership, millage and election campaigns, and the Michigan Federation of Teachers Convention (1963).
1 linear foot.

THE NEWSPAPER GUILD

National Office
THE NEWSPAPER GUILD. *Papers, 1933–69.*
Organized as the American Newspaper Guild in 1933, the group has recently changed its title to The Newspaper Guild. Many of the files consist of correspondence with local guilds and cover such topics as contracts, strikes, and negotiations. Proceedings, International Executive Board minutes, constitutions, National Labor Relations Board cases, circular letters and notices, organizer and staff representative reports, and Heywood Broun Award entry files are also contained in the collection.
23 1/2 linear feet; 171 volumes [80 linear feet unprocessed].

Locals
THE NEWSPAPER GUILD LOCAL 22 (DETROIT). *Papers, 1933–60.*
The Detroit Newspaper Guild papers include office files from 1934 to 1957, and include records of all negotiations and contracts, transcripts of meetings with publishers, elections, and arbitration awards. The Guild at one time included employees of the Detroit *Times*, Detroit *Free Press*, Associated Press, United Press International News Service, and the *Michigan Catholic*.
25 linear feet; [28 linear feet unprocessed].

THE NEWSPAPER GUILD LOCAL 32 (BOSTON). *Papers, 1934–58.*
The collection is comprised of correspondence between the Boston Guild and the national office, and also between smaller guilds in the Boston area or units of the Boston local from 1934–58, and deals with organizing, contracts, negotiations, policy questions, letters of Jonathan Eddy of the ANG, financial reports (1938–58), minutes of local meetings, the New England District Council [ANG] (1945–57), national convention material (1947–57), national and local Guild elections (1947–57), and grievance materials (1949–58).
22 linear feet [unprocessed].

THE NEWSPAPER GUILD LOCAL 47 (ST. LOUIS). *Papers, 1933–66.*
Files relating to the activities of The Newspaper Guild in the St. Louis, Missouri, area. Minutes, reports, correspondence, and other papers discuss such topics as strikes, lockouts, and negotiations.
10 1/2 linear feet.

THE NEWSPAPER GUILD LOCAL 51 (MILWAUKEE). *Papers, 1935–63.*

The Milwaukee Newspaper Guild was chartered on May 15, 1935. The files consist of contracts, correspondence, reports, handbills, and other items on negotiations, arbitrations, strikes (1936–62); ANG convention *Proceedings* and *Officers' Reports* (1944–63, but not all years); extensive local financial records (1954, 1959, 1961, 1962); and manuals from the ANG on collective bargaining, organizing, and administration.
22 linear feet [unprocessed].

UNITED AUTO WORKERS

Departments

UAW ACCOUNTING DEPARTMENT. *Papers, 1945–54.*
Monthly financial reports of the International Union.
1 linear foot.

UAW AGRICULTURAL IMPLEMENT DEPARTMENT. *Papers, 1946–69.*
Correspondence, reports, minutes, grievances, press releases, agreements, notes, contracts, and clippings relating to contract negotiations and grievance and arbitration cases with International Harvester Corporation (1950–68), John Deere Company (1946–64), Caterpillar Tractor (1957–67), and Allis Chalmers (1961–66); minutes and reports of Agricultural Implement conferences (1956–65); and miscellaneous general office files (1952–69). Correspondents include Pat Greathouse, Emil Mazey, Walter Reuther, Brendan Sexton, and Arthur Shy.
33 linear feet; [60 linear feet unprocessed].

UAW CHRYSLER DEPARTMENT. *Papers, 1938–47.*
Correspondence with the many UAW locals at the Chrysler Corporation, mostly concerning grievances over seniority, classification, and rates of pay, with some discussion of the Homer Martin-UAW split.
7 linear feet.

UAW COMMUNITY RELATIONS. *Papers, 1953–66.*
Files from the office of Mrs. Mildred Jeffrey include correspondence and papers on community meetings and projects; COPE activities; and citizens' groups, such as Citizens for Michigan and Citizens for Schools. There is also material on out-state and out-of-state CIO councils, and on consumer councils.
1 1/2 linear feet [unprocessed].

UAW CONVENTIONS. *Papers, 1951–53.*
Delegate lists, votes per local, credentials, and some routine correspondence for the 1951 and 1953 UAW International conventions.
8 linear feet.

UAW EDUCATION DEPARTMENT. *Papers, 1948–62.*
Through a variety of means, the Education Department of the UAW carries out its charge of developing and implementing programs of labor

education for members of the union. This collection represents some of the files of the Education Department for the period noted and reflects the wide range of topics considered in the UAW's educational program, including adult education resources, the role of church and labor, collective bargaining techniques, co-ops, education conferences, fair employment practices, housing, citizenship, and summer schools. The materials consist of correspondence, notes, outlines, proceedings, and various pamphlets.
29 1/2 linear feet.

UAW EDUCATION DEPARTMENT: EDWARD COFFEY FILES. *Papers, 1951–57.*
This collection represents a part of the office files of Mr. Coffey, a one-time assistant director of the Education Department of the UAW. The papers illustrate the wide range of programs developed by the Education Department. Church and labor relationships; summer schools; educational conferences; work with universities; fair employment practices; and recreation and governmental programs affecting labor and other areas are discussed. *4 linear feet.*

UAW EDUCATION DEPARTMENT: VICTOR REUTHER FILES. *Papers, 1946–49.*
Victor Reuther served as director of the UAW Education Department during the last half of the 1940s. This collection represents a portion of his files for that period. Among the subjects covered are UAW summer schools and European labor unions. Correspondents include Hubert Humphrey, Walter Reuther, Brendan Sexton, and Norman Thomas.
1 1/2 linear feet.

UAW FORD DEPARTMENT. *Papers, 1941–48.*
Correspondence, notes, agreements, reports, and minutes relating to contract negotiations between Ford Motor Company and the UAW Ford Department, National Ford Council, sub-councils, and National Negotiating Committee; correspondence between the Ford Department and Ford local unions, UAW regional offices, and other UAW departments; and general office files consisting of correspondence, reports, hearings, memoranda, staff reports, and miscellaneous materials. Subjects include NLRB and War Labor Board cases against Ford Motor Company, and local and national contract issues. Major correspondents are George Addes, Ken Bannon, Harry Bennett, John S. Bugas, James B. Carey, Malcolm Denise, Norman Matthews, Emil Mazey, Philip Murray, Victor Reuther, Walter Reuther, Maurice Sugar, R. J. Thomas, and Leonard Woodcock.
9 linear feet.

Collections

UAW GENERAL MOTORS DEPARTMENT. *Papers, 1938–64.*
The collection encompasses correspondence, minutes, speeches, agreements and proposed agreements, membership records, strike bulletins, demands and proposals of local unions, union security petitions, and lists of plants certified by the NLRB. Subjects include contract negotiations and demands of local unions, grievance cases of local unions, membership and union shop campaigns, and the General Motors strike of 1945–46. Correspondents include W. H. Anderson, Thomas Johnstone, John Livingston, Homer Martin, Emil Mazey, Walter Reuther, and Charles Wilson.
15 linear feet.

UAW INTERNATIONAL AFFAIRS DEPARTMENT. *Papers, 1955–65.*
Correspondence, reports, minutes, clippings, and other documents of the UAW International Affairs Department under the directorship of Victor Reuther. The files pertain to the work of the UAW abroad, particularly through such groups as the International Confederation of Free Trade Unions and the International Metalworkers Federation. There are also materials dealing with the problems of labor in individual countries and the work of the UAW in attempting to assist in the resolution of the difficulties.
55 linear feet [unprocessed].

UAW INTERNATIONAL EXECUTIVE BOARD. *Papers, 1942–48.*
Minutes of regular and special meetings of the UAW Executive Board for the period indicated. Included are some verbatim reports; others are merely summaries.
6 linear feet.

UAW PUBLIC RELATIONS DEPARTMENT. *Papers, 1938–53.*
Clippings and press releases, correspondence, memoranda, reports, and financial papers collected by the UAW Public Relations Department. Subjects include Michigan political affairs (1940–52), American Brass Company strike (1938), civil rights, war production and the War Labor Board, General Motors Strike (1946), the Urban League, and Henry Wallace and the Progressive Party (1945–53). Correspondents include John Dancy, Norman Matthews, and Walter Reuther.
15 linear feet.

UAW PUBLIC RELATIONS DEPARTMENT: FORD MOTOR COMPANY. *Papers, 1937–42.*
Correspondence, press releases, clippings, notes, handbills, and speeches pertaining to the early struggle for unionization at Ford Motor Company

(1937–42); reports, hearings and decisions, press releases, and miscellaneous papers relating to NLRB cases against Ford Motor Company (1937–41). The materials were collected by the UAW Public Relations Department during the campaign to organize the Ford Motor Company. Subjects include Harry Bennett and the Ford Service Department, Henry Ford, John L. Lewis, and the Homer Martin controversy. Among the correspondents are Maurice Sugar and Edward Levinson.
1 1/2 linear feet.

UAW PUBLIC REVIEW BOARD. *Papers, 1957 – early 1960s.*
The Public Review Board was established by the UAW in 1957. This board, comprised of leaders from religious, judicial, and academic communities, represents the final step in grievances filed by a member against the UAW if the aggrieved does not wish to appeal to the International Convention. Decisions of the Public Review Board are binding upon the union. These particular files contain cases heard by the Review Board from its inception to the early 1960s.   *10 linear feet.*

UAW RADIO DEPARTMENT. *Papers, 1949–64.*
Scripts of UAW-sponsored morning, afternoon, and evening radio programs: *Eye Opener* (1954–64), *Shiftbreak* (1957–64), and *Labor Views the News* (1950–52 and 1957); scripts of television programs: *Ballot Box* (1954), *Meet the UAW* (1955–56), and *Telescope* (1957).
33 linear feet.

UAW RECREATION DEPARTMENT. *Papers, 1945–50.*
Correspondence, minutes and reports on National Committee for Fair Play in Bowling; F.D.R. labor camps; and UAW children's camps. Correspondents include Hubert Humphrey, Emil Mazey, and Walter Reuther.
1 linear foot.

UAW RESEARCH AND ENGINEERING DEPARTMENT. *Papers, 1940–53.*
The collection comprises correspondence with local unions (1940–51), and UAW regional directors and International representatives (1944–50); correspondence with individuals, civic and labor organizations and UAW departments (1940–53); general office and subject files consisting of reports, memoranda, speeches, contracts, press releases, correspondence, statistical data, and miscellaneous items (1941–53); questionnaires regarding war production and wartime employment (1940–43); and miscellaneous contracts and reports (1942–50). The materials were collected by the Research and Engineering Department, which supplies information and

technical assistance to local unions, UAW departments, officers, and International representatives. It prepares economic analyses and reports of industrial trends, and assists in the preparation of resolutions, testimony, pamphlets, and other publications. Correspondents are Prentiss M. Brown, Carl Haessler, Richard Leonard, Emil Mazey, Victor Reuther, Walter Reuther, Maurice Sugar, Nat Weinberg, and James Wishart, on topics such as Labor's Non-Partisan League; the Smith Act; and wartime labor, price, and production controls.   *19 linear feet.*

UAW SECRETARY-TREASURER: EMIL MAZEY. *Papers, 1947–52.*
Activities of UAW Executive Board members and officers, and departments and councils are among the subjects of these files kept by Mr. Mazey as secretary-treasurer of the UAW, a position to which he was elected in 1947. Included also are the official election roll call documents from the 1947 convention and correspondence with financial secretaries of the many UAW locals. Appeal Board cases involving local union disputes of all kinds, and a short file of regional business and reports are followed by a series of alphabetically listed general files and an added local union file. Subjects include post-war seniority problems of women and veterans, exemptions for Mennonites and Seventh-day Adventists, defense employment, and union financial matters. The collection has letters of George Addes, Richard Gosser, John Livingston, Walter Reuther, R. J. Thomas, and A. L. Zwerdling.   *32 linear feet.*

UAW SOCIAL SECURITY DEPARTMENT. *Papers, 1939–65.*
The Social Security Department of the UAW administers pension, health, employment security, and insurance programs. These files pertain to the Department's work in health-care legislation, including Medicare and Blue Cross-Blue Shield contracts. Among health care bills discussed are the Kerr-Mills Bill, the Forand Bill, and the King-Anderson Bill. Correspondents include Wilbur Cohen, Nelson Cruikshank, and Walter Reuther.
17 linear feet.

UAW STUDEBAKER-PACKARD DEPARTMENT. *Papers, 1950s.*
Financial statements, agreements, and other files kept by this now-defunct department of the UAW.
1 1/2 linear feet [unprocessed].

UAW UNEMPLOYMENT COMPENSATION DEPARTMENT. *Papers, 1945–55.*
Hearings, determinations, correspondence, petitions for hearings, briefs, court transcripts, and related papers pertaining to individual and group

appeals on contested unemployment compensation claims, in which the Unemployment Compensation Department acted as interested party and agent for the claimants. *6 linear feet.*

UAW VETERANS DEPARTMENT. *Papers, 1943–47 (predominantly 1945–46).*
Correspondence and mimeographed material covering conferences, apprenticeship, fair employment practices, seniority, disabled veterans, and the creation and co-ordination of UAW regional and local veterans committees. Among the correspondents are George Addes, Tracy Doll, Emil Mazey, Louis Rabaut, Victor Reuther, August Scholle, Maurice Sugar, and R. J. Thomas. *3 1/2 linear feet.*

UAW WAR POLICY DIVISION. *Papers, 1941–46 (predominantly 1943–44).*
Correspondence, reports, speeches, notes, newspaper clippings, publicity material, and minutes on: shortage of critical materials; employment stabilization; job transfers; utilization of labor; job training programs; alien workers; rationing; allied relief; housing; price and rent control; child care; discrimination; counseling; education; fair employment practices; reconversion; post-war planning; and veterans. Correspondents include George Addes, Nelson Cruikshank, John Edelman, Arthur Elder, Sidney Hillman, Mildred Jeffrey, Walter Reuther, George Romney, Dorothy K. Roosevelt, August Scholle, Maurice Sugar, R. J. Thomas, and Leonard Woodcock. *16 1/2 linear feet.*

UAW WASHINGTON OFFICE. *Papers, 1935–64.*
Correspondence, reports, minutes, and other records from the office maintained in Washington, D.C. by the UAW. The files pertain to the union's activities in legislation, politics, and other areas of concern to labor in the broad field of government. Among the specific topics covered are the Office of Price Administration (1943–46); the Office of Price Stabilization (1951–53); consumer affairs; elections (1945–59); postwar Europe; the General Motors Strike (1945–46); rent controls; the Taft-Hartley Act; and tax legislation. *100 linear feet [unprocessed].*

Regions

UAW REGION 1-B LEADERSHIP INSTITUTE. *Papers, 1970.*
Notes, course outlines, and other materials used in the Sixteenth Annual Region 1-B Leadership Institute held July 19–24, 1970. Subjects covered include collective bargaining in 1970 and the political elections of 1970. *1/2 linear foot.*

Collections

UAW REGION 1-D. *Papers, 1958–59.*
Region 1-D includes the western and northern counties of Michigan. Local unions and their problems with management, financial audits, organizational efforts, routine disputes, and appellate decisions are discussed. Correspondents include Emil Mazey, Walter Reuther, Ken Robinson, and various International representatives.
18 1/2 linear feet; [52 linear feet unprocessed].

UAW REGION 1-E.
Region 1-E has jurisdiction over UAW locals in a portion of western Wayne, southern Oakland, and all of Monroe and Washtenaw counties, Michigan. The collection consists of twelve linear feet of general files for Region 1-E and six linear feet of material from the Region's Education Department.
18 linear feet [unprocessed].

UAW REGION 7 (CANADA). *Papers, 1937–65.*
Office files for the UAW Canadian regional office representing all UAW members in Canada. Included are minutes, reports, leaflets, correspondence, and similar documents concerned with all phases of UAW activity, including organizing drives, unemployment relief, grievances, and U.S. and Canadian relations.
73 linear feet [unprocessed].

UAW REGION 7: TORONTO SUB-REGION. *Papers, 1941–68.*
Correspondence; minutes; press releases; notes; organizational publicity; agreements and proposed agreements; wage classification records; decisions of arbitrators; legal briefs; newspaper clippings; and published material form the collection. Subjects include Region 7 (1941–68), District Council negotiations (1942–65), grievance cases (1942–68), labor-management disputes settled by government agencies (1941–66), and the UAW International (1941–58). Among the correspondents are George Addes, George Burt, John Eldon, Edward Levinson, Thomas MacLean, Emil Mazey, Dennis McDermott, Victor Reuther, Walter Reuther, Paul Siren, and Frank Winn.   *41 linear feet.*

UAW REGION 9. *Papers, late 1950s – early 1960s.*
Correspondence, agreements, and other office files of the UAW regional office responsible for New Jersey, eastern Pennsylvania, and upstate New York. Included are files pertaining to local unions within the region, sub-regional offices, and the International Union.
120 linear feet [unprocessed].

Locals

LOCAL 5. *Papers, 1937–65.*
Local 5, established in 1933 as AFL Federal Labor Union 18310, services the Studebaker Corporation in South Bend, Indiana. General office files (1943–65) include correspondence, minutes, clippings, reports, constitutions, and miscellaneous papers as well as correspondence, minutes, reports, and other papers of Local 5 officers and committees, UAW departments and councils, and county and state industrial union councils (1945–65); agreements, contracts, and grievances (1937–65); and correspondence, minutes, contracts, and reports pertaining to health insurance, pension plans, and Supplemental Unemployment Benefits (SUB) (1940–65). *14 1/2 linear feet.*

UAW LOCAL 6. *Papers, late 1950s.*
Grievances, correspondence, and miscellaneous office files for UAW Local 6, representing workers at the International Harvester plant in Melrose Park, Illinois.
20 linear feet [unprocessed].

UAW LOCAL 7. *Papers, January–May 1950.*
Local 7 is the bargaining agent for the workers of the Chrysler Jefferson Assembly Plant, Detroit. This entire collection deals with the Chrysler Strike of 1950, and includes agreements, bulletins, leaflets, newspaper clippings, correspondence, handbills, minutes, proposal agreements, and a calendar of union gains.
1/2 linear foot.

UAW LOCAL 9. *Papers, 1933–63.*
Local 9 serves as the bargaining agent for employees of the Bendix Products Corporation of South Bend, Indiana. The correspondence, minutes, clippings, reports, and other items contained in this collection cover strikes (including the first sit-down in the auto industry staged by Local 9); factionalism; political action; community services; fair employment practices; and pension plans. Among the correspondents are George Addes, James Carey, F. J. Dillon, David Dubinsky, William Green, Robert LaFollette, John L. Lewis, William Knudsen, Homer Martin, Sherman Minton, Frank Morrison, Walter Reuther, and R. J. Thomas.
48 1/2 linear feet.

UAW LOCAL 14. *Papers, 1940s–1950s.*
Local 14 is an amalgamated local in Toledo, Ohio, representing workers at several plants. The major unit serviced by Local 14 is the Chevrolet

Collections

Transmission Plant. These papers consist of minutes, correspondence, and other office files.
45 linear feet [unprocessed].

UAW LOCAL 25. *Papers, 1933-39.*
UAW Local 25 (General Motors) in St. Louis, Missouri, began as AFL Federal Labor Union No. 18386. The collection includes minutes of regular, special, and closed Executive Board meetings of both unions (1933-39); membership lists, and some miscellaneous minutes of groups such as the Central Trade and Labor Union of St. Louis and vicinity (1935).
1 reel of microfilm.

UAW LOCAL 27. *Papers, 1951-69.*
Local 27 is an amalgamated local located in London, Ontario, servicing thirteen units, among them General Motors Diesel, Kelvinator, Minnesota Mining and Manufacturing, Fruehauf Trailer, and Bendix Westinghouse. Correspondence, grievances, minutes, and other items cover union education, the Labour College of Canada, Medicare, and the New Democratic Party. Two of the more prominent correspondents are George Burt and Donald McDonald.
4 1/2 linear feet.

UAW LOCAL 51. *Papers, 1940s-1950s.*
Local 51 serves as the bargaining representative for the Plymouth Assembly Plant of the Chrysler Corporation in Detroit. More recently it has also come to represent workers at the Mound Road Engine Plant of the same company. Minutes, correspondence, grievances, and other office files reflect topics such as the American Committee for Protection of Foreign Born; Chrysler strike of 1950; factionalism; dispute between Local 51 and the UAW International Executive Board (1949); civil rights; political activity; social security; the Sam Sweet case; and the problems of labor in World War II. Correspondents include Richard Frankensteen, Victor Reuther, Walter Reuther, and R. J. Thomas.
15 1/2 linear feet [unprocessed].

UAW LOCAL 53. *Papers, 1958-64.*
The papers include legal briefs and decisions, union leaflets, and arbitration awards, and deal with wage negotiations and job classifications, mostly at Eaton Manufacturing Company, and Yale and Towne Manufacturing Company in Chicago, Illinois.
2 1/2 linear feet [unprocessed].

United Auto Workers

UAW LOCAL 57. *Papers, 1933–69.*
Local 57, which services the Fort Wayne Works of the International Harvester Company, has among its records correspondence, minutes, and leaflets, covering factional struggles, the war effort, agreements, seniority, pensions, and NLRB cases. Correspondents include George Addes, John Brophy, F. J. Dillon, Adolph Germer, William Green, Homer Martin, Wyndham Mortimer, Philip Murray, Walter Reuther, and R. J. Thomas.
3 1/2 linear feet.

UAW LOCAL 75. *Papers, 1934–66.*
Local 75 represents the workers at the American Motors (formerly Nash-Kelvinator) plant in Milwaukee, Wisconsin. Included in the collection are minutes of the executive board, management meetings, and general membership meetings; correspondence with UAW International and Region 10, Nash-Kelvinator and American Motors, membership and general; negotiations and contract files; Joint Council (Federal Labor Unions 19059, 18785, and 19008) minutes; committee reports; bulletins; and published reports.   *35 linear feet [unprocessed].*

UAW LOCAL 80. *Papers, 1939–61.*
Local 80 minutes (1941–61), agenda and minutes of meetings with Gemmer Manufacturing Company (1942–56), grievances (1939–60), agreements, reports, correspondence, pamphlets, handbills, and miscellaneous materials collected by Local 80, which serviced the Gemmer Manufacturing Company in Detroit until the company moved from the Detroit area. Subjects include the War Labor Board, PAC, contract negotiations and collective bargaining, and the Michigan Labor Mediation Board.
9 linear feet.

UAW LOCAL 108. *Papers, 1943–61.*
Local 108 services the Polar Ware Company of Sheboygan, Wisconsin. These files, however, represent the period when the workers at this plant were represented by Local 166 of the United Electrical Workers. Minutes, newsletters, bulletins, and correspondence cover day-to-day local union business and the 1961 strike against Polar Ware.
1/2 linear foot.

UAW LOCAL 133. *Papers, 1941–60.*
Reports, agreements, form letters, handbills, clippings, and miscellaneous material collected by Local 133, which services the Fafnir Bearing Company of New Britain, Connecticut.
1/2 linear foot.

Collections

UAW LOCAL 135. *Papers, 1949—50.*
The papers cover contract negotiations between Local 135, Grand Rapids, Michigan, and the American Seating Company, from October 27, 1949 to May 5, 1950.
2 linear feet.

UAW LOCAL 142. *Papers, 1945—54.*
Local 142 was the bargaining unit for the former Kaiser-Frazer Corporation Plant at Willow Run, Michigan. Correspondence, minutes, proceedings, election notices, reports, and grievance records on contract negotiations (1949—50), cooperative housing projects, and social security and retirement material (1948—54). Correspondents include George Addes.
7 linear feet.

UAW LOCAL 154. *Papers, 1935—64.*
Minutes of the Hudson Motors bargaining agency (1935) and papers of subsequent union interest. The Hudson Strike of 1951, the merger of Hudson and Nash-Kelvinator, the transfer of jobs to Wisconsin, and the termination of production by American Motors in plants serviced by Local 154 are discussed by correspondents Roy Abernathy, Tracy Doll, Norman Matthews, Emil Mazey, Ken Morris, Walter Reuther, and Leonard Woodcock.
1 linear foot.

UAW LOCAL 157. *Papers, 1936—65.*
Local 157 is the tool and die local servicing a number of companies in western Detroit and the surrounding area. The collection is comprised of correspondence, minutes, agreements, reports, and other papers of the company units which comprise the local; and correspondence, agreements, election material, minutes, and general office files of Local 157. Correspondents include Ed Carey, Jerome Cavanagh, George Edwards, Martha Griffiths, Philip Hart, Emil Mazey, Victor Reuther, Walter Reuther, Arthur Vandenberg, G. Mennen Williams, and Leonard Woodcock.
17 linear feet.

UAW LOCAL 174. *Papers, 1939—55.*
Local 174, an amalgamated local, services numerous plants on the west side of Detroit. The files of this union include correspondence, clippings, manuals, booklets, photos, umpire decisions, collective bargaining papers, agreements, and War Labor Board proceedings.
21 linear feet.

UAW LOCAL 190. *Papers, 1958–62.*
Local 190 serviced the Packard Company in Detroit until the company went out of existence. The collection contains minutes and financial records.
1 reel of microfilm; [12 linear feet unprocessed].

UAW LOCAL 199. *Papers, 1944–64 (predominantly 1950–64).*
The collection contains correspondence, minutes, financial records, membership records, agreements, and grievance records. Local 199 is the bargaining agent for McKinnon Industries, a subsidiary of General Motors in St. Catherines, Ontario. Since 1940, Local 199 has been affiliated with the Canadian Congress of Labour. Labor-management contract negotiations (1951–64), strikes (1955–61), and Canadian UAW Council (1950–63) are discussed in the correspondence of George Burt, John Livingston, Emil Mazey, and Leonard Woodcock.
15 linear feet.

UAW LOCAL 200. *Papers, 1948–64.*
Correspondence, minutes, resolutions, reports, arbitration hearings, clippings, and other materials collected by Local 200, which services the Ford Motor Company of Canada in Windsor, Ontario. Subjects include the suspension of the United Electrical Workers (UE) from the Canadian Congress of Labour, and Local 200's strike in 1951. Correspondents include Ken Bannon, George Burt, M. J. Coldwell, C. S. Jackson, Solon Low, Paul J. J. Martin, Emil Mazey, A. R. Mosher, Arthur Reaume, and Walter Reuther.
4 1/2 linear feet; 2 scrapbooks.

UAW LOCAL 212. *Papers, 1937–55.*
Local 212 services plants of Briggs Manufacturing Company and Chrysler Corporation of Detroit. The collection is comprised of general correspondence and Local 212 officers' correspondence (1937–48); office files (1937–55) consisting of reports, correspondence, memoranda, clippings, and miscellaneous papers; agenda, minutes, and notes from membership, council, Executive Board, plant, committee and stewards' meetings (1937–55); correspondence, reports, notes, and financial records of the financial secretary (1937–54); contracts, agreements, correspondence, reports, and other papers pertaining to wage rates, seniority, apprenticeships, work standards, and contract negotiations (1937–55); and grievance materials (1937–53). Subjects include pre-World War II anti-war organizations, Battle of the Overpass, Briggs strike of 1939, communist issue

(1948), factional issues within the UAW, Labor's Non-Partisan League, Homer Martin controversy, Tom Mooney, organizing of Ford Motor Company, Political Action Committee (PAC) in the 1950s, public housing, Progressive Party (1948), and the War Labor Board. Major correspondents are George Addes, John Dingell, Homer Ferguson, Gerald R. Ford, Richard Frankensteen, Emil Mazey, Blair Moody, Ken Morris, Louis Rabaut, Walter Reuther, August Scholle, R. J. Thomas, Arthur Vandenberg, and G. Mennen Williams.
30 1/2 linear feet.

UAW LOCAL 216. *Papers, 1937—67.*
Local 216 serves as the bargaining agent for employees of the General Motors plant in South Gate, California. The collection contains minutes not only of Local 216 bodies, but also of the Los Angeles CIO Council, the California CIO Council, and the UAW National General Motors Council. Among the topics covered are the GM Strike of 1945—46, war production, and union factionalism. Correspondents include George Addes, Thurman Arnold, Sheridan Downey, Hiram Johnson, William Knowland, Homer Martin, Walter Reuther, and R. J. Thomas.
16 linear feet; 3 scrapbooks.

UAW LOCAL 230. *Papers, April 1946 and March—April 1957.*
Strike bulletins, reprints, and clippings from this Chrysler plant local in Los Angeles.
44 items; [10 linear feet unprocessed].

UAW LOCAL 239. *Papers, 1948—69.*
Office files of the UAW local servicing the Baltimore, Maryland, Fisher Body plant. Correspondence, minutes, financial records, and other items cover such topics as political action, bargaining, alleged racial discrimination in the plant, and factional issues. Among the correspondents are Thomas Alesandro, Frank Fitzsimmons, Arthur Goldberg, George Meany, Madalyn Murray, Joseph Tydings, and most UAW international officers.
11 linear feet.

UAW LOCAL 240. *Papers, 1938—55.*
Amalgamated Local 240 represents salaried and office employees of several companies in Windsor, Ontario, the largest comprising Ford of Canada offices in Windsor. Minutes, briefs, umpire decisions, and other materials cover such topics as grievances, insurance plans, salaries, and job classifications.
1 linear foot.

UAW LOCAL 248. *Papers, 1936—56.*
Correspondence, clippings, pamphlets, flyers, press releases, radio scripts, and newsletters collected by UAW Local 248, Allis-Chalmers Manufacturing Company in West Allis, Wisconsin. Subjects include organizing activities; strikes of 1939, 1941, and 1946—47; the trial of local leadership in 1948; election of local leadership in 1948; election of local officers and delegates; negotiations and contracts; arbitration proceedings; minutes of the local Executive Board, UAW-CIO Joint Council, Allis-Chalmers Council, Milwaukee County CIO, and Wisconsin State Industrial Union Council. Major correspondents are Robert Buse, Harold Christoffel, Matthew Kelly, Harvey Kitzman, Walter Reuther, and Charles M. Schultz.
24 linear feet [unprocessed].

UAW LOCAL 280. *Papers, 1946—61 (predominantly 1948—59).*
UAW Local 280 was the bargaining agent for Continental Motors Corporation, Continental Aviation and Engineering Corporation, and the Engine Plant of Kaiser Corporation of Detroit. Correspondence, agreements, proposed agreements, minutes, grievance records, rate classification records, petitions to the Wage Stabilization Board, and transcripts of the Joint Pension Plan Board comprise the collection. The closing of the Kaiser Engine Plant (1954) and other matters are discussed by Alvin Bentley, Edgar Kaiser, Norman Matthews, Emil Mazey, and Leonard Woodcock.
2 linear feet.

UAW LOCAL 341. *Papers, 1937—61.*
Local 341 serviced the Marmon-Herrington Company of Indianapolis, Indiana. The collection contains minutes (1937—61), general office files (1937—60), contracts, and other documents. Subjects include arbitration of grievances, NLRB, and the War Labor Board. Among the correspondents are George Addes, George D. Aiken, George Burt, Homer Capehart, A. W. Herrington, William Jenner, Emil Mazey, Walter Reuther, and R. J. Thomas.
1 1/2 linear feet.

UAW LOCAL 397. *Papers, 1937—38.*
Minutes of the first meetings of Local 397, Coach and Body, Ltd. of Brantford, Ontario.
1/2 linear foot.

UAW LOCAL 399. *Papers, 1949—68.*
Minutes, pension agreements, and copies of the local's bulletin *Shield* (1958—63) are included among the papers of Local 399, organized in New

Collections

Toronto, Ontario, in 1951 to service Anaconda American Brass, Ltd. The Canadian UAW Council, the Canadian Labour Congress, and working conditions are discussed. Some minutes of Local 110, CCL (1949–50), are in the collection. *1/2 linear foot.*

UAW LOCAL 400. *Papers, 1942–62.*
Local 400 is the bargaining agent for the Ford Motor plants and facilities in Highland Park, Utica, and Mount Clemens, Michigan, and also for the Michigan Proving Grounds of the Ford Motor Company. Minutes, correspondence, reports, speeches, circulars, and grievance records deal with the Allis-Chalmers strike; Reuther-Thomas factionalism; fair employment practices; Ford negotiations (1947); merger of the Wayne County (Michigan) AFL and CIO; portal-to-portal pay; retirement and pension plans. Correspondents include George Addes, Ken Bannon, Albert Cobo, Edward Connor, George Edwards, Homer Ferguson, Philip Hart, Norman Matthews, Emil Mazey, Louis Miriani, Ken Morris, William Oliver, Victor Reuther, Walter Reuther, R. J. Thomas, and Arthur Vandenberg.
31 linear feet.

UAW LOCAL 410. *Papers, 1937–59.*
Until the late 1950s Local 410 represented employees of the Midland Steel Corporation in Detroit. Included are correspondence, minutes, handbills, and reports pertaining to cooperation between locals during the UAW's early years, the National War Labor Board, fair employment practices, local elections, and collective bargaining. Correspondents include George Addes, Norman Matthews, and Walter Reuther. *10 1/2 linear feet.*

UAW LOCAL 444. *Papers, 1956–61.*
General office files consisting of correspondence, minutes, notes, leaflets, and miscellaneous materials collected by Local 444, which services the Chrysler Corporation in Windsor, Ontario.
1/2 linear foot.

UAW LOCAL 595. *Papers, 1946–48.*
Minutes of meetings on negotiation of local strike issues (1946); a time-study report; and correspondence collected by Local 595, which services the General Motors plant in Linden, New Jersey.
62 items.

UAW LOCAL 599. *Papers, 1935–66.*
Buick Local 599 of Flint, Michigan, was originally organized in 1935 as AFL Federal Labor Union 18512. The collection consists of the files of

the local's Education Department, the Bargaining Committee, and a general office file. Included are minutes of the Executive Board, the Bargaining Committee, membership meetings, and meetings of other smaller local committees. Among the subjects covered are the development of Local 599, elections, and fair employment practices. Correspondents include John Livingston and Walter Reuther.
5 linear feet.

UAW LOCAL 600. *Papers, 1942–50.*
Executive Board minutes, business correspondence, and committee reports are included, in addition to clippings and posters.
2 1/2 linear feet [unprocessed].

UAW LOCAL 602. *Papers, 1937–62.*
Correspondence, minutes, clippings, grievances and umpires' decisions, agreements, financial reports, seniority books, and memoranda collected by UAW Local 602, which services the Fisher Body plant in Lansing, Michigan. Subjects include the Homer Martin controversy, Local 602 Social Building Club, NLRB election (1940), and strike (1945). Correspondents include George Addes, Charles Chamberlain, Patrick V. McNamara, Emil Mazey, Philip Murray, Walter Reuther, and R. J. Thomas.
20 linear feet.

UAW LOCAL 650. *Papers, 1937–64.*
Correspondence, minutes, proposed agreements and demands, grievance records, seniority records, and wage and rate classifications of Local 650, the bargaining agent for the Reo Motor Company, Lansing, Michigan, and, until 1938, a branch of Local 182, an amalgamated union of all the workers in Lansing. In February 1939, the Reo branch of Local 182 applied to the UAW Executive Board for a separate charter; the request was granted and Local 650 was established. Subjects include Local 182 strike (1946), dispute between Reo Motors and Wayne Keeney (1946–47), and strike (1951). Among the correspondents are George Addes, Richard Frankensteen, Homer Martin, Victor Reuther, Walter Reuther, August Scholle, and R. J. Thomas.
13 linear feet.

UAW LOCAL 662. *Papers, 1934–65.*
Local 662 services the General Motors, Delco-Remy Division plant in Anderson, Indiana. Minutes, correspondence, handbills, and other items reflect not only the activities of Local 662, but also of UAW Women's Auxiliary 203. Among the subjects covered are UAW summer schools; the

Collections

merger of the AFL and CIO in Indiana; and the Perfect Circle Strike of 1955.
2 linear feet; 1 volume.

UAW LOCAL 664. *Papers, 1939–61.*
Local 664 is the bargaining agent for Fisher Body, Chevrolet, and the Prophet Company, North Tarrytown, New York. Correspondence, agreements, appeal cases, and newspaper clippings review the Homer Martin controversy, strikes, Civil Rights Defense Committee, and General Motors National Council and Sub-Council organizations. Correspondents include George Addes, Martin Gerber, Allan Haywood, John Livingston, Walter Reuther, and R. J. Thomas.
1/2 linear foot.

UAW LOCAL 678. *Papers, 1948–68.*
Local 678 (now merged with Local 239) was a Baltimore, Maryland, local representing the General Motors Assembly Division. Membership lists (1948–68), seniority status (1956), and new hires (1952–57); minutes of the Executive Board (1948–68), the Baltimore AFL-CIO meetings (1960–68), and the Maryland and District of Columbia AFL-CIO Executive Board (1957–68); correspondence with local union officers and committee chairmen; financial reports (1949–68); employment status reports (1956–64) and local contract agreements (1951–68); and the 1961 strike are among the topics covered. Major correspondents are Daniel Brewster, Edward A. Garmatz, Albert J. Mattes, Emil Mazey, Roy Reuther, Walter Reuther, and Leonard Woodcock.
20 linear feet.

UAW LOCAL 742. *Papers, 1941–54.*
Amalgamated UAW Local 742 serviced Briggs Manufacturing and other companies and is now part of UAW Briggs Local 212. Correspondence, minutes, and records of meetings are included, also pension material and other union business. The Harry Bridges and Sam Sweet cases are discussed in some files, as is the Committee on Fair Employment Practices [FEPC] and the Political Action Committee [PAC]. Correspondents are George Addes, Melvin Bishop, George Edwards, Homer Ferguson, Walter Reuther, and others.
10 1/2 linear feet.

UAW LOCAL 833. *Papers, 1897–1965 (predominantly 1933–60).*
Correspondence, motions, briefs, transcripts, affidavits, exhibits, pamphlets, boycott resolutions, radio scripts, daily strike newsletters, con-

tracts, and negotiation files of UAW Local 833, the bargaining agent for employees of the Kohler Company, Kohler, Wisconsin. The papers in this collection deal mainly with the 1954–60 strike and boycott against the Kohler Co., the National Labor Relations Board case growing out of the strike, and the McClellan Committee hearings investigating the UAW and the Kohler strike specifically. Other subjects covered are the 1934–41 strike of AFL Federal Labor Union 18545 against the Kohler Co., the Kohler Workers Association, the UAW organizing drive, and silicosis. Important correspondents are: Paul Douglas, James R. Hoffa, Irving Ives, Walter J. Kohler, Jr., James E. Murray, William Proxmire, Carl Sandburg, and Alexander Wiley.
51 linear feet; 18 scrapbooks.

UAW LOCAL 870. *Papers, 1940–70.*
Local 870 represents the Ford Motor Company of Dallas, Texas. Correspondence, notices, minutes, statements, and other forms concern the Local's finances (1944–70), grievances (1941–61), the National Negotiating Committee (1949), compensation claims (1947–49), and the Texas State Industrial Union Council (1942–51). Among the correspondents are George F. Addes, Ken Bannon, Richard T. Leonard, Emil Mazey, Victor Reuther, and Walter Reuther.
5 linear feet [unprocessed].

UAW LOCAL 887. *Papers, 1939–65.*
Correspondence, National War Labor Board [NWLB] briefs, minutes, and other materials cover the work of Local 887, representing workers at the North American Aviation plant in Los Angeles. Topics include NWLB hearings on the unionization of office and technical employees in 1943, and contract negotiations (mid–1940s to mid–1950s).
1/2 linear foot; [8 linear feet unprocessed].

UAW LOCAL 889. *Papers, 1943–65.*
A white-collar amalgamated union, Local 889 was established in 1940, serving Chrysler-related plants and suppliers in southeastern Michigan. Papers include central office files, minutes and correspondence, grievances, seniority lists, and other items.
35 linear feet.

UAW LOCAL 932. *Papers, 1937–64 (predominantly 1940–61).*
Local 932 is a UAW-affiliated body representing workers at the Minneapolis Moline, Inc. plant in Minneapolis, Minnesota. Most of the material actually deals with Local 932's predecessor, United Electrical Radio and

Collections

Machine Workers of America-CIO, Local 1146. The collection includes correspondence, reports, and minutes relating to UE activities such as negotiations, union elections, factionalism, and political lobbying during the period 1938–55. There is also material on the inter-union struggle between the UAW and UE for the right to represent the agricultural implement workers. Among the correspondents are Julius Emspak and James Matles.
11 linear feet.

UAW LOCAL 988. *Papers, 1947–64.*
Minutes of general membership and executive board meetings for Local 988, which represents employees of the International Harvester plant in Memphis, Tennessee. In addition to the minutes, the collection contains proposed by-law revisions, grievances, and correspondence regarding the placing of an administratorship over the local in 1960 by the International Union.
1 linear foot.

UNITED FARM WORKERS

National Offices

UNITED FARM WORKERS. *Papers, 1959–71.*
Correspondence, reports, minutes, memoranda, legal documents, clippings, notes, leaflets, newsletters, publications of the Farm Worker Press, and miscellaneous materials collected by the United Farm Workers (formerly the United Farm Workers Organizing Committee), which was formed in 1966 with the merger of the National Farm Workers Association, an independent organization founded in 1962 by Cesar Chavez, and the Agricultural Workers Organizing Committee (AFL-CIO). Subjects include AWOC strikes (1959–65), Agricultural Workers Freedom to Work Association, California Rural Legal Assistance, Cesar Chavez's fast for nonviolence (1968), contracts with wine and table grape growers, the DiGiorgio Corporation arbitration and representation election, employment of Mexican nationals, the grape strike and boycotts, living and working conditions of farm workers, the merger of the National Farm Workers Association and the Agricultural Workers Organizing Committee (1966), National Farm Workers Association first organizational meeting and constitutional convention (1962), pesticides and occupational health and hazards, the Pilgrimage to Sacramento (1966), Senate hearings on migratory labor, and the UFWOC strike in Texas. Correspondents include Edmund G. Brown, Ernesto Galarza, Wayne C. Hartmire, Robert F. Kennedy, William Kircher, Thomas Kuchel, Walter Reuther, Paul Schrade, Jesse Unruh, Harrison Williams, and Willard Wirtz.
27 linear feet; [120 linear feet unprocessed].

UNITED FARM WORKERS ORGANIZING COMMITTEE: TEXAS BRANCH. *Papers, 1960–71.*
Correspondence, reports, clippings, and leaflets relating to the activities of the Texas branch of the United Farm Workers Organizing Committee (1967–71); and clippings and leaflets pertaining to Antonio Orendain and the Hanford (California) Community Service Organization (1960–64). The materials were collected by Mr. Orendain and the Texas branch of UFWOC in McAllen, Texas. Subjects include the Community Service Organization; farm workers' strike in Rio Grande City/Starr County, Texas; Field Foundation's legal services grant; the National Farm Workers Service Center (including its medical and legal facilities); and the UFWOC-Texas radio program, "La Voz del Campesino." Correspondents include Cesar Chavez, Reynaldo de la Cruz, Bishop Patricio Flores, and Bishop Humberto Medeiros.   *1/2 linear foot.*

Boycott and State Offices

UNITED FARM WORKERS: BOSTON BOYCOTT OFFICE. *Papers, 1966–71.*
Files concerned with the national consumer boycott of California grapes in the Boston area. Correspondence, clippings, and other records document such topics as the boycott of grapes and lettuce and the false labeling of California grapes. Letters from Cesar Chavez are included in the collection.
6 1/2 linear feet.

UNITED FARM WORKERS: NEW YORK BOYCOTT OFFICE. *Papers, 1965–70, (predominantly 1967–70).*
Correspondence, reports, financial records, memoranda, clippings, legal documents, leaflets, newsletters, and miscellaneous printed material collected by the New York City Boycott Office of the United Farm Workers Organizing Committee (AFL-CIO), on the various aspects of the boycott of California table grapes (1967–70). Subjects include the Agricultural Workers Freedom to Work Association, California Rural Legal Assistance, consumer suits against chain stores, Department of Defense purchases of grapes, false labeling of grapes, Giumarra strike and boycott, National Labor Relations Act, pesticides and the Federal Food and Drug Administration, secondary boycotts, and the Senate Subcommittee on Migratory Labor. Correspondents include Timothy Costello, Charles Goodell, Wayne C. Hartmire, Jacob Javits, William Kircher, John V. Lindsay, Frank O'Connor, and William Ryan.
9 1/2 linear feet.

UNITED FARM WORKERS: OTHER BOYCOTT AND STATE OFFICES. *Papers, 1968–70.*
Correspondence, press releases, news clippings, newsletters, leaflets, broadsides, and photographs concerning the activities of the local and state offices of Arizona, Chicago, Chicago Heights (Illinois), Cleveland, Columbus (Ohio), Denver, Detroit, Hawaii, London (England), Los Angeles, Monmouth (New Jersey), Milwaukee, New York State, New Orleans, Northridge (California), Ohio, Pacoima (California), Philadelphia, San Fernando (California), San Jose (California), Seattle, and Stark County (Ohio).
10 linear feet.

OTHER ORGANIZATIONS

AMERICAN CIVIL LIBERTIES UNION: MICHIGAN CHAPTER. *Papers, 1955–66.*
Correspondence, reports, minutes, press releases, newspaper clippings, and published material. Among the subjects are censorship, academic freedom, church-state relations, civil rights, police conduct, House Un-American Activities Committee, and deportation cases. Correspondents include Charles Lockwood, Ernest Mazey, and Rolland O'Hare.
22 linear feet; [54 linear feet unprocessed].

AFL-CIO. *Papers, 1916–52.*
Four reels of microfilm obtained from the records department of the AFL-CIO. Specifically filmed were correspondence files between the AFL and the national offices of the AFT (1916–52); ALPA (1938–52), and UAW (1938–48).
4 reels.

ANN ARBOR TEACHERS ASSOCIATION. *Papers, 1911–68.*
Minutes (1911–68), correspondence, financial papers, reports, salary schedules, clippings, memoranda, and miscellaneous materials collected by the Ann Arbor (Michigan) Teachers Association. Established in 1911 as the Ann Arbor Teachers Club, it now serves as the professional organization and bargaining agent for teachers in the Ann Arbor School District. Subjects include teacher certification, salary negotiations, school board elections, unionism vs. professionalism, busing of pupils, and legislation relevant to education.
8 linear feet; [10 linear feet unprocessed].

ASSOCIATION OF CATHOLIC TRADE UNIONISTS OF DETROIT. *Papers, 1938–68 (predominantly 1938–56).*
Correspondence, speeches, newspapers and clippings, pamphlets, and handbills. The Association of Catholic Trade Unionists of Detroit was a liberal Roman Catholic group organized in 1938 to strengthen the trade union movement along Christian lines. The main project of the Detroit chapter was the publication of the *Michigan Labor Leader,* which eventually became the *Wage Earner.* The paper took a leading role in the campaign against communism. In addition to publishing the newspaper, the ACTU promoted schools in which problems of religion and labor were studied. Members of the Association (which included some Protestants) came from a variety of local unions in the Detroit area. Subjects include CIO (1939–

45); Wayne County CIO Council (1942–46); Michigan CIO Council; UAW local unions, especially Ford Local 600; AFL-CIO unions, including Bakery Workers, Brotherhood of Carpenters, Construction Workers, Brotherhood of Electrical Workers, United Electrical Workers, Furniture Workers, Mine Mill and Smelter Workers, Packinghouse Workers, Typographical Workers, United Auto Workers, and Woodworkers; Ford Strike (1949); General Motors Strike (1945); organization of Ford Motor Company (1940–41); and organization of General Motors (1939–45). Correspondents include George Addes, Richard Deverall, Tom Doherty, Henry Ford II, Richard Frankensteen, Owen Knox, Victor LoPinto, Edward Cardinal Mooney, Lucien Nedzi, Ben Probe, Walter Reuther, Paul Ste.-Marie, and Paul Weber.   *19 1/2 linear feet.*

CALIFORNIA MIGRANT MINISTRY. *Papers, 1939–70 (predominantly 1950–70).*
Correspondence, reports, memoranda, speeches, minutes, clippings, pamphlets, and newsletters collected by the California Migrant Ministry, an agency of the Southern and Northern California Council of Churches, and an affiliate of the Migrant Ministry of the National Council of Churches. The California Migrant Ministry provides various services for farm workers and their families. Subjects include the Delano Grape Strike, grape boycotts, labor organizing among farm workers, national and state legislation for farm workers, Public Law 78 and braceros, rural housing and poverty, and worker-priest programs. Correspondents include Edmund G. Brown, Cesar Chavez, John Connally, Clair Engle, Ernesto Galarza, John F. Kennedy, Thomas Kuchel, George Murphy, James Roosevelt, Harrison Williams, and Willard Wirtz.   *21 linear feet.*

CIGAR MAKERS UNION NO. 130. *Papers, 1885–87.*
Minute book, 1885–87. This union was located in Saginaw, Michigan.
1 volume.

CITIZENS' CRUSADE AGAINST POVERTY. *Papers, 1964–70.*
The files of a non-partisan coalition of organizations and individuals dedicated to eradicating poverty from the U.S. Two of its principal activities were the Citizens' Board of Inquiry on the Child Development Group of Mississippi and the Citizens' Board of Inquiry into Hunger and Malnutrition in the United States. Other topics covered include the Office of Economic Opportunity, the Southern Rural Action Program, and training programs to organize the poor. Correspondents include I.W. Abel, Saul Alinsky, Walter Reuther, Sargent Shriver, and Whitney Young.
4 linear feet.

CITIZENS FOR MICHIGAN. *Papers, 1959–62.*
Articles of incorporation, constitution, and by-laws; correspondence; minutes; press releases and newsletters; mailing lists; speeches; and newspaper clippings of this independent, non-profit organization, established in 1959 to study the current and anticipated needs of the state of Michigan and to seek ways to implement programs. George Romney was chairman of this organization from its inception until it ceased operations in 1962. Subjects include Executive Committee and Board of Directors, Michigan Constitutional Convention (1960–62), and study reports of members of Citizens for Michigan. Correspondents include Eugene Black, Philip Hart, Clare Hoffman, John Lesinski, Robert McNamara, and Charles Potter.
11 1/2 linear feet.

CIVIL RIGHTS CONGRESS OF MICHIGAN. *Papers, 1935–54.*
Correspondence, minutes, financial records, petitions, speeches, legal documents, index case files, press releases, newspaper clippings, bulletins, and pamphlets. The Civil Rights Congress was organized in 1935, and, until 1937, aided the cause of labor; protected academic freedom; and attacked police brutality, censorship, the Black Legion, the Ku Klux Klan, fascism, and discrimination. In 1938, its name was changed to the Civil Rights Federation and the group then turned to problems concerning discrimination against blacks and political minorities. Subjects include strikes, police brutality, discrimination, the Black Legion, the Ku Klux Klan, fascism, political freedom, the Dies Committee, the House Un-American Activities Committee, the Smith Act, Fair Employment Practices Commission, poll tax, anti-lynching, Gerald L.K. Smith, Father Coughlin, the Rosenberg case, and the Scottsboro Boys. Correspondents are Roger Baldwin, Charles Beard, Ruth Benedict, Frank Boas, Frank Couzens, Tracy Doll, Ernest Goodman, Dashiell Hammett, David Henry, Granville Hicks, Edward Jeffries, Estes Kefauver, Milton Kemnitz, Owen Knox, Robert LaFollette, Patrick McNamara, Vito Marcantonio, Homer Martin, A.G. Mezerick, Frank Murphy, Stanley Nowak, William Patterson, Harper Paulson, Louis Rabaut, Ann Shore, and Robert Weaver.
47 linear feet.

COMMUNICATIONS WORKERS OF AMERICA LOCAL 4000. *Papers, 1930–68.*
Executive Board minutes, correspondence, publications, and mimeographed material concerning the general activities of the union, and factionalism within the local relating to affiliation with the national Communications Workers of America.
24 linear feet [unprocessed].

Collections

CONGRESS OF INDUSTRIAL ORGANIZATIONS: OFFICE OF THE PRESIDENT. *Papers, 1940-56 (predominantly 1953-55).*
Files of the CIO under the presidency of Walter Reuther divided into five series: President, Walter Reuther; Assistant to the President, Victor Reuther; European Office and International Affairs; Legislative; and Housing Committee. Correspondence, reports, minutes, and other records cover a wide range of topics including the AFL-CIO merger (1955); CIO Conventions and executive board meetings (1953-55); housing, labor, and foreign policy; foreign trade unions; the Taft-Hartley Act (1952-54); and assistance to underdeveloped countries. Correspondents include all major labor and political figures of the period.
50 linear feet [unprocessed].

CONGRESS OF INDUSTRIAL ORGANIZATIONS: DEPARTMENT OF EDUCATION AND RESEARCH COLLECTION. *Papers, 1945-55.*
Papers, 1945-55.
The office files of George T. Guernsey, associate director in charge of education for 1945-55, under directors Kermit Eby and Stanley Ruttenberg. In the collection are packets of educational materials for education directors and worker education programs; pamphlets; songbooks; and material on labor films, union summer schools, conferences, and other topics. Correspondents include Dorothy Bendix, James B. Carey, Kermit Eby, Brownie Lee Jones, Joseph Kowalski, Victor Reuther, Lawrence Rogin, Stanley Ruttenberg, and Brendan Sexton.
5 1/2 linear feet.

CONGRESS OF INDUSTRIAL ORGANIZATIONS: OFFICE OF THE SECRETARY-TREASURER. *Papers, 1935-60,*
PART I – JAMES B. CAREY PAPERS, 1935-55. *71 linear feet.*
Correspondence, reports, minutes, transcripts, press releases, speeches, and other materials from the office of James Carey, secretary-treasurer of the CIO from 1938 to 1955. Mr. Carey served as chairman of the CIO Civil Rights Committee and secretary-treasurer of the Philip Murray Memorial Foundation. He was the CIO representative to many international conferences, held a number of advisory positions with U.S. government agencies, and was on the executive boards of many private organizations. The topics cover a wide range of CIO activities. Among these are attempts to reunite the AFL and the CIO from 1937 to 1942 and again in 1955; Harry Bridges; communism in the labor movement; financial affairs of the CIO; International Confederation of Free Trade Unions and World Federation of Trade Unions; disputes within electrical workers' unions; CIO and Latin America; labor in World War II; and political action. Other subjects are the

Canadian-American Conference on Foreign Policy (1951); civil rights; European recovery programs; foreign aid; housing and rent control; price and wage regulations; Social Security; and the United Nations. Correspondents include nearly every major labor figure for the period. Others, whose letters are found in the collection, are Alben Barkley, Chester Bowles, Clifford Case, Emmanuel Celler, Everett Dirksen, Paul Douglas, Arthur Goldberg, Averell Harriman, Leon Henderson, Paul Hoffman, Cordell Hull, Hubert Humphrey, John F. Kennedy, Fiorello LaGuardia, Herbert Lehman, Archibald MacLeish, John McCormack, Warren Magnuson, James Mitchell, Wayne Morse, Westbrook Pegler, Francis Perkins, Eleanor Roosevelt, Franklin D. Roosevelt, Leverett Saltonstall, Francis Cardinal Spellman, John Steelman, Edward Stettinius, Stuart Symington, Harry S. Truman, Oswald Garrison Villard, and Sumner Welles.

PART II — GEORGE L.P. WEAVER PAPERS, 1941–60. *48 1/2 linear feet.*

George Weaver, in addition to serving as assistant secretary-treasurer of the CIO, also held at various times the positions of assistant to the president of the United Transportation Service Employees Union; director of the CIO's Civil Rights Committee; assistant to the chairman of the National Security Resources Board; and member of the Committee to Reorganize the Reconstruction Finance Corporation. Mr. Weaver also played leading roles in the senatorial and presidential campaigns of Stuart Symington. Correspondence, reports, minutes, notes, and other materials cover his work in these areas. In addition to labor topics, the Weaver papers cover Americans for Democratic Action; civil rights; Atlantic Conference of 1959; tin missions to Bolivia and southeast Asia (1951–52); housing; defense; manpower; McCarran-Walter Immigration Bill; NAACP; and the Taft-Hartley Act. Besides leading labor figures, the correspondents include Alben Barkley, Paul Butler, Emmanuel Celler, Clark Clifford, Jonathan Daniels, Charles Diggs, Paul Douglas, Arthur Goldberg, Averell Harriman, Hubert Humphrey, Jacob Javits, Lyndon Johnson, Thurgood Marshall, John McClellan, Richard Nixon, Adam Clayton Powell, William Rogers, Franklin Roosevelt, Elmo Roper, Leverett Saltonstall, Stuart Symington, Robert Weaver, Walter White, Roy Wilkins, and Whitney Young.
119 1/2 linear feet.

DETROIT COMMISSION ON COMMUNITY RELATIONS. *Papers, 1942–69.*
The Commission on Community Relations was established by the City of Detroit to make recommendations to improve governmental services affecting racial relations, and to promote understanding between the races. Minutes, correspondence, and case studies document the Commission's

Collections

efforts to achieve these goals. Topics covered include discrimination in housing, the 1943 race riots, southern migration into Detroit, police-community relations, and school redistricting.
22 linear feet.

DETROIT COMMITTEE TO END THE WAR IN VIETNAM. *Papers, 1957–68.*
This collection is comprised of minutes, newspapers, open letters, and reports. It includes the Detroit Branch minutes (1962–66); the Detroit Executive Committee minutes (1960–66); the *Michigan Militant Newsletter* (1959–60); *Youth Discussion Bulletin;* and open letters and reports which cover the Michigan Mobilization Committee and November Days (1966).
2 linear feet.

DETROIT COUNCIL OF CHURCHES. *Papers, 1920–69.*
Organized in 1919, the Detroit Council of Churches represents more than 800 churches in the metropolitan Detroit area. The collection covers two main areas of the Council's work: Christian education and social-political action. Among the topics covered are civil rights, fluoridation, housing, indecent literature, religion, and public education. Correspondents include Jerome Cavanagh, Emanuel Celler, James Farmer, Robert Griffin, Philip Hart, Luther Hodges, Patrick McNamara, and George Romney.
16 1/2 linear feet.

DETROIT EDUCATION ASSOCIATION COLLECTION. *Papers, 1914–68 (predominantly 1957–67).*
Correspondence, reports, minutes, constitutions, awards, petitions, publicity material, drafts of articles, notes, posters, press releases, newsletters, calendar of meetings, bound journals, scrapbooks, and newspaper clippings of the Detroit Education Association and its predecessor, the Detroit Teachers Association. Subjects include DEA collective bargaining election contests with the Detroit Federation of Teachers (1963–66); DEA budget presentations to the Board of Education (1955–64); DEA constitutional revision (1963–64); DEA contract negotiations with the Board of Education (1961–67); DEA lobbying activities with the Michigan Legislature (1955–65); DEA membership campaigns (1959–66); Michigan Education Association Board of Directors meetings (1963–67); MEA Representative Assembly (1964); MEA regional conferences (1960–64); MEA Teachers Institute Day (1964); National Education Association conventions (1959–66); Detroit school millage campaigns (1959–63); Detroit Teachers retirement programs (1951–65); education

Other Organizations

proposals for Detroit public schools (1958); Livonia Education Association (1962–63); and Michigan Constitutional Convention (1961–62). Correspondents include Samuel M. Brownell, Charles Diggs, John Dingell, Martha Griffiths, Thaddeus M. Machrowicz, Patrick V. McNamara, George Romney, Harold Ryan, and Robert Waldron.
24 1/2 linear feet.

DETROIT INDUSTRIAL MISSION. *Papers, 1954–58.*
The Detroit Industrial Mission is a church group exploring the relationship of the church to factory workers and the place of the church in daily industrial life. The papers include correspondence, reports, project evaluations, and various papers by project members.   *2 linear feet.*

DETROIT TEACHERS ASSOCIATION: WAYNE STATE UNIVERSITY CHAPTER. *Papers, 1933–63.*
Financial papers and membership lists (1933–63), constitution and bylaws (1938), minutes (1941–42), and correspondence (1947–48, 1963), collected by the Wayne State University Chapter of the Detroit Teachers Association (later the Detroit Education Association).   *1/2 linear foot.*

FAIR HOUSING CAMPAIGN IN BIRMINGHAM, MICHIGAN. *Papers, 1968.*
Correspondence, printed informational material, newspaper clippings, and memorabilia of a group of volunteers who worked for the passage of Ordinance 692, which disallowed discrimination in the sale or lease of real estate in Birmingham, Michigan. Correspondents include Kent Mathewson, Mary Augusta Rogers, and George Romney.
1/2 linear foot.

THE GI UNDERGROUND PRESS AND AMERICAN SERVICEMEN'S UNION. *Papers, 1969–71.*
Press releases, newsletters, and other items from the files of *Broken Arrow,* a newspaper of the GI Underground Press and the American Servicemen's Union, an alliance for the exchange of views on social and political events. Topics covered include attitudes of servicemen towards the war in Viet Nam, military injustice, student protest and military boycotts, and antiwar demonstrations.
2 linear feet.

GRAND RAPIDS EDUCATION ASSOCIATION. *Papers, 1907–67.*
Correspondence, clippings, financial papers, reports, and agreements of the Grand Rapids (Michigan) Education Association (1964–66); reports from

Collections

the Michigan Education Association (1965–66); proceedings, correspondence, reports, handbooks, and surveys of the Grand Rapids Board of Education (1955–66); reports, budgets, resolutions, and surveys of the National Education Association (1965–67); and minutes (1907–34) and newsletters (1933–63) of the Grand Rapids Teachers Club. The materials were collected by the Grand Rapids Education Association, founded in 1907 as the Grand Rapids Teachers Club. Subjects include teacher salaries, negotiations, elections, and professional problems.
4 linear feet; 2 scrapbooks.

INDUSTRIAL WORKERS OF THE WORLD. *Papers, 1905–72.*
Founded in 1905, the IWW numbered among its members (known popularly as Wobblies) lumberjacks, miners, farmhands (especially migrant workers), sailors, and workers in textile mills. The files include proceedings, trial records and evidence, newspapers, pamphlets, and correspondence. Subjects of interest include the Centralia Conspiracy; criminal syndicalism; the Everett Massacre; Free Speech fights; organization of farm workers; pacifism and patriotism during World War I; labor conditions; the controversy between craft and industrial unionism; government raids and seizures; trials of various members; foreign IWW administrations; strikes; political prisoners; and information on such figures as Vincent St. John, William D. Haywood, Joe Hill, and Elizabeth Gurley Flynn. Correspondents include T.J. Bogard, Arthur Boose, Richard Brazier, A.S. Embree, William D. Haywood, Claude Irwin, Joyce Kornbluh, John A. Law, George Lucas, Albert Prashner, Rudolf Rocker, Vincent St. John, Nicolaas Steelink, Fred W. Thompson, William Unger, Walt Westman, and Claire Whitaker.
80 linear feet; 45 reels of microfilm.

JEWISH LABOR COMMITTEE. *Papers, 1949–62.*
Correspondence, reports, press releases, publications, memoranda, clippings, and miscellaneous materials collected by the Jewish Labor Committee, which was organized by Detroit Jewish workers and labor organizations in 1934 to fight totalitarianism abroad and discrimination at home. Among topics discussed are civil rights, NAACP, discrimination in housing and employment, bombings in the South, school prayer issue, and Soviet anti-semitism. Correspondents include Charles C. Diggs, Jr., Martha Griffiths, John Hannah, Adolph Held, Herbert Hill, William Oliver, William T. Patrick, Jr., August Scholle, Neil Staebler, and G. Mennen Williams.
5 linear feet.

JOINT COMMITTEE ON LIBRARY SERVICE TO LABOR GROUPS.
Papers, 1946–66 (predominantly 1948–63).
Mostly correspondence, drafts of publications, and minutes and reports. The Committee on Library Service to Labor Groups was established in 1945 to encourage and assist public libraries to develop specialized services useful to labor. Throughout its history, the Committee has received support from the American Library Association, the AFL, the CIO, and the AFL-CIO. Subjects relate to labor education. Correspondents include Frank Henson, Myles Horton, and Brownie Lee Jones.
5 linear feet.

KENOSHA LABOR. *Papers, 1933–66.*
Kenosha Labor is the newspaper of the labor movement in Kenosha, Wisconsin. The papers of this journal include materials on UAW Local 72 at American Motors in Kenosha; strikes; the Trade Union Unity League; WPA; and the Wisconsin Employment Relations Board.
1/2 linear foot.

LABOR'S NON-PARTISAN LEAGUE. *Papers, 1938–42.*
Mostly convention material from the Michigan area, including proceedings, programs, delegate lists, and other items.   *1/2 linear foot.*

LIVONIA EDUCATION ASSOCIATION. *Papers, 1945–68.*
Correspondence; minutes; reports; memoranda; contracts; procedure manuals; clippings; reference material; and publications of educational organizations comprising the files of the Livonia (Michigan) Education Association, established in 1945 as the Livonia Township Teachers Club, which serves as the professional organization and bargaining agent for teachers in the Livonia School District. Subjects include school board and school millage elections, teacher strikes (1964–65; 1967–68), and unionism vs. professionalism. Correspondents include Lynn Bartlett, Raymond Dzendzel, Martha W. Griffiths, Philip Hart, Sander Levin, and George Romney.   *15 linear feet.*

MICHIGAN AFL-CIO. *Papers, 1939–58.*
Correspondence, memoranda, reports, clippings, resolutions, minutes, notes, court decisions, hearings, pamphlets, press releases, posters, and miscellaneous materials comprising the general office files of Michigan CIO Council presidents John Gibson and August Scholle (1943–54); Michigan CIO secretary-treasurers John Gibson, Ben Probe, and Barney Hopkins (1939–54); the files of Tom Downs relating to his work as Michigan CIO

Collections

Council representative, state legislative representative of the CIO, and member of the Michigan Employment Security Commission (1947–54); the editor's files and financial records of the *Michigan CIO News* (1939–52); the Michigan CIO Education Department's general files (1946–55): Fair Employment Practices Committee files (1946–49): Radio Council files (1948–51), and files of summer schools and training institutes (1946–54); miscellaneous financial records, Executive Board minutes, correspondence, and miscellaneous materials of the Michigan Federation of Labor prior to its merger in 1958 with the Michigan CIO Council (1940–58). Subjects include AFL-CIO merger, anti-labor legislation, civil rights, election campaigns, equal rights for women, farm labor and farmers' unions, federal wage and hours legislation, Ford Strike (1949), importation of Mexican farm workers, Labor's League for Political Education, legislative apportionment and redistricting, McCarran-Walter Act, peacetime draft controversy (1945–47), Progressive Party/Henry Wallace campaign (1948), public housing and rent control, unemployment and workmen's compensation legislation, use of prisoners of war in the Michigan lumber industry, and workers education. Correspondents include James B. Carey, Gerald R. Ford, Martha Griffiths, Philip Hart, Hubert Humphrey, Patrick V. McNamara, Walter Reuther, George Romney, Franklin D. Roosevelt, Robert Taft, Maurice Tobin, Harry S. Truman, Arthur Vandenberg, Roy Wilkins, G. Mennen Williams, Leonard Woodcock, and many other prominent people active in politics, civil rights, labor, business, education, and civic affairs.
103 linear feet; [200 linear feet unprocessed].

MICHIGAN AFL-CIO: LANSING OFFICE. *Papers, 1930–63 (predominantly 1952–56).*
Reference files consisting primarily of clippings and some press releases, biographical material, voting records, correspondence, legislative records, and notes on individuals, unions, organizations, Michigan state departments and agencies, topics of current interest, and elected and appointed local, state, and national officials. The materials were collected by the Lansing office of the Michigan CIO Council and Michigan AFL-CIO. Topics include Bricker Amendment, Michigan state budgets, Albert Cobo, FEPC, education, Dwight Eisenhower, election recounts, guaranteed annual wage, health care, housing, Michigan Constitutional Convention, Frank McKay, Kohler Company, Patrick McNamara, Michigan Farm Bureau, migrant labor, Walter Reuther, George Romney, Eleanor Roosevelt, legislative reapportionment, Robert Taft, taxes, and Wayne County.
19 linear feet.

Other Organizations

MICHIGAN COMMISSION ON DISPLACED PERSONS. *Papers, 1937–65.*
Correspondence, minutes, reports, clippings, memoranda, speeches, resolutions, press releases, immigrant and refugee arrival lists, and miscellaneous materials relating to the Michigan Committee on Displaced Persons (1946–51), the Michigan Commission on Displaced Persons (1949–60), the Michigan Committee on Immigration (1951–64), wartime aliens and naturalized citizens (1940–47), refugee records (1953–65), and "Interpreter Releases" (1937–64). The materials were collected by the Michigan Commission on Displaced Persons and Refugees. Subjects include licensing of immigrant physicians; wartime aliens; the McCarran-Walter Act; and other legislation affecting immigrants and refugees. Among the correspondents are John Dingell, Paul Douglas, Homer Ferguson, Hubert Humphrey, Jacob Javits, Estes Kefauver, Herbert Lehman, Blair Moody, Roy Reuther, George Romney, Arthur Vandenberg, and G. Mennen Williams.
23 1/2 linear feet.

MICHIGAN CONSTITUTIONAL CONVENTION. *Papers, 1961.*
State of Michigan Constitutional Convention, 1961, Official Record (2 volumes); *Journal of the Constitutional Convention,* (1961); "Constitution of the State of Michigan" (a workbook); *Financial Report of the State of Michigan,* Part 2; *A Comparative Analysis of the Michigan Constitution,* Volume 1; and papers of the Michigan Institute of Local Government, collected by Lillian Hatcher, a Democratic delegate to the Convention.
1 1/2 linear feet.

MICHIGAN WELFARE LEAGUE. *Papers, 1916–65.*
The League is interested in physical and mental health, mental retardation, juvenile and adult corrections, family and child welfare, public assistance, recreation and group work, special education, aging, youth problems, migrant labor, and human relations. Minutes, newsletters, correspondence, and other documents reflect the League's work in these areas. Among the correspondents are Jerome Cavanagh, Anthony Celebrezze, Philip Hart, Walter Heller, Patrick McNamara, George Romney, George Smathers, Robert Weaver, and Leonard Woodcock.
30 linear feet.

MINERS FOR DEMOCRACY. *Papers, 1941–73 (predominantly 1969–72).*
The files of the reform group within the United Mine Workers whose activities led to the ouster of former president Tony Boyle. Correspondence, dispositions, transcripts, briefs, and campaign materials relate to

health and safety in coal mines and the UMW elections of 1969 and 1972. Correspondents include Herman Benson, Cesar Chavez, Thomas Eagleton, Jacob Javits, Claiborne Pell, and George Shultz.
31 1/2 linear feet.

NATIONAL ASSOCIATION FOR THE ADVANCEMENT OF COLORED PEOPLE: DETROIT BRANCH. *Papers, 1943–66 (predominantly 1961–65).*
Correspondence, reports, speeches, minutes, press releases, civil rights complaint forms, legal affidavits, newspaper clippings, and published material. Subjects include Detroit race riot of 1943; civil rights complaints (1960–66); membership campaigns (1960–65); and scattered records concerning police brutality and discrimination in housing, employment, and education (1960–66). Correspondents include members of the Detroit Common Council (1960–65), Al Barbour, James Del Rio, John Dingell, George Edwards, Ray Girardin, James Hare, Philip Hart, Herbert Hill, Arthur Johnson, Robert Kennedy, Thurgood Marshall, Wade McCree, Patrick McNamara, Clarence Mitchell, Lawrence O'Brien, Adam Clayton Powell, Roy Reuther, George Romney, Philip Rutledge, Horace Sheffield, Otis Smith, John Swainson, Robert Tindal, Edward Turner, James Wadsworth, Robert Weaver, Roy Wilkins, G. Mennen Williams, Myra Wolfgang, and Leonard Woodcock.
16 1/2 linear feet; [22 linear feet unprocessed].

NATIONAL CAMPAIGN FOR AGRICULTURAL DEMOCRACY. *Papers, 1967–70.*
The files of this educational and lobbying organization contain correspondence, minutes, reports, news releases, research files, news clippings, leaflets, and public hearing transcripts concerning efforts to obtain legislation and develop public opinion beneficial to agricultural workers.
14 1/2 linear feet.

NATIONAL SHARECROPPERS FUND. *Papers, mid–1950s–mid–1960s.*
Minutes, reports, correspondence, and other items document the work of the National Advisory Council on Farm Labor and the National Advisory Committee on Agricultural Life and Labor.
37 linear feet [unprocessed].

OWOSSO EDUCATION ASSOCIATION. *Papers, 1914–68.*
Correspondence, reports, contract negotiations and agreements, minutes, newspapers, newsletters, and published material collected by the Owosso (Michigan) Education Association which evolved from the Owosso Teach-

ers Club. Subjects include contract negotiations and relationship of the Owosso Education Association with the Michigan Education Association.
3 linear feet.

PEOPLE'S SONG LIBRARY. *Papers, 1940–70 (predominantly 1940–55).*
The People's Song Library is comprised of songs collected by the Almanac Singers (1941–43); People's Songs, Inc. (1946–49); People's Artists, Inc. (1950–57); and Sing Out, Inc. (1958–70). Scores, songbooks, and lyrics by Aaron Copland, Woody Guthrie, Joe Hill, "Leadbelly" Ledbetter, Alan Lomax, Phil Ochs, Tom Paxton, Malvina Reynolds, Peggy and Pete Seeger, Josh White, and lesser-known and some anonymous authors dealing with civil rights, the Cuban Revolution, election songs of the 1940s, labor, pacifism, and war. Included are traditional folksongs and some of more recent vintage.
10 linear feet

RUBBER, CORK, LINOLEUM AND PLASTIC WORKERS OF AMERICA. *Papers, 1933–67.*
Pamphlets, reports, press releases, and proceedings pertaining to the minimum wage in the rubber industry, collective bargaining, organizing, and labor in politics.
2 1/2 linear feet.

SAGINAW FEDERATION OF LABOR. *Papers, 1917–41.*
Files from the Saginaw (Michigan) Federation of Labor. Included are minutes for 1926–41, and minutes of an affiliated body, Carpenters Local 334 for 1917–38. Other items include miscellaneous correspondence, financial statements, and membership applications.
1 1/2 linear feet.

UNITED COMMUNITY SERVICES. *Papers, 1887–1938.*
The collection is comprised of material relating to the work of charitable and health care groups before most of their activities were centralized under other organizations such as United Community Services. Included are correspondence, minutes, financial records, reports, and case files of organizations such as the Associated Charities of Detroit, Detroit Community Union, European Relief Council, Detroit Society for the Study and Prevention of Tuberculosis, the Red Cross, and the Michigan Fresh Air Society.
24 linear feet; [30 volumes unprocessed].

Collections

UNITED TRANSPORT SERVICE EMPLOYEES. *Papers, 1944–66.*
Clippings, reports, correspondence, and reports of articles relating to writings and other activities of Willard S. Townsend, founder and president of the International Brotherhood of Red Caps (1938), which later became the United Transport Service Employees (CIO). The collection has material on Mr. Townsend and also on civil rights, blacks in labor and the Korean War, and history of the UTSE.
1/2 linear foot.

WAYNE COUNTY AFL-CIO. *Papers, 1918–63.*
Correspondence, minutes, reports, clippings, and other materials of the Wayne County, Michigan, AFL-CIO. The files cover the sit-downs of the 1930s, formation of the CIO, labor in the Depression, the Soviet Union and American labor, the AFL-CIO merger of 1955, political action, Great Lakes Strike of 1948, Great Lakes Seaway, loyalty boards, and the Teamsters Union. Among the correspondents are Prentiss Brown, William Comstock, James Couzens, Lauren Dickinson, Homer Ferguson, Frank Fitzgerald, Henry Ford II, Fred Green, William Green, Alex Grosbeck, Sidney Hillman, Lyndon Johnson, Harry Kelly, Huey Long, Frank Martel, Frank Murphy, Kim Sigler, Upton Sinclair, Harry S. Truman, Arthur Vandenberg, Murray D. Van Wagoner, and G. Mennen Williams.
36 1/2 linear feet; [26 linear feet unprocessed].

WAYNE COUNTY AFL-CIO: EDUCATION COMMITTEE. *Papers, 1963–67.*
Correspondence, minutes, proclamations, and publicity material relating to labor education, for both members of the labor movement and the general public. Several files concern Labor Education Week (1964 to 1967). Other topics are consumer education, libraries, and the Speakers Bureau. Correspondents are Al Barbour, Clarence Hilberry, and Carroll Hutton.
1/2 linear foot.

WAYNE COUNTY AFL-CIO: PRESIDENT'S OFFICE. *Papers, 1951–67.*
Correspondence, reports, minutes, clippings, and other items from the office files of the president of the Wayne County, Michigan, AFL-CIO. The bulk of the files relate to Al Barbour's service as president from 1958 to 1967. Among the subjects covered are civil rights, manpower development, poverty programs, political activities, and the industrial development of Detroit and Michigan. Correspondents include Jerome Cavanagh, John Conyers, Charles Diggs, Arthur Goldberg, Philip Hart, Hubert Humphrey, Lyndon Johnson, John Kennedy, Eugene McCarthy, George Romney, and G. Mennen Williams. *36 1/2 linear feet.*

Other Organizations

WAYNE STATE UNIVERSITY STAFF ASSOCIATION. *Papers, 1956–69.*
Newsletters, memoranda, salary schedules, annual reports, collective bargaining agreements, constitutions and by-laws, notices, and minutes collected by the University Staff Association (the Office Personnel Association, 1956–63), which represents the University's clerical and technical employees.
1/2 linear foot.

WORKERS' DEFENSE LEAGUE. *Papers, 1936–65.*
This collection of correspondence, press releases, newspaper clippings, speeches, trial briefs and transcripts, and published pamphlets and leaflets, thoroughly documents the WDL's efforts to obtain justice for labor organizers, government critics, victims of racial and economic discrimination, and conscientious objectors, through established, legal processes.
100 linear feet [unprocessed].

UNPROCESSED COLLECTIONS

The following collections have not been completely arranged and described:

Adamcyk, Stephen
Anderson, Alfred and Rose
AFT Garden City, Michigan
AFT Hawaii
AFT San Francisco
ALPA Dallas
ALPA Governmental Affairs Department
ALPA Los Angeles Legal Office
ALPA New York Legal Office
ALPA Personnel Department
ALPA Retirement and Research
ALPA San Francisco
Betts, W.W.
Bordner, Robert
Brock, Stewart
Calhoun, Arthur
Christenson, Edith
Citizens for a United Detroit
Collins, Vernon
Chrapkiewicz, Joseph
Daniel, Berthe and Franz
Daniel, Mrs. Cuthbert
Davidson, Ben
Davis, William
Dillard, Ernest
Dolgoff, Sam
Drake, James
Drob, Judah
Edwards, Hagburt
Eklund, John
Employers Association of Detroit
Fantozy, Sam
Fishlow, David
Forsen, Clemens
Gentile, Charles
Glaberman, Martin and Jessie
Glicman, Henry
Hatcher, Raymond
Henderson, Lettisha
Henkelman, William
Henney, Westray
Herstein, Lillian
Hill, James
Hoffman, S.L.
Hood, Raymond
IWW Minneapolis
Iron Molders Union of North America
Kahn, Mark
Kanter, Irving
Keane, Jay
Kincaid, Charles
Kleinman, Rose
Lane, Layle
Leab, Daniel
Lederle, Arthur
Lefkowitz, Abraham
Lindsay, C.Z.
Lipton, Howard
Llewellyn, Percy
Majerus, Ray
Mason, Gabriel
McGough, Mary
Miles, Isadore
Miller, Jack
Montgomery, George
Myerscough, Tom
Organization of Architectural and Engineering Employees: Detroit Chapter
Ovington, Mary White

Unprocessed

Parker, Paul
Pilch, Alex
Pragen, Otto
Rand, Don
Reisman, Mrs. Harry
Reuss, Richard
Rigby, Charles
Rugh, Jack
Ryan, William
Salandini, Father Victor
Schick, David
Schnapper, M.B.
Smith, Norman
Smith, Stanton and Nancy
Stevens, Don
Strachan, Stuart
Swan, Joseph
Taft, Philip
Thoman, Tony
UAW Bookstore
UAW Community Action Program
UAW Competitive Shops Department—Pat Greathouse
UAW Die Casting Department
UAW Library
UAW Local 309
UAW Local 506
UAW Local 653
UAW Local 904
UAW Local 1088
UAW Local 1139
UAW Local 1444
UAW Organizing Department— Pat Greathouse
UAW Region 1A
UAW Region 1B
UAW Region 3
UAW Region 6
UAW Region 10
UAW Saginaw, Michigan Sub-Region
UAW Skilled Trades Department
UAW Women's Department
Verri, Albert
Vinitsky, A. Randall
Wayne County Employees Local 771
Wayne State University Professional and Administrative Association
Weil, Truda
Wheeler, Doris
Whitty, Michael
Williams, John

PART II
Oral History Interviews

ORAL HISTORY INTERVIEWS

In the fall of 1959, the Institute of Labor and Industrial Relations at the University of Michigan and Wayne State University began an oral history project on the unionization of the automobile industry. For further information on this project, readers may consult Jack W. Skeels's article, "Oral History Project on the Development of Unionism in the Automobile Industry" (*Labor History,* Spring 1964). Transcripts of interviews with 133 persons are available for study by qualified researchers.

Another oral history project recently completed deals with the role of blacks in organized labor. Thirty-two interviews have been transcribed and are available.

Additionally, the Archives has purchased 14 oral history transcripts from the New York Times/Columbia Oral History Program. A listing of these interviews is contained in this section of the guide.

Prospective users of oral history materials particularly are urged to contact the Archives in advance of their visit. Procedures for the use of transcripts held by the Archives are as follows:

1. Transcripts will be available to the following classes of persons:
    a. Regular academic faculty at a recognized college or university engaging in objective scholarly research dealing with the subject matter of the transcripts.
    b. Graduate students working on a thesis topic dealing with the subject matter of the transcripts and working under academic supervision.
2. Requests for use of the material shall be made in the following way:
    a. The individual will fill out the applicable parts of the "Oral History Interview Form."
    b. Graduate students additionally shall present a letter from their supervisory professor, indicating the need to use the material and the nature of the thesis topic.
    c. All persons shall execute the "Oral History Transcript Use Contract."
3. Use of the transcript material shall be limited in the following way:

a. No individual shall remove the transcript from the library.
b. The transcripts shall not be microfilmed or reprinted.
c. The transcripts are not available for inter-library loan.
d. All users of this material shall agree in writing to abide by the above regulations by executing the "Oral History Transcript Use Contract."
4. Procedures on using quotations from transcripts:
a. If an excerpt or quotation from the transcripts is to be published, the author must submit the name and address of the publisher so that the latter can be informed of the possibility of libelous statements in the transcripts. This is a condition stipulated in the "Oral History Transcript Use Contract" and required by all users.

The entries for each transcript below consist of the interviewee's name followed by a brief notation of the topics and personalities discussed. The last line of each entry indicates the number of pages in the transcript and the date of the interview.

UNIONIZATION OF AUTO INDUSTRY

ADDES, GEORGE
Toledo Auto-Lite Strike (1934); suspension of five top International officers (1938); NRA and labor; AFL in auto industry; establishment of accounting and bookkeeping systems for UAW.
41 pp. *June 1960.*

ADKINS, LOUIS
UAW in Janesville, Wisconsin, Fisher Body Plant; growth of UAW Local 95. 17 pp. *August 1961.*

ANDERSON, JOHN W.
AFL in auto industry; strikes at Briggs (1933), Murray Body (1933), GM (1937), Yale and Towne (1937), Ford (1941); factionalism in UAW; MESA; UAW-GM Council; discrimination in auto plants; Cadillac Square demonstration against Taft-Hartley Act; Reuther shooting; skilled trades; labor education.
252 pp. *February* and *May 1960.*

BANNON, KEN
Ford-Rouge Plant 10-Day Strike (1941); UAW Convention (1946); pre-

union working conditions in Ford-Rouge Plant; UAW Local 600; Ford Highland Park Plant; Ford pension plan.   24 pp. *February 1963.*

BARTEE, JOHN
Organizing in Indiana and Caterpillar Tractor, Peoria, Illinois; Flint sit-downs; 1936 UAW Convention.
28 pp. *April 1961.*

BECKMAN, CHARLES
Organizing of Cleveland-Fisher Body; AFL in auto industry; Cleveland-Fisher Body strikes of 1932, 1937, and 1939; Homer Martin split; Toledo "Rump" Convention (1937); UAW 1939 Convention, Cleveland; Cleveland Auto Workers Council; move for international auto union; incentive plan; black auto workers; labor and politics.
29 pp. *July 1961.*

BENI, J. A.
Growth of UAW Local 72; Nash Strike (1939); piece-work; early grievance procedures; war production; Local 72 and the community.
23 pp. *March 1963.*

BERNDT, RAYMOND H.
Organizing of Studebaker, South Bend; Martin-CIO split; Indiana State CIO; "Labor Bookshelf" plan; pre-union working conditions at Studebaker; movement for international auto union; war production; UAW Region 3.
28 pp. *May 1963.*

BISHOP, MERLIN
Kelsey-Hayes and Fisher Body strikes (1937); labor education; Brookwood Labor School; UAW summer schools; Cadillac Square demonstration (1938); Ford Hunger March; labor songs.
48 pp. *March 1963.*

BRAMS, STANLEY
Midland Steel (1936) and Kelsey-Hayes (1937) strikes; Flint sit-downs; outsider's view of UAW factionalism; evaluation of UAW conventions.
40 pp. *November 1959.*

BULLY, NORMAN
Homer Martin-CIO split; Reuther vs. Thomas; labor-management relations in peace and war; no-strike pledge; wildcat strikes; discipline at GM.
31 pp. *October 1961.*

BURT, GEORGE
Organizing of Chrysler, GM and Ford in Canada; GM-Oshawa, Ontario strike (1937); labor-government relations in Canada; fringe benefits; organizing agricultural implement workers in Canada.
38 pp. *April 1963.*

CAREY, ED
Organization of Chrysler; Chrysler Sit-Down; work of a UAW International representative; UAW and politics.
13 pp. *April 1963.*

CASE, ARTHUR
Early UAW-AFL activities in Flint; Flint Sit-Down; GM Tool and Die Strike of 1939; UAW-AFL vs. UAW-CIO; Rank and File Caucus; Unity Caucus; company unions; communism in unions; *Flint Weekly Review;* race relations in plants; UAW conventions of 1937, 1943, and 1947.
51 pp. *August 1960.*

CLEVELAND, JAMES
Organizing of Chevrolet plants; 1939 Tool and Die Strike; GM Strike of 1946; UAW-AFL vs. UAW-CIO; Reuther-Thomas conflict; UAW conventions of 1937, 1939, 1941, and 1947; piecework, shop conditions, and union gains; Allis-Chalmers delegates; race relations in plants; Graham Tool Company; Farm Equipment merger; outline of a local union officer.
45 pp. *October 1961.*

COLEMAN, RICHARD
Organizing the Twin Coach Company, Kent, Ohio; organizing in Ohio and California; Hercules Motor Strike, Canton, Ohio; Douglas Aircraft Sit-Down; Progressive Caucus; Martin-CIO split; UAW conventions of 1936, 1939, and 1940; Wolman Board; Central Labor Union, Akron.
27 pp. *July 1960.*

CONWAY, CHARLES
Organizing of Fisher Body-Chevrolet in St. Louis; Flint Sit-Down; St. Louis Fisher Body-Chevrolet Strike of 1937; Martin-CIO split; UAW Convention of 1937; NRA and auto industry; Wolman Board; anti-union activity; labor's attitude on Franklin Roosevelt.
46 pp. *April 1961.*

CONWAY, JACK
Growth of UAW Local 6; organizing Buick Aviation Engine Plant, Melrose

Park, Illinois; effect of UAW factionalism on local unions; UAW conventions 1944, 1947; collective bargaining; no-strike pledge.
24 pp. *March 1963.*

COOK, ALEXANDER
Flint-Fisher Body organizing; Fisher Body Strike (1930); Martin-Dillon split; Auto Workers Union; NRA; MESA; Auto Labor Board; UAW in Toledo.
44 pp. *August 1960.*

COUSER, JAMES
Drive to organize Ford-Rouge Plant; Ford Strike (1941); factionalism in Local 600; Wayne County Tool and Die Council; communism and red-baiting; Unemployment Council of 1958; communists in auto unions.
24 pp. *November 1960.*

CRANEFIELD, HAROLD
J.I. Case Strike, Racine (1934); Flint Sit-Down; NLRB; NRA; Depression in Wisconsin; Wisconsin Industrial Union; LaFollette Civil Liberties Committee; industrial espionage; Supreme Court, labor and the New Deal.
25 pp. *May 1963.*

DAVIDOW, LARRY
Wadsworth Manufacturing Company strikes (1919 and 1930); Fisher Body Strike (1921); Flint and Chrysler sit-downs; Martin vs. CIO; Socialist Party; Auto Workers Union; Communist Party; skilled trades in auto industry; courts and labor; Dingman's Welfare Club.
37 pp. *July 1960.*

DE CAUX, LEN
Flint sit-downs; Allis-Chalmers Strike (1944); North American Aviation Strike (1941); UAW conventions of 1936, 1937, 1939, and 1941; Brookwood Labor College; Independent Labour Party; IWW; International Seamen's Union; early CIO; labor journalism; communism and the left in unions; 1940 election.
64 pp. *March 1961.*

DI GAETANO, NICK
Chrysler Sit-Down; Chrysler Strike (1950); Chrysler Flying Squadrons at Ford-Rouge Plant (1941); Chrysler Industrial Union; UAW-Wayne County Educational Committee; activities on behalf of Sacco-Vanzetti.
75 pp. *April* and *May 1959.*

Oral History Interviews

DITZEL, JOSEPH
Organizing in Toledo, Ohio, and Saginaw, Michigan; Toledo-Chevrolet Strike (1935); Flint sit-downs; GM Strike (1945-46); Progressive and Unity caucuses; Martin split; UAW conventions of 1936; 1937; 1939 (Cleveland); 1946; and 1947; no-strike pledge; communist influence in UAW.
39 pp. *September 1960.*

DOHERTY, JAMES
Organizing in St. Louis-GM plants; Flint sit-downs; St. Louis Fisher Body-Chevrolet Strike (1937); Martin-CIO split; 1937 UAW Convention; NRA; Wolman Board; anti-union activity; labor's attitude towards Franklin D. Roosevelt.   46 pp. *April 1961.*

DOLL, TRACY
Flint sit-downs; Hudson Strike (1937); UAW factionalism (1939); UAW Convention, Cleveland (1939); incentive wages; Associated Auto Workers of America; Wayne County CIO Council; Michigan State Legislature.
60 pp. *April 1961.*

DORNETTO, DOMINIC
Organizing of Allis-Chalmers by United Electrical Workers; Richmond Radiator organizing; 1941 Allis-Chalmers Strike; Local 613 and United Electrical Workers Split; 1949 UAW Convention; company union; communism in United Electrical Workers; UAW merger with Allis-Chalmers workers; collective bargaining gains; white-collar unions.
26 pp. *April 1961.*

ELDON, JOHN
AFL in the auto industry; organizing locals in Windsor, Canada, area; problems of UAW Education Department; educating new union members; equal pay for equal work; leadership training; pre-union working conditions; left-wing groups in auto industry.
34 pp. *March 1960.*

FAGAN, FRANK
Organizing of Murray Body; Murray Body strikes of 1929 and 1937; Martin vs. CIO; IWW; Auto Workers Union; the New Deal and the growth of unions.   31 pp. *February 1963.*

FERRAZZA, JESS
Briggs organizing campaign; Briggs strikes of 1933, 1937, and 1939;

Homer Martin vs. CIO; UAW Local 742; black workers in auto industry; no-strike pledge.
28 pp. *May 1961.*

FERRIS, JOSEPH
Organizing of Briggs; Flint sit-downs; Briggs strikes of 1937 and 1939; Homer Martin-CIO split; working conditions in Briggs; Depression and auto industry; Franklin D. Roosevelt; Dingman's Welfare Association; anti-union activities; no-strike pledge; War Labor Board.
49 pp. *May 1961.*

FOSTER, BERT
Organizing of Cleveland-Fisher Body; Cleveland-Fisher Body Sit-Down (1936); 1939 Tool and Die Strike; 1945-46 GM Strike; Homer Martin vs. CIO; 1939 UAW Convention; shop conditions before unions; NRA; AFL and auto unions; MESA; picketing and strike breaking; Allied Industrial Union.
24 pp. *July 1960.*

FRANCIS, EVERETT
Organizing of Flint-Fisher Body 1; Flint sit-downs; Fisher Body Strike (1934); GM Tool and Die Strike (1939); GM Strike 1945-46; Homer Martin vs. UAW-CIO; UAW conventions of 1935, 1939, 1941; *Flint Weekly Review;* skilled work in auto industry; NRA; Flint Federation of Labor; Wolman Board; LaFollete Civil Liberties Committee; UAW locals 156 and 501; Wagner Act.
80 pp. *October 1961.*

FRANKENSTEEN, RICHARD
Organizing of Chrysler, Motor Products, Briggs, Thompson Products, Detroit Stove Works, Ford, and aircraft industry; strikes at Motor Products, Midland Steel, Kelsey-Hayes, and North American Aviation; Martin vs. CIO; Lovestone faction; Progressive vs. Unity Caucus; Thomas vs. Reuther; 1936, 1939, and 1941 UAW conventions; Dodge Works Council; Auto Labor Board; LaFollette Civil Liberties Committee; industrial espionage; War Labor Board; Battle of the Overpass; race relations in auto plants and UAW; incentive pay.
100 pp. *October* and *November 1959.*

FREITAG, ELMER
Organizing of North American Aviation; North American Strike (1941);

rank-and-file grievances before union; National Defense Mediation Board; House Un-American Activities Committee.
16 pp. *June 1960.*

FURAY, MORT
Organization of paint companies in Detroit; Kelsey-Hayes Sit-Down; American Brass Company Strike (1937); trimmers in Detroit body plants; National Union for Social Justice; Mine, Mill and Smelter Workers; housing; Renters and Consumers League; Labor's Non-Partisan League; UAW Spring Council.
33 pp. *April 1960.*

GALLAGHER, DANIEL
Organizing of Timken-Axle Detroit, Federal Screw Company, and westside Detroit; Timken Sit-Down; Martin vs. UAW-CIO; 1939 UAW Convention; pre-union shop conditions; company unions; methods of a union organizer; anti-union activities; New America; Labor's Non-Partisan League.
51 pp. *January 1960.*

GANLEY, NAT
Organization of Packinghouse and Poultry Workers in Detroit (early 1930s); strikes at Motor Products (1935), GM (1945-46), Square D (1950s); Flint sit-downs; Unity vs. Progressive Caucus; Martin-CIO split; Reuther vs. Thomas, Frankensteen, and Addes; UAW conventions of 1936-44, 1953, and 1955; Scenery Painters Union; Trade Union Unity League; Auto Workers Union; growth of industrial unions; Unemployment Council movement; third parties; Michigan Commonwealth Federation; communism and labor.
77 pp. *April 1960.*

GELLES, CATHERINE
Literature distribution at Ford-Rouge Plant; Battle of the Overpass; Bohn Aluminum Sit-Down (1936); Federal Screw (1938) and Ford (1941) strikes; role of women in union movement; political action; community service.
20 pp. *July 1961.*

GENSKE, WILLIAM
Flint-Fisher Body 1 organizing campaign; Flint sit-downs; 1939 GM Tool and Die Strike; Martin-CIO split; 1939 and 1943 UAW conventions; pre-union shop conditions; race relations in automobile industry.
43 pp. *July 1960.*

GERMER, ADOLPH
Organizing in Illinois coal mines; Rubber and Auto Workers organization; coal strike of 1894; Colorado Fuel and Iron Strike; Flint sit-downs; strikebreaking in Colorado; Ludlow Massacre; socialism and World War I; NRA; rise of CIO; IWW; World Federation of Trade Unions; International Woodworkers of America.   29 pp. *November 1960.*

GOMON, JOSEPHINE
Briggs Strike (1933); Mayor's Unemployment Committee, Detroit (1932); Ford Hunger March; Thrift Garden Project; housing and black employment at Ford-Willow Run.
34 pp. *December 1959.*

GRANT, MURVEL
Organizing of Gemmer Manufacturing Company; wildcat strikes; Gemmer Strike (1958); Homer Martin split; company unions; pre-union working conditions; war production; seniority; arbitration; closing and transfer of Gemmer Manufacturing Company.
43 pp. *April 1962.*

GREATHOUSE, PAT
Organizing of Chicago Ford and Dodge plants; organizing of farm equipment and aircraft workers; Republic Steel Strike (1937); 1941 and 1942 UAW conventions; pre-union working conditions; UAW-Farm Equipment merger; Allis-Chalmers local; work of UAW administration and officers.
30 pp. *May 1963*

GREGORY, STANLEY
Flint sit-downs; Martin-CIO split; Fisher Body Employees Union; UAW Local 95; pre-union shop conditions; industrial espionage.
13 pp. *March 1963.*

HAESSLER, CARL
UAW factional disputes; Association of Catholic Trade Unionists; Harry Bennett; communism in the labor movement; the Catholic Church and labor; the Federated Press; Richard Frankensteen; racketeering and labor; Flint sit-downs and GM strikes of 1939 and 1945-46; Sidney Hillman; Richard Leonard; John L. Lewis; Jay Lovestone; Homer Martin; Emil Mazey; Wyndham Mortimer; Philip Murray; North American Aviation strike (1941); Roy, Victor, and Walter Reuther; R.J. Thomas; UAW Conventions (1936-59); *United Auto Worker;* labor and World War II.
267 pp. *November 1959* and *October 1960*

HAGGARD, FRED
Organizing of Pontiac-Fisher Body; Flint sit-downs; GM Tool and Die Strike of 1939; Martin vs. CIO; Railroad Brotherhood; pre-union shop conditions; Oakland County CIO Council.
27 pp. *July 1961.*

HALL, ED
Organizing of Seaman Body, GM, and Ford; Seaman Body Strike (ca. 1934); Flint sit-downs; Homer Martin vs. UAW-CIO; Unity and Progressive caucuses; 1936, 1937, and 1939 UAW conventions; Wolman Board; industrial espionage; White Motor local.
41 pp. *October 1959.*

HAMMOND, MATTHEW
Tool and die shop organizing; MESA Tool and Die strike (1933); effect of UAW factionalism on tool and die locals; Michigan Commonwealth Federation; Reuther "500 planes a day" plan; Tool and Die Manufacturers Association; apprentice-journeyman relations; UAW President's Committee. 64 pp. *March 1961.*

HARRIS, RICHARD
Organizing of Dodge and Herron-Zimmer Moulding; Motor Products strike; Kelsey-Hayes, Flint, and Chrysler sit-downs; NRA and labor; Wolman Board; pre-union shop conditions; company union; anti-union activities; AIWA; MESA; AFL Auto Workers; communists and auto workers.
35 pp. *November 1959.*

HATTLEY, JOSEPH
Fisher Body and Chrysler organizing; strikes at Motor Products (1935), Chrysler (1939), GM (1946), Chrysler (1950 and 1958); Flint sit-downs; Martin-CIO split; Reuther vs. Thomas; 1936, 1939, 1941, and 1946 UAW conventions; Woodworkers Union; anti-union activity; AFL Auto Local 7; AIWA; company unions; Dingman's League; collective bargaining; war production; pensions.
49 pp. *August 1961.*

HUGHES, ARTHUR
Organizing of Chrysler, especially Dodge; Chrysler strikes of 1937, 1939, 1950, and 1958; Homer Martin vs. UAW-CIO; Chrysler Works Council; LaFollette Civil Liberties Committee; AIWA; anti-union activity; collective bargaining; pension and welfare plans; production standards; reconversion.
37 pp. *March 1963.*

HUMPHREYS, WILLIAM
Organizing Campbell, Wyant and Cannon Foundry; Growth of UAW Local 539, Muskegon, Michigan; drive to organize Caterpillar Tractor, Peoria, Illinois; housing for minority groups in Muskegon; blacks and communism.
30 pp. *July 1961.*

HURST, JACK
Organizing in aircraft industry, especially North American; North American strike (1953); working conditions in aircraft industry; International Association of Machinists.
19 pp. *April 1961.*

INGRAM, R.C.
Norwood, Ohio-Chevrolet organizing; Norwood-Chevrolet strikes (1935 and 1937); Flint sit-downs; 1936 UAW Convention; pre-union shop conditions; Federal Local 19940.
14 pp. *April 1961.*

INNIS, FOREST
Unionization of WPA workers, Bendix, Chrysler, and Briggs; Bendix Sit-Down; Progressive vs. Unity Caucus; Homer Martin and his opponents; 1936, 1937, and 1939 UAW conventions; NRA; AFL and mass production industries; Depression anti-union activities; Anderson, Indiana labor conditions; Bendix company union.
26 pp. *March 1963.*

JENSEN, MARTIN
Attempts to organize Ford (late 1930s); Ford Strike (1941); UAW factionalism; pre-union working conditions in Ford-Rouge plant; NLRB trial, Ford Motor Company (1937); seniority system; UAW Local 600 grievance and umpire system; first Ford contract.
116 pp. *November 1960.*

JOHNSON, CLAYTON
Organizing by AFL in Flint-Fisher Body; Flint-Fisher Body 2 Sit-Down (1937); Martin-CIO split; Battle of Bull's Run; company unions; UAW education program; "Victory Through Equality of Sacrifice."
23 pp. *June 1961.*

JOHNSON, LESTER
Organizing of Fisher Body, Detroit; strikes at Motor Products, Graham Paige and Fisher Body (1921); 1920 Auto Workers Convention; Auto

Workers Union; work conditions before unions; International Organization of Machinists; Carriage and Wagon Workers, AFL; Socialist Party; IWW; communism and auto workers; industrial espionage.
29 pp. *June 1959.*

KANTER, ROBERT
Cadillac Motor and Timken Axle organizing; strikes at Cadillac Motor (1937), Federal Screw (1938), American Brass (1938); labor education; industrial espionage; Battle of the Overpass; incentive pay plans.
27 pp. *April 1963.*

KITZMAN, HARVEY
J.I. Case Company organizing and strikes of 1933, 1945-47, 1959, and 1960; WPA; Racine Workers Committee; Wisconsin Industrial Union Council; communism and labor; collective bargaining; UAW and Farm Implement merger.   28 pp. *March 1963.*

KLASEY, TOM
Organizing of Flint-Chevrolet; Toledo-Chevrolet Strike (1935); Flint sit-down; GM Tool and Die Strike (1939); Homer Martin-CIO split; 1934 Conference of Federal Auto Locals; 1936 UAW Convention; IWW; AFL and auto industry; Wolman Board; company unions; anti-union activity; formation of CIO; LaFollette Committee; UAW-WPA unions.
50 pp. *September 1960*

KLUE, LEONARD
Organizing Michigan Steel Tube Products; strikes at Michigan Steel Tube in 1941, 1946, 1947, and 1950; communists and UAW; company spies; "slow-downs"; war production; no-strike pledge; bargaining process.
48 pp. *May 1961.*

LADUKE, THEODORE
Organization of Flint-Chevrolet; Flint sit-down; GM Tool and Die Strike (1939); political groups with the UAW; Martin vs. UAW-CIO; 1936 UAW Convention; 1939 UAW-AFL Convention; Industrial Mutual Association; pre-union shop conditions; MESA; AFL and auto workers; company unions; NRA; Auto Labor Board; early grievance procedure.
35 pp. *August 1960.*

LEACH, RUSSELL
Organizing Murray Body; UAW right- and left-wing elements; Society of

Tool and Die Craftsmen; bargaining in skilled trades; tool and die apprentice training; labor and communism.
34 pp. *July 1961.*

LEE, ED
Ford organizing drive; Ford Strike (1941); Local 600 and communism; Labor Day parades; blacks and Local 600.
43 pp. *April 1961.*

LEGGAT, AL
Allis-Chalmers Strike; pro/anti Reuther forces; Ford Hunger March; *Ford Facts*; Ford pension proposals; Camp Atterbury incident; Michigan CIO.
80 pp. *December 1959.*

McCRACKEN, ELIZABETH
MESA organizing work; strikes of tool and die workers (1933); strikes at Motor Products (1935), Michigan Tool Company (1936), Kelvinator (1937); Auto Labor Board; AIWA; KKK; MESA compared with other unions.
38 pp. *December 1959.*

McDANIEL, JOHN
Organizing of Packard and Gemmer Manufacturing Company; wildcat strikes; Gemmer Strike (1958); Homer Martin split; 1939 UAW Convention, Cleveland; company mergers; women workers; war production; company unions; black employees; local elections; arbitration; closing of Packard and Gemmer plants.
35 pp. *May 1961.*
43 pp. *April 1962.*

McGILL, JOHN
Buick organizing; Flint sit-downs; GM Tool and Die Strike (1939); AFL vs. CIO in UAW; Unity and Progressive caucuses; Reuther vs. Thomas and Addes; 1939 and 1946 UAW conventions; UAW Local 156; Flying Squadrons; Equality of Sacrifice program; Rank and File Caucus; wildcat strikes.
27 pp. *July 1960.*

MANFRED, FRANK
Organizing in Kelsey-Hayes and Ford; Kelsey-Hayes, Midland Steel and Flint sit-downs; strikes at Hygrade Meat, Timken-Axle, and Ford; Homer Martin vs. UAW-CIO; Progressive and Unity caucuses; 1936 and 1937

UAW conventions; Depression conditions in auto plants; NRA; company unions; industrial espionage; Battle of the Overpass.
59 pp. *June 1960.*

MANNING, MICHAEL
Kelsey-Hayes organization; strikes at Bower Roller Bearings (1933), and Hupmobile (1934); AFL vs. CIO in auto industry; Martin-CIO split; 1934 National Conference of Auto Workers Locals; 1937 UAW Convention; NRA; Wolman Board; LaFollette Committee; AIWA.
56 pp. *July 1960.*

MARQUART, FRANK
Socialist Party and auto unions; ACTU; labor education; production standards; grievance process; UAW Local 212; UAW Local 600; growth of UAW departments.
59 pp. *February 1960* and *September 1961.*

MATTHEWS, NORMAN
Unionization of Packard Motor Company; GM Strike (1945-46); Chrysler strikes of 1948, 1950, and 1955; race relations in auto industry; collective bargaining in auto industries; Community Chest.
21 pp. *March 1963.*

MATTSON, JOSEPH
Organizing of Durkee Atwood Company and Ford Minnesota plants; Martin vs. UAW-CIO; 1939 and 1940 UAW conventions; IWW; NRA; Federal Local 19827; Minnesota State CIO Council; UAW District Council
17 pp. *July 1961.*

MERRELLI, GEORGE
Organizing of Chevrolet Gear and Axle; GM Tool and Die Strike (1939); GM Strike (1945-46); attempt to return UAW to AFL; 1939 UAW Convention, Cleveland; GM Council; pension and health plans; umpire system; election of Walter Reuther.
17 pp. *February 1963.*

MERRILL, RUSSELL
AFL organizing of Studebaker, South Bend; CIO in auto industry; suspension of five top UAW officers; Homer Martin-CIO split; UAW conventions of 1935, 1936, 1937, and 1939; early negotiations with Studebaker;

seniority procedures; grievance procedures; move for international auto union; rise of CIO.   36 pp. *May 1963.*

MICHENER, LEWIS
UAW-CIO on the West Coast; organizing of Ford and aircraft industry; North American Aviation Strike (1941); suspension of five top International officers; Martin-CIO split; UAW 1939 Cleveland Convention; pre-union working conditions in auto industry; IAM vs. UAW in aircraft industry; war production.
37 pp. *June 1960.*

MILEY, PAUL E.
Working conditions, Fisher Body, Cleveland (1920s); importance of trimmers in UAW; general impact of Depression; organization of F.L.U. No.18614; NRA and Auto Labor Board; Cleveland movement for an autonomous international (1934–36); Toledo Auto Lite Strike (1934); 1935 UAW-AFL Convention; 1936 South Bend Convention; Cleveland Fisher Body Sit-Down (1936).
39 pp. *July 1961.*

MONTGOMERY, ANDREW
AFL in Pontiac auto plants; organizing in Pontiac after Flint sit-downs; Homer Martin split; pre-union working conditions in Pontiac Motor; war production; UAW Local 653 elections; speed-up; merit pay; women employees.   18 pp. *July 1961.*

MORRIS, KEN
Strikes at American Brass (1938), Briggs (1939), GM Tool and Die (1939); Martin-CIO split; Reuther vs. Thomas; UAW 1939 Convention, Cleveland; protection of women's job rights at close of World War II; UAW Local 212; Kefauver investigation.
52 pp. *June 1963.*

MORTIMER, WYNDHAM
AFL in Cleveland auto plants; organizing in Cleveland-White Motor, Flint, and aircraft industry; Atlanta-GM (1936), Flint sit-downs and North American Aviation (1941) strikes; Progressive and Unity caucuses; First Conference of Auto Industry Federal Locals; 1935 AFL Convention; UAW conventions of 1935, 1936, 1937, and 1939; Cleveland movement for an international auto union; Wolman Board.
82 pp. *June 1960.*

NOWAK, STANLEY
Organizing of Polish American Auto Workers; Ternstedt Slow-Down Strike (1937); Martin meeting with West Side Detroit delegation, Eddystone Hotel; UAW Convention (1937); collective bargaining (1930s); campaign for State Senate (1938).
24 pp. *June 1960.*

ODDIE, JAMES
Organizing of Gemmer Manufacturing Company; wildcat strikes; Gemmer Strike (1958); Homer Martin split; company unions; pre-union working conditions; war production; seniority; arbitration; closing of Gemmer's Detroit plant.
43 pp. *April 1962.*

O'DONOHUE, CLAYTON
Gemmer Manufacturing Company unionization; Gemmer Strike (1958); Martin-CIO split; company unions; war production and peacetime conversion; arbitration; problems resulting from plant closing.
43 pp. *April 1962.*

O'HALLORAN, CYRIL
Organizing Los Angeles area auto plants and aircraft industry; North American Aviation Strike; communist influence in California UAW locals; AFL vs. CIO in auto industry; production standards; collective bargaining.
27 pp. *June 1960.*

OLIVER, WILLIAM
Organizing Ford-Highland Park; 1943 UAW Convention; Detroit race riots; black women at Ford-Highland Park; Cutter-Grinder case; "Lady in Red Slacks" case; UAW Fair Practices Department; fight against congressional filibuster; housing.
23 pp. *March 1963.*

O'MALLEY, PATRICK
CIO in Cleveland auto plants; organizing of White Motor; factionalism; communist influence in UAW; early working conditions in White Motor; piecework system; labor spies; war production.
17 pp. *July 1961.*

PAGANO, JOSEPH
AIWA; Hudson Industrial Workers of America; organizing of Ford Motor Company; Hudson Sit-Down (1937); Ford Strike (1940); wildcat strikes in

World War II; communists and UAW; UAW conventions (1937 and 1939), Cleveland; pre-union working conditions; Labor's Non Partisan League; UAW administratorships.
45 pp. *May 1960.*

PALMER, F.D. "JACK"
Organizing in Flint (early 1930s); Flint Fisher Body Plant 1 (1930), Flint sit-downs, GM Tool and Die (1939), and GM (1945) strikes; Martin-CIO split; company unions; shop steward system; UAW-GM Department; no-strike pledge; labor in Flint politics; election of Walter Reuther to UAW presidency; cost of living clause.
43 pp. *July 1960.*

PANZNER, JOHN
IWW in Nevada mining areas and Detroit auto plants; organizing by AFL and CIO in auto industry; Mesabi Range Strike (1916); Flint sit-downs; working conditions in Detroit (late 1800s); Socialist Party in Michigan; war production.
46 pp. *April 1959.*

PAYNE, WILLIAM
UAW organizing in San Francisco Bay region; Ford-Richmond, California strike (1937); 1941 Ford contract; war production and peacetime reconversion; labor relations at Ford; speed-up; committeeman system.
16 pp. *April 1961.*

PEPPLER, ORRIN
MESA and UAW in Detroit job shops; Buel Die and Machines Company Strike; Martin split; Detroit job shops during Depression; UAW Tool and Die Council; apprentice programs; war production; tool and die grievances; journeymen's cards.
34 pp. *March 1961.*

PICONKE, JOSEPH
MESA in Detroit; AIWA; organizing of Hudson; Hudson strikes (1939); Chrysler strike (1937); Progressive and Unity caucuses; Martin-CIO split; UAW conventions (1937 and 1939), Cleveland; bonus system.
34 pp. *April 1960.*

PODY, LEON
Communist organizing in early 1930s and their role in the Briggs strike (1933); Briggs strike and the activities of the committee in charge of the

strike; working conditions in auto plants in early 1930s, especially metal finishing; IWW in Detroit and auto plants; role of ex-Briggs strikers in Murray Body strike (1933); relief problems in Murray and Briggs strikes; role of foreign language and ethnic groups; work stoppage (sit-in) at Hudson Connor Avenue Body shop (1934); AFL in auto plants (1934); murder of organizer (AFL) John Bailey.
42 pp. *November 1959* and *January 1960*.

POPLAWSKI, Adam
AIWA; AFL in Packard; amalgamation of AIWA and UAW; Packard "Racial" Strike (1943); Progressive and Unity caucuses; Reuther vs. Addes; UAW Convention (1936); pre-union working conditions; Packard Works Council; bonus system; job classifications; war production; local elections; black auto workers.
33 pp. *May 1960*.

PRATO, GENE
Ford organizing drive; Ford Strike (1941); Ford-Rouge plant working conditions; arbitration and umpire system; Liberty Legion; war production.   37 pp. *January 1963*.

PURDY, EDWARD
Organizing Fruehauf Trailer Company; Martin-CIO split; dues checkoff; Detroit East Side Small Locals' Caucus; wildcat strikes and no-strike pledge; war production; farm equipment merger.   29 pp. *July 1961*.

QUILLICO, WALTER
Ford organizing drive; Ford Strike (1941); housing and recreational problems at Willow Run Bomber Plant; growth of UAW Local 600; politics and Local 600; *Ford Facts*.   38 pp. *February 1960*.

RAYMOND, PHILIP
Organizing by Auto Workers Union (1920s); AFL in auto industry; organizing of Ford; strikes in Detroit auto plants (1920s), Flint-Fisher Body (1929), Briggs (1933), Grand Rapids Kelsey-Hayes (1933); background of Auto Workers Union; labor spies; company unions.
25 pp. *January 1960*.

REUTHER, MAY
Strike at Federal Screw (1938); AFT in early 1930s; UAW Local 174; preparing printed material for and aiding in strikes; success of UAW.
22 pp. *May 1963*.

REUTHER, VICTOR

Organizing of Kelsey-Hayes; Reuther as an organizer in Anderson, Indiana; Homer Martin split; Kelsey-Hayes Strike (1936); Flint sit-downs; UAW Convention (1940); early life; world tour (1933–35); UAW education programs; war production; communists in UAW; CIO in Europe.
50 pp. *March 1963.*

RICHARDSON, HERBERT

Attempt to organize Flint-Fisher Body (early 1930s); AFL in Flint; Flint-Fisher Body Number 1 Strike (1930); First National Council of Automotive Workers (1934); negotiations (early 1930s); Washington Conference (1934); company unions; UAW-AFL National Council; Wolman Board; move for international auto union.
25 pp. *July 1960.*

RINGWALD, JOHN

Organizing Chevrolet Forge Plant, Detroit; Ford organizing drive; Progressive and Unity caucuses; UAW conventions (1937 and 1939), Cleveland; labor and communists.
16 pp. *June 1960.*

ROHAN, ARTHUR

Carriage, Wagon and Automobile Workers-AFL; organizing on the West Coast (1920s); Racine, Wisconsin, organizing (early 1930s); strike in New York City body shops (1919); United Automobile, Aircraft and Vehicle Workers conventions (1919 and 1926); working conditions in auto industry (mid-1900s); workers education.
39 pp. *August 1961.*

ROLAND, JAMES

Organizing of Toledo auto plants (early 1930s); strikes at Toledo-Auto Lite (1934) and Toledo-Chevrolet (1935); working conditions in Toledo (early 1930s).   18 pp. *September 1960.*

ROSS, HARRY

Organizing Dodge and Ford; Dodge Sit-Down (1937); Ford Strike (1941); UAW factionalism; industrial espionage; Auto Labor Board; AFL Federal Labor unions; AIWA.
78 pp. *July 1961.*

RUSSO, PAUL

AFL in Kenosha, Wisconsin; CIO in Wisconsin auto plants; Kenosha-Nash

Sit-Down (1933); UAW conventions (1935 and 1936); pre-union working conditions; movement for an international auto union.
21 pp. *April 1960.*

SAGE, SAM
Trade Union Unity League and Auto Workers Union; AIWA; AFL Federal Labor Union at Briggs; MESA; Wayne County CIO Council; wildcat strikes; war production; Michigan Commonwealth Federation; labor and Democratic Party; Detroit municipal elections.
49 pp. *July 1960.*

SAHORSKE, FRANK
Organizing of the unemployed and farm implement workers in Racine, Wisconsin; organizing in Rockford, Illinois, and Chicago areas; Wisconsin Industrial Union; strikes at J.I. Case (1934–35 and 1936); UAW Convention (1936); International Molders Union; company unions.
23 pp. *August 1961.*

SCHILLING, WALTER
Organizing of Fisher Body and Chevrolet plants in St. Louis; Flint sit-downs; strike at St. Louis GM plants (1937); Martin-CIO split; UAW Convention (1937); NRA and auto industry; Wolman Board; anti-union activity; labor's attitude toward Franklin Roosevelt.
46 pp. *April 1961.*

SHAFFER, LEO
GM strike (1945-46); Reuther vs. Addes, Thomas; results of factionalism on UAW; communists and UAW; UAW conventions (1946 and 1959); local elections; UAW-GM Department; Committee for Democratic Action in the UAW.
39 pp. *November 1960.*

SIMONS, BUD
Auto workers union; organizing Hayes Ionia Company, Grand Rapids; AFL in Flint-Fisher Body; Flint-Fisher Body Strike (1930); Flint sit-downs; UAW Local 156; Black Legion and auto unions.
73 pp. *September 1960.*

SMITH, SAMUEL
UAW Convention (1939), Cleveland; communist issue in UAW.
20 pp. *October 1959.*

SOUTHWELL, HARRY
MESA organizing, Universal Products; Martin-CIO split; Reuther vs. Addes; company unions; operation of amalgamated locals; war production.
28 pp. *April 1963.*

SPETH, ROY
Seaman Body Strike; UAW conventions (1935 and 1936); early development of a UAW local; steward system; Wisconsin State Industrial Union Council; local and state elections.
27 pp. *March 1963.*

STEVENSON, WILLIAM
MESA in Detroit tool and die shops; Tool and Die Strike (1933); GM Tool and Die Strike (1939); UAW Skilled Trades Department; war production; "Up-Graders."
31 pp. *July 1961.*

SWANSON, CARL
AFL and CIO organizing in Flint; strikes: Toledo-Chevrolet (1935), Flint sit-downs, GM (1945-46); Martin Progressives vs. Unity Caucus; UAW conventions of 1937, 1939, and 1940; Wolman Board; grievance procedures; war conversion; incentive plans; relations with Flint city government.   46 pp. *August 1960.*

TAPPES, SHELTON
Ford organizing drive; struggle for black rights; UAW's WPA Department; Battle of the Overpass; blacks and unions (late 1930s).
24 pp. *July 1961*

TAYLOR, I. PAUL
Organizing by Auto Workers Union; AWU strikes (mid-1900s); Fisher Body Strike (1920); Detroit Labor Forum (1920s); role of socialists in AWU; IWW and AWU relations.
12 pp. *November 1960.*

THOMAS, R.J.
AIWA; organization of Ford; Chrysler Sit-Down; North American Aviation Strike; Homer Martin controversy; UAW conventions (1936, 1937, and 1939); Auto Labor Board; early bargaining at Chrysler; merger of AIWA and UAW; war production; blacks in auto industry; no-strike pledge; tenure as UAW president.   36 pp. *March 1963.*

THOMPSON, HUGH

AFL in auto industry; organizing in Anderson, Indiana and Oshawa, Ontario; strikes at Anderson-Guide Lamp (1936–37), Murray Body (1933), Seaman Body (1934), South Bend-Bendix, Atlanta-GM (1936); First Conference of Auto Locals (1934); UAW conventions (1935 and 1936); blacklisting; AFL-Detroit Office; Auto Labor Board; company unions; AFL National Council; labor spies; development of UAW seal.
41 pp. *March 1963.*

TUTTLE, FRANK

Chrysler Sit-Down; Progressive and Unity caucuses; UAW Convention (1939), Cleveland; blacklisting; labor spies; Black Legion; collective bargaining.
26 pp. *April 1959.*

VEGA, ART

Organizing of Briggs; working conditions before unions; speed-up; bonus systems.
12 pp. *April 1961.*

VESS, RAYMOND

Organizing of Pontiac Motor; Pontiac-Fisher Body Strike (1937); GM Strike (1945-46); Martin-CIO split; 1943 UAW Convention; NLRB election (1939); foundry work; automation; war production; upgrading; black employees; women workers; bonus plan; no-strike pledge; speed-up.
36 pp. *October 1961.*

WALLEMANN, FRANK

Organizing of St. Louis GM plants; Flint sit-downs; St. Louis-GM Strike (1937); Martin-CIO split; 1937 UAW Convention; NRA; Auto Labor Board; Federal Local 18386; anti-union activity.
46 pp. *April 1961.*

WILSE, JACK

Organizing in Cleveland auto plants; Cleveland-Fisher Body Sit-Down (1937); Murray Ohio Strike (1945-46); seniority; time study.
20 pp. *July 1961.*

WOODCOCK, LEONARD

Organizing in Detroit Gear and Axle and western Michigan; strikes at Motor Products (1933, 1934, and 1935); Briggs Strike (1933); GM Tool and Die Strike (1939); Martin split; Reuther vs. Addes; UAW conventions

(1943 and 1944); Wolman Board; CIO education classes; no-strike pledge; pattern bargaining.
45 pp. *April 1963.*

YAEGER, CHARLES
Organizing GM Truck, Pontiac; strike at GM Truck (1937); Martin vs. Reuther; UAW conventions (1937 and 1939), Cleveland; local union financial procedures; finances of international unions; dues structure; officers' salaries.
29 pp. *April 1963.*

YENNEY, ELMER
Organizing Janesville-Chevrolet; strike at Janesville-Chevrolet (1937); Martin-CIO split; piecework; company unions; Wolman Board; labor spies; war production; work standards; UAW and the community.
24 pp. *April 1961.*

YOST, LAWRENCE
Ford organizing drive; Flint sit-downs; communist influence in UAW; Reuther vs. Addes; 1944 UAW Convention; pre-union working conditions in Ford; UAW Education Program; war production; no-strike pledge; pension programs; UAW in Kaiser-Frazer and Chrysler; grievance procedures.
72 pp. *November 1960.*

ZAREMBA, JOHN
AFL in auto industry; AIWA; Dodge Sit-Down (1937); Flint sit-downs; working conditions in Dodge-Main prior to union; bonus system; company unions; stool pigeons.
30 pp. *August, September, October 1961.*

BLACKS AND THE LABOR MOVEMENT

ALBRIER, FRANCES
One of the first black female members of the Boilermakers Union. Problems of black women welders in entering craft unions; A. Philip Randolph and Brotherhood of Sleeping Car Porters; Executive Order 8802 and policies of Boilermakers Union towards minorities.
27 pp. *November 1968.*

BATTLE, ROBERT
President, Trade Union Leadership Council, and second vice-president, UAW Ford Local 600. Ford Motor Company and employment of blacks; Ford Organizing Drive; origins of TULC (Trade Union Leadership Council) and of NALC (Negro American Labor Council); relationship of UAW and TULC; blacks and apprenticeship training.
102 pp. *March 1969.*

BILLUPS, JOSEPH
Youth and early labor experiences in IWW and Autoworkers Union; International Labor Defense; Detroit and the Scottsboro case; the black and the Communist Party; Ford Organizing Drive; Nat Turner Clubs.
47 pp. *October 1967.*

BILLUPS, MR. AND MRS. JOSEPH
Mr. Billups was one of earliest black members of UAW Ford Local 600, and his wife was active in organizing UAW auxiliaries. Pre-UAW auto unionism; the black and left-wing activities; Detroit during the Depression; Unemployed Councils; Nat Turner Clubs; Ford Hunger March; Ford Organizing Drive.
16 pp. *September 1967.*

BLEDSOE, MRS. GERALDINE
Former director of Equal Employment Opportunity, Michigan Employment Security Commission. CIO and the black community; Detroit NAACP; Reverend Charles Hill; civil rights organization in the decade, 1935–45.
10 pp. *1970.*

COLES, JOSEPH
Black Democratic leader, former assistant director Detroit Commission on Community Relations. Sweet trials; black political shift from Republican

to Democratic Party; Detroit city government in relation to blacks; housing; Sojourner Truth Riot; Detroit Race Riot (1943); Mayor Jeffries; UAW and black political activities.
30 pp. *July 1970.*

CROCKETT, GEORGE
Detroit Recorder's Court; youth and education; activities as attorney for FEPC; experiences as executive director, UAW's Fair Practice Committee; blacks and Detroit politics.
42 pp. *March 1968.*

DADE, CANON MALCOLM
St. Cyprian's Presbyterian Evangelical Church, Detroit. Ford Motor Co. and the black Church; Ford organizing drive; relationship of UAW to black community.
48 pp. *September 1969.*

DI GAETANO, NICK
Detroit, UAW Local 7 retiree. Ethnic groups among Detroit workers; IWW; blacks in the auto plants and in the UAW.
16 pp. *June 1968.*

DOTY, EDWARD L.
Black unionist, Chicago, Illinois. Discrimination in Chicago area building trades, especially in electricians' and plumbers' unions; organization of all-black Consolidated Trades Council.
19 pp. *November 1967.*

GRIGSBY, SNOW
Black church and labor leader, former post office employee. Race relations in Detroit following World War I; organization and activities of Detroit Civic League, particularly in opening jobs for blacks.
15 pp. *March 1967.*

HATCHER, RAY
Deputy Director, Detroit Regional office, Housing and Urban Development Department. Detroit Urban League in the early 1940s; discrimination in housing; Sojourner Truth and Detroit Race Riots of 1942 and 1943; Royal Oak Township's efforts to become self-sufficient, all black community.
70 pp. *1970.*

HILL, REVEREND CHARLES
Late pastor of Hartford Ave. Baptist Church, Detroit. Ford Motor Co. and the black church; Ford Organizing Drive; blacks and unions; expansion of housing opportunities for blacks; Detroit Race Riot (1943); black political activities in Detroit.
43 pp. *May 1967.*

JONES, MRS. DOROTHY
Presently faculty member, Rutgers State University. United Federation of Teachers; Dr. Kenneth Clark; Northern school desegregation; Ocean-Hill, Brownsville episode; Black Caucus of AFT; Al Shanker.
30 pp. *July 1968.*

LATTIMORE, WILLIAM
Federal Mediation and Conciliation Service. Organization of Local 3, UAW; "Dirty Nickel" Strike of Dodge foundry workers; black caucus at UAW, Grand Rapids Convention (1944); UAW factionalism and the black.
11 pp. *August 1967.*

LEVER, JACK
Former labor educator and organizer. Cooperatives; Organizing in IAM; IAM and black workers; Brookwood Labor College; Ben Fletcher, IWW, the Longshoremen's Association; Steelworkers Organizing Committee.
22 pp. *May 1968.*

LIVINGSTON, DAVID
President, District 65, Distributive Workers of America. Distributive Workers; Textile Workers Union; organizing of black and Puerto Rican workers.
38 pp. *April 1969.*

McPHAUL, ARTHUR
Former executive director, Civil Rights Congress of Michigan. Ford Organizing Drive; life in black community in 30s; Black Legion; police brutality; National Negro Congress; Reverend Charles Hill; Sojourner Truth Riot; Civil Rights Federation; Civil Rights Congress.
30 pp. *1970.*

MAKI, ELEANOR
American Youth Congress; Civil Rights Federation and Civil Rights Congress; Sojourner Truth housing episode; AFT in the 1930s and 1940s.
30 pp. *1970.*

MARQUART, FRANK

Former labor educator, UAW. Ford hiring after $5.00 per day wage announcement in 1914; black workers and Ford; radicalism in the pre-World War II period; Proletarian Party; blacks and communism; UAW educational activities.
18 pp. *July 1968.*

MASON, HODGES

One of the first black presidents of a UAW local (Bohn Aluminum). Participation of blacks in sit-down strikes; 1938 strike at Bohn Aluminum; blacks and left-wing activities; UAW conventions, especially 1937, 1942, 1943; organizing at Ford Rouge Plant, factionalism in UAW (late 30s and 40s.)
62 pp. *November 1967.*
Placing the first black women in war production work in the Detroit area in 1942.
18 pp. *February 1968.*

NEELEY, JAMES

International representative, UAW, at time of death in 1969. Upgrading black workers in war production jobs in Detroit area in 1940s; hate strikes at Packard Motor Co.; 1943 Race Riot, role of the union; nature of "Negro" jobs; first contacts with union; views on separatism.
18 pp. *September 1967.*

OSMAN, ARTHUR

Former president, District 65, Distributive Workers of America. Conditions in dry goods industry in New York in early 1930s; AFL-CIO split in later 30s; organizing of black workers in the industry; adoption of hiring hall system and policy on sending black job applicants; democratic practices in the union; changing racial make-up of union; opposition to union checkoff; relationships with clothing industry unions and with Teamsters; racism in unions.
77 pp. *July 1968.*

RASKIN, JACK

Former executive secretary, Civil Rights Congress of Michigan. Civil Rights Congress and its predecessor organizations in 1940s and early 1950s; interest in racial problems; Sojourner Truth project; National Workers League; infiltration at neighborhood improvement association meetings;

National Negro Congress; Reverend Charles Hill; Judge George Crockett; Race Riot (1943); Haywood Patterson.
40 pp. *1970.*

RICHARD, ZELINE
Detroit Board of Education employee, prominent in leadership of New Caucus of AFT. Growth of Detroit Federation of Teachers; national AFT conventions, 1964 to date; "Racism in Education" Conference (1966); role of Ed Simpkins in AFT; school decentralization; emergence of New Caucus; Detroit Federation and its response to needs of black teachers; Al Shanker and the N.Y. situation; attitudes of blacks towards unions.
52 pp. *March 1969.*

ROBERTSON, GEORGE
President, UAW Local 235, Detroit. Experiences as production worker at Chevrolet Gear and Axle in late 1940s; attitude of local union toward grievances of black workers, then and now.
7 pp. *November 1967.*

SHEFFIELD, HORACE
UAW administrative assistant. Organizing campaign at Ford; involvement of NAACP on union's side; the black and left-wing political activities; UAW Conventions and the question of a black board member, especially in 1943, 1959, and 1962; organization of TULC and its subsequent development; NALC and its relation to TULC; A. Philip Randolph; role of black caucuses; League of Revolutionary Black Workers; blacks in UAW and other unions; blacks in the skilled trades.
37 pp. *July 1968.*

SIMMONS, LE BERON
Practicing Detroit attorney. Origins of Civil Rights Congress of Michigan; Sojourner Truth episode; National Negro Congress; police brutality in the 1930s; work as assistant prosecutor.
16 pp. *1969.*

SMITH, BERNIE
Retired Probate Court clerk. Black life in Detroit in early 1900s; organization of Detroit Urban League; black politics at turn of century; Dr. Ames; reactions to black influx of World War I; Elijah McCoy; the Sweet case; John Donery; Forrester Washington; St. Matthews Church and Father Daniel.
36 pp. *June 1969.*

TAPPES, SHELTON

Assistant director, UAW Fair Practices Department. Automobile industry before unionization; "Negro" jobs in the industry; Ford Organizing Drive; role of black in growth of Local 600; black caucuses in the UAW; history of Fair Practices Department.
91 pp. *1968.*

WHITBY, BEULAH

Social worker, former assistant director, Detroit Commission on Community Relations. Employment with YWCA; meeting of trains carrying migrants from South; casework with Detroit welfare department; Detroit in Depression; Muslims; Sojourner Truth episode; 1943 Race Riot; role of left-wing activitists; The Inter-racial Commission; NAACP, Urban League, and the black community.
41 pp. *September 1969.*

NEW YORK TIMES/COLUMBIA UNIVERSITY PROGRAM

The following interviews have been purchased by the Archives and are available on microfiche:

Roger Baldwin
John Brophy
William H. Davis
Julius Emspak
Albert Hayes
Benjamin F. McLaurin
Harry L. Mitchell
A. J. Muste
John O'Hara
William Pollock
Max Schachtman
Norman Thomas
Eva MacDonald Valesh
Roy Wilkins

INDEX

This index contains subjects and personal names mentioned in the entries for each collection, as well as the titles of each collection. The oral history section of the Guide has not been indexed. Readers may wish to consult *Preliminary Index to the United Automobile Workers Oral History,* compiled by the Institute of Labor and Industrial Relations, University of Michigan-Wayne State University, 1967.

Abel, I. W., 120
Abernathy, Ralph, 37
Abernathy, Roy, 108
Abner, Willoughby, 21
Abortion, 34
Academic freedom, 91, 119
Accidents: airlines, 89
Acme Paints: jurisdictional disputes, 36
Adamcyk, Stephen, 134
Addes, George, 21-22, 44, 47, 62-63, 69, 71, 73, 75, 80-81, 85, 99, 102-5, 107-8, 110-15, 120
Adult corrections, 129
Adult education: 32, 91, 99; UNESCO, 66
Africa: labor movement, 86; workers' education, 79
Aged: problem of, 60, 92
Aging, 129
Agreements: airlines, 74
Agricultural Implement conferences: UAW, 98; UAW, 1947, 83
Agricultural implement industry: UAW, 76. *See also* UAW Agricultural Implement Department
Agricultural labor, 40
Agricultural Workers Freedom to Work Association, 117, 118
Agricultural Workers Organization: 1915, 57
Agricultural Workers Organizing Committee: 54, 117; National Farm Workers Association merger (1966), 117; strikes (1959-65), 117
Agriculture: 52, 82; Department of, 76
Aguirre, J. M., 30
Agency for International Development: Uganda Mission, 53
Aid: to European refugees, 52; to parochial schools, 55

Aid to Dependent Children, 70
Aiken, George D., 26, 111
Aircraft evaluations, 87
Aircraft industry: organizing, 27, 59-60, 80; UAW, 39; wage rates, 58
Air Line Pilots Association (ALPA), 38-39, 72, 74: affiliation with AFL, 87; AFL (1938-52), 119; American Air Line Pilots, 88; Atlanta, 90; Caribbean, 89; Chicago, 89; Cincinnati, 79; committees, 87; conventions, 39; elections, 39; Flight Engineers Union, 90; formation, 88; grievances, 88; insurance, 74; "key men," 79; negotiations, 39, 55, 89-90; organizing, 79; pensions, 74; political activity, 87; San Francisco, 90; seniority, 88; split with airline stewards and stewardesses (1960), 24; strikes, 39, 88, 90
ALPA Board of Directors, 87
ALPA Contracts Administration Dept., 87-88
ALPA Dallas Joint Council, 134
ALPA Delta Council 43, 89
ALPA Denver Joint Council, 89
ALPA Employment Agreements Dept., 87
ALPA Engineering and Air Safety Dept., 87
ALPA Executive Board, 88
ALPA Executive Committee, 88
ALPA Governmental Affairs Dept., 134
ALPA Insurance Study Committee, 87
ALPA Legal Dept., 88
ALPA Los Angeles Joint Council, 89
ALPA Los Angeles Legal Office, 134
ALPA Miami Joint Council, 89-90
ALPA Military Affairs Committee, 39
ALPA Minneapolis Joint Council, 90
ALPA New York Joint Council, 90

ALPA New York Legal Office, 134
ALPA O'Hare Joint Council, 90
ALPA Organizational Structure Study Committee, 38, 87
ALPA Pan American Council 56, 90
ALPA Personnel Department, 134
ALPA Physical Standards Committee, 87
ALPA President's Dept., 88
ALPA Professional Standards Committee, 87
ALPA Public Relations Dept., 89
ALPA Retirement and Research Dept., 134
ALPA San Francisco Joint Council, 134
ALPA Seattle Joint Council, 90
ALPA Southern Council 112, 90
ALPA Stewards and Stewardesses Division, 89
Airline stewards and stewardesses: split with ALPA (1960), 34
Air Line Stewards and Stewardesses Association: 89; Transport Workers Union, 90
Airlines: accidents, 89; agreements, 74; arbitration, 74; crew complements, 87; federal regulations, 88; flight attendants, 89; government policy, 88; hijackings, 80; interchanges, 87; mergers, 87-90; negotiations, 73; noise abatement, 89-90; pensions, 87; route changes, 88; schedules, 89; strikes, 74, 88-89; third crew member, 88; training, 87; working conditions, 88; working hours, 88
Air mail: legislation, 87
Airports, 87
Air safety, 39, 73-74, 87, 89-90
Air traffic control, 87
Alaska Air Lines, 90
Albion Malleable Iron Company: NLRB election, 51
Alesandro, Thomas, 110
Aliens: wartime, 129; workers, 103
Alinsky, Saul, 31, 120
Allegheny-Ludlum Steel Corp.: organizing, 56
Allied Industrial Workers-AFL: relations with UAW, 30
Allied Relief, 103
Allis-Chalmers: strike, 112; strikes (1939, 1941, 1946-47), 111; strike (1947), 80; UAW, 98, 111
All-weather flying, 87
Almanac Singers, 131
Amalgamated Clothing Workers: 84; Detroit, 53; organizing, 82
American Air Line Pilots, 88
American Bowling Congress: discrimination, 66
American Brake Company: strike (1938), 100
American Civil Liberties Uuion: 43, 59, 64; Michigan chapter, 43, 119

American Committee for the Protection of the Foreign Born, 106
American Federation of Labor (AFL): ALPA affiliation, 87; ALPA (1938-52), 119; AFT (1916-52), 119; auto industry, 29, 38, 43, 45, 56, 61; CIO merger, 112, 114, 128, 130; CIO merger (1937-42), 122; Detroit, 56; education, 41; Federal Labor Unions, 107; UAW (1938-48), 119
AFL Education Committee, 26
AFL-Congress of Industrial Organizations (AFL-CIO): 71; Baltimore, 114; Maryland and District of Columbia, 114; merger, 37; Michigan, 75; United Farm Workers, 54; United Farm Workers, coordination with, 37; voter registration (1962, 1964), 70
AFL-CIO Industrial Union Dept., 29, 71
AFL-CIO Region 22, 37
American Federation of State, County and Municipal Workers (AFSCME): 30; factionalism, 77; Michigan, 86
AFSCME Council 7, 23
AFSCME Council 77, 31
AFSCME Local 26, 31
American Federation of Teachers (AFT), 26, 41-42, 50, 52, 58-59, 64, 68, 73, 79, 83: AFL (1916-52), 119; budgets, 91; Chicago, 50; collective bargaining, 92-93; communications, 91; communism, 26, 42, 50, 91-92; CIO affiliation (1938), 91; constitution, 92; contracts, 91; conventions, 91-94; defense cases, 91; East Detroit, 94; Ecorse, Mich., 95; elections, 91; factionalism, 91; finances, 92; Garden City, Mich., 134; grievances, 92; Hamtramck, 95; Hawaii, 134; history, 92; locals, 91-92; membership drives, 93; Michigan Federation of Teachers, 93; National Education Association, 64; organizing, 92; Pittsburgh, 94; political action, 92; public relations, 91; St. Louis, 94; St. Paul, Minn., 93; San Francisco, 93, 134; segregated locals, 92; strikes, 92; Toledo, 94; Washington, D.C., 63; Wayne State University, 62, 95. *See also* Teachers
AFT Executive Council, 91-92
AFT International Relations Committee, 26
AFT Local 28, 93
AFT Local 61, 93
AFT Local 250, 94
AFT Local 400, 94
AFT Local 420, 94
AFT Local 698, 94
AFT Local 1052, 95
AFT Local 1295, 95
AFT Local 1425, 95
AFT locals: charters, 92
AFT President's Dept., 92

American Guardian, 22
American Labor Party: 84 New York (1919-20), 31
American Miners Association, 83
American Motors: 35; Kenosha, Wis., 127; plant closing, 108; UAW, 107
American Newspaper Guild, 96. *See also* The Newspaper Guild
American Seating Company: UAW, 108
American Servicemen's Union, 125
American Slav Congress, 65
American Socialist Monthly, 69
American Teacher, 58
Americans for Democratic Action: 123; New York, 74
Ameringer, Oscar, 22
Amnesty: draft resisters, 43
Anaconda American Brass, Ltd.: UAW, 112
Anarchism, 24
Anderson, Alfred, 134
Anderson, Ind.: sit-down, 50, 70, 73; UAW, 81, 113
Anderson, John, 22
Anderson, Mary, 71
Anderson, Rose, 134
Anderson, W. H., 100
Ann Arbor Teachers Association, 119
Ann Arbor Teachers Club, 119
Anti-communism, 36
Anti-labor legislation, 128
Anti-left legislation, 45
Anti-lynching, 121
Anti-papism, 26
Anti-religion, 59
Anti-semitism: Soviet Union, 126
Anti-union activities: teachers, 73; textile industry, southern, 40
Anti-war demonstrations, 125
Anti-war groups: pre-World War II, 109
Anti-war movements, 91
Appeal cases: UAW, 102
Apportionment: legislative, 128
Apprenticeships: 47, 50; UAW, 103
Appropriations: Michigan Senate, 56
Arbitration: 30; airlines, 74; Canada, 75; The Newspaper Guild, 97
Arizona: UFW boycott, 118
Armed forces: discrimination, 59
Arnold, Thurman, 110
Artists, Engineers, Chemists, and Technicians, Federation of, 25
Asia: workers' education, 79
Asia, southeast: tin mission (1951-52), 123
Associated Charities of Detroit, 131
Associated Press: The Newspaper Guild, 96
Association of Catholic Trade Unionists, 30
Association of Catholic Trade Unionists of Detroit, 119-20
The Astors, 65

Atlanta: ALPA, 90; UAW, 89
Atlantic Conference (1959), 123
Atomic energy, 60
Attorney General's Office, Michigan, 63
Aurora-Caterpillar: organizing, 76
Austin, Richard 22, 35, 55-56
Automation, 44, 52
Automobile industry: AFL, 29, 38, 45, 56, 61; organizing, 25, 27, 40, 58, 82-83; organizing, Indiana, 70; private detectives, 25; sit-downs (1936-37), 82; strikes, 45; strikes (1930 s), 40. *See also* UAW
Automobile insurance, 85
Automobile Labor Board, 38, 43, 45, 61
Automobile prices, 84
Automobile unions: early organizing, 27; 1930s-40s, 27. *See also* UAW
Automobile Workers Union of Trade Union Unity League, 56
Automotive Industrial Workers Association, 43, 62, 85
Aviation: international, 74
Axtelle, George, 26
Bailey, John M., 63
Baker, Charles, 23
Bakery Workers, 120
Baldwin, Roger, 32, 55, 121
Ballot Box, 101
Baltimore: AFL-CIO, 114; UAW, 110, 114
Bank Holiday, 54
Bannon, Ken, 27, 62, 99, 109, 112, 115
Barber-Colman: organizing, 76
Barbour, Al, 32, 130, 132
Barker, Mary, 26
Barkley, Alben, 123
Bartlett, Lynn, 127
Baskin, Alex, 23
Basso, Joseph, 23
Battle of the Overpass, 40, 109
Baxter, Warner, 23
Bayh, Birch, 53, 81
Beard, Charles, 121
Beasley, Olive, 23
Beffel, John, 23-24
Behncke, David, 39, 74, 79, 88
Belli, Melvin, 36
Bendix: labor relations, 69; strikes, 105; UAW, 105
Bendix, Dorothy, 122
Bendix Westinghouse: UAW, 106
Benedict, Ruth, 121
Bennett, Harry, 99, 101
Benson, Herman, 24, 130
Bentley, Alvin, 111
Benton, William, 84
Berry Brothers: organizing, 36
Bethune, Mary, 67
Betts, W. W., 134
Bishop, Dorothy Hubbard, 24
Bishop, Melvin, 44, 114
Bishop, Merlin, 24

171

Black Cabinet, 39
Black, Eugene, 41, 121
Black, Hugo, 88
Black Legion: 58, 121; Citizens Committee, 62
Black Press, 39
Blackburn, Sam, 25
Blacks: employment in government, 67; Ford, 50; labor, 132; presidential campaign of 1968, 39; voting, 67
Blackwood, Ben, 58
Blaich, John, 25
Blankenhorn, Ann, 25
Blankenhorn, Heber, 25, 34
Blossom, F. A., 79
Blue Cross, 102
Blue Shield, 102
Bluestone, Irving, 25
Blume, Peter, 25
Boas, Frank, 121
Boeing: negotiations, 61
Bogard, T. J., 126
Bolivia: tin mission (1951-52), 123
Bollens, Jack, 30
Bombings: southern United States, 126
Boose, Arthur, 126
Borchardt, Selma, 26, 50
Bordner, Robert, 134
Borg-Warner Company, 30
Boston: TNG, 96; UFW, 118
Bowles, Chester, 40, 84, 123
Bowling: National Committee for Fair Play, 101
Boycotts: Giumarra, 118; grape, 117-18, 120; Kohler, 115; lettuce, 118; military, 125
Boyd, Knickerbocker, 81
Boyle, Tony, 129
Braceros, 120
Braden, Anne, 65
Braden, Carl, 65
Brandeis, Louis, 83
Brantford Coach and Body, Ltd.: UAW, 111
Brazier, Richard, 126
Brewer, George, 26
Brewer, Grace, 26
Brewster, Daniel, 114
Bricker Amendment, 128
Brickley, James H., 85
Bridges, Harry, 114, 122
Briggs: 50; strike (1933), 56, 61; strike (1939), 42, 109; UAW, 109, 114
Britain: socialism, 47
British colonialism, 30
Brock, Stewart, 134
Broken Arrow, 125
Brooke, Edward, 39
Brooklyn Society of Ethical Culture, 52
Brookwood Labor College, 33, 42, 70, 79
Broomfield, William, 33

Brophy, John, 37, 41-42, 56, 62, 75, 80, 107
Broun Award, 96
Brown, Basil, 38
Brown, Edmund, 37, 49, 117, 120
Brown, Ivan, 26-27
Brown, James H., 27
Brown, Joe, 27
Brown, Prentiss, 50, 102, 130
Brown, Roy, 27-28, 60-61
Brown, William T., 79
Brownell, Samuel M., 125
Bruff, John, 57
Brundage, Slim, 23
Bryn Mawr Summer School for Workers, 29
Budgets: Michigan, 33, 128
Buffalo: hotel waiters (1917), 60
Bugas, John S., 99
Buick: UAW, 112
Burkart, Robert, 28
Burt, George, 28, 75, 104, 106, 109, 111
Burton, John, 28
Buse, Robert, 111
Busing, 119
Butler, Paul, 123
Calhoun, Arthur, 134
California: Communist Party, 78; CIO, 37, 110; labor movement, 83; political campaigns (1953-68), 37
California Conference of Machinists, 27
California Migrant Ministry, 120
California Rural Legal Assistance, 117-18
Callaghan, Frank, 30
Calumet, Michigan: copper strike, 55
Calverton, V. F., 32
Campus disputes, 49
Canada: arbitration, 75; labor, 42; Labour College, 106; UAW, 28, 42, 75, 109, 112; UAW organizing, 104; U.S. auto trade agreements (1969, 1970), 75; U.S. relations, 104
Canadian-American Conference on Foreign Policy (1951), 123
Canadian Congress of Labour: United Electrical Workers suspension, 109
Canadian Labour Congress, 75, 112
Capehart, Homer, 111
Capper, Arthur, 26
Carey, Ed, 32, 108
Carey, James, 40-42, 55, 75, 83-84, 99, 105, 122, 128
Caribbean: ALPA, 89
Carlstrom, Lawrence, 28
Carpenters Union, 120
Carpenters Local 334, 131
Case, Clifford, 123
Casey, Jack, 28
Caterpillar Tractor: UAW, 98
Catholic University: School of Social Action, 30

172

Cavanagh, Jerome, 22, 28-29, 32-34, 68, 81-82, 85, 108, 124, 129, 132
Cedervall, Tor, 29
Celebrezze, Anthony, 129
Celler, Emmanuel, 123-24
Censorship, 119
Center for Community Change, 71
Centralia conspiracy, 126
Certification: teachers, 68, 119
Chain stores: consumer suits, 118
Chalmers, W. Ellison, 29
Chamberlain, Charles, 113
Chaplin, Ralph, 24
Charity, 131
Charters: AFT locals, 92
Chase, Alice, 79
Chatfield, Leroy, 29
Chavez, Cesar: 29, 31, 34, 49, 92, 117-18, 120, 130; fast (1968), 117
Chemical workers, 36
Chevrolet: UAW, 105-6, 114
Chevrolet Gear and Axle, 66
Chiakulas, Charles, 29-30
Chicago: ALPA, 89; AFT, 50; Greek community, 30; politics, 30; teachers, 83; UAW, 33, 106; UFW boycott, 118
Chicago Heights (Illinois): UFW boycott, 118
Child care, 103
Child Development Group of Mississippi, 120
Child labor, 82
Child labor law: Texas, 40
Child Welfare League, 41
Children: social and economic conditions, 25; UAW, 101; welfare, 129
China: Committee to Aid, 63
Chrapkiewicz, Joseph, 134
Christenson, Edith, 55, 134
Christian Brothers: UFW negotiations, 29; representation election, 29
Christie, J. C., 73
Christman, Elizabeth, 71
Christoffel, Harold, 111
Chrysler: 37, 50; Imperial plant, 67; labor relations, 67; negotiations, 51; organizing, 85; stockholders' suits, 36; strike (1937), 85. *See also* auto industry strikes, sit-downs; strike (1939), 42, 85; strike (1950), 105-6, strike, Los Angeles (1957), 47; UAW, 98, 105, 109-10, 112, 115
Chudleigh, H. E., 30
Church: labor movement, 99, 125
Churches, 124
Church-state relations, 119
Ciccone, Louis, 30
Cigar Makers Union Number 130, Saginaw, Mich., 120
Cincinnati: ALPA, 79
Citizens: naturalized, 129
Citizens Advocate Center, 71

Citizens Committee for Equal Opportunity, 35
Citizens Crusade Against Poverty, 71, 120
Citizens for Michigan, 35, 98, 120
Citizens for Schools, 98
Citizens for a United Detroit, 134
Civil aviation: use by military, 89
Civil Aviation Administration, 88
Civil disorders, 28
Civil liberties: 34, 40, 74; Detroit, 65
Civil rights: 36-37, 40, 44, 46-47, 49, 55, 60, 63, 68, 70-71, 73, 76, 79, 85, 91-92, 100, 106, 119, 123-24, 126, 128, 130, 131; Conference for the Protection of, 63; CIO Committee, 123; Detroit, 65; Detroit education, 72; Mississippi, 74
Civil Rights Congress of Michigan, 121
Civil Rights Defense Committee, 114
Civil Rights Federation, 85, 120
Civil Service, 55
Civil War Centennial, 63
Clancy, Father Raymond, 30
Clark, Joseph, 40
Clark, Mark, 81
Clark, Ramsey, 39, 49
Clerical workers: Wayne State University, 133
Cleveland: IWW, 29; UFW boycott, 118
Clifford, Clark, 123
Clothing industry: conditions, 1920s-30s, 25
Coal miners: health, 130; safety, 130
Coal mining: conditions (1920s-30s), 25; government administration (1946), 45; organizing, 83; southern Illinois, 47; working conditions, 65
Cobb, Alton, 31
Cobo, Albert, 112, 128
Coffey, Ed, 99
Cogen, Charles, 50, 52, 73, 92
Cohen, David, 31
Cohen, Joseph, 23
Cohen, Wilbur, 42, 102
Coit, Eleanor, 32
Coldwell, M. J., 109
Coleman, McAlister, 22
Collective bargaining: 71; AFT, 92-93; farm workers, 49; pilots, 88; rubber industry, 131; teachers, 64, 94; techniques, 99; UAW, 64, 103
College: teachers, 91
Collier, John, 31-32
Collier, Phyllis, 31
Collier, William Armistead, Jr., 31-32
Collins, Vernon, 134
Collins, Virgil, 32
Collins, William, 38, 45, 62, 72
Colonialism: British, 30
Colorado Federation of Teachers, 73
Colorado Labor Council, 73

173

"Colored Division," Democratic National Committee (1932-40), 66-67
Columbus: UFW boycott, 118
Commission on Community Relations, Detroit, 35
Commission on Equal Employment Opportunity, President's, 39
Committee on Militarism in Education, 41
Committee on Political Education (COPE), 29-30, 70, 73, 98
Commons, John R., 29
Commonwealth College, 55
Communications Workers of America Local 4000, 121: factionalism, 121
Communism: 24, 45, 59, 79; AFT, 26, 42, 50, 91-92; labor movement, 38, 119, 122; UAW, 109
Communist Party: CIO, 57; education, 78; Michigan, 44-45; New England, 78; Pittsburgh, 78; Southern California, 78; Wisconsin, 78
Communist Party of the United States, 78
Communists at Work, 58
Community Health Authority, 68
Community involvement: labor, 46
Community organizations: Chicago, 31; Detroit, 31
Community relations, 46
Community service organizations: Hanford, California, 117
Community services: Detroit, 77; UAW, 105
Community Union Center: Chicago, 29
Community unions, 30
Company unions, 38, 42, 45
Compensation: unemployment, 102-3, 128; workmen's, 40, 44, 128
Competitive shops: UAW, 47
Comstock, William, 130
Conger, Lyman, 28
Congress of Industrial Organizations (CIO): 42, 57, 71, 119; AFL merger, 112, 114, 122, 128, 130; AFL merger (1937-42), 122; AFT proposed affiliation (1938), 91; California, 110, California, southern, 37; Civil Rights Committee, 123; Communist Party, 57; conventions, 122; councils, 98; Executive Board (1953-55), 122; finances, 122; formation, 45, 130; Illinois, 45; Indiana, 41; Latin America, 122; Los Angeles, 72, 110; Michigan, 49, 75, 120, 127; Milwaukee, 111; Missouri, 45; New Orleans (1939) 69; organizing, 58; UAW, 69; Wayne County, 44, 70, 84-85, 120; Wisconsin, 111; women's auxiliaries, 76
CIO Department of Education and Research, 122
CIO Office of the President, 122

CIO Office of the Secretary-Treasurer, 122-23
CIO Political Action Committee, 49
CIO Region 13, 37
Congress: United States, 37
Congressmen: United States, 29
Connally, John, 120
Connecticut: politics, 84
Connole, A. B., 58
Connor, Edward, 32, 36, 112
Conscientious objectors, 133
Conservation, 40, 78, 82
Constitution: AFT, 92; UAW, 67
Constitutional Convention. *See* Michigan Constitutional Convention
Construction workers, 120
Consumers: affairs, 64, 103; councils, 98; chain store suits, 118; education, 132
Consumers League, 82
Continental Air Lines, 89
Continental Aviation: UAW, 111
Continental Motors: UAW, 111
Contracts: AFT, 91; TNG, 96
Controls: rent, 123, 128; wages, 84, 123
Conventions, ALPA, 39, 87; AFT, 91-94; CIO, 122; Democratic National (1964), 49; Michigan Federation of Teachers (1963), 95; National Farm Workers Association (1962), 117; NEA (1959-66), 124; Socialist Party (1936, 1938), 40-41; TNG, 96-97; UAW, 64, 98; UAW (1936), 56, 79; UAW (1937), 41; UAW (1946, 1953, 1957, 1959, 1961), 77; UAW (1947-53), 84
Convention Investigating Committee: report to UAW International Executive Board (1947), 34
Conyers, John, Sr., 33
Conyers, John, Jr., 22, 34, 36, 132
Cooper, John Sherman, 26
Co-operative colonies, 32
Cooperatives: 40, 64, 94, 99; housing, 108
Coordinating Council on Human Relations, Detroit, 62
Copeland, William, 33
Copland, Aaron, 131
Copper mining: strike at Calumet, Mich., 55
Corrections: adults, 129; juveniles, 129
Cost of living, 40
Costello, Timothy, 118
Cote, Edward, 33
Coughlin, Father Charles, 31, 42, 56, 59, 62, 73, 121
Council of Churches: Detroit, 35; Michigan, 35
Counseling, 103
Counts, George, 26
Coup: Greece, 1967, 30
Court: reorganization, 55

Cousens, Leon, 33
Couser, James, 33-34
Couzens, Frank, 121
Couzens, James, 43, 132
Cowley, Malcolm, 32
Craft unionism: vs. industrial unionism, 126
Craig, Roger, 34
Cranefield, Harold, 34
Credit unions, 40, 42, 77
Crime: waterfront, New York and New Jersey, 82
Criminal code: revision, 46
Criminal law, 41
Criminal syndicalism, 82, 126
Crockett, George, 34, 62
Crosby, Jack, 34-35
Crouch, Paul, 23
Cruikshank, Nelson, 102-3
Cuban revolution, 131
Current, Gloster, 35, 67
Cushman, Edward, 35
Cuttle, Raymond, 35
Cyprus: 29; trade unions, 30
D'Agostino, John, 35
Dallas, Texas: night school (1901), 40; politics, 40; UAW, 115
Dancy, John C., 76, 100
Daniel, Berthe, 134
Daniel, Mrs. Cuthbert, 134
Daniel, Franz, 134
Daniels, Jonathan, 123
Dann, Sol, 36
Davidson, Ben, 134
Davis, Jerome, 50, 92
Davis, William, 134
Day, Walter, 36
Dayan, Moshe, 36
Dearden, John Cardinal, 35
Debs, Eugene, 22, 26, 47
Debs, Katherine, 26
Defense: 123; employment, 102; production, 71
Defense cases: AFT, 91
Defense Department: grape purchases, 118
de la Cruz, Reynaldo, 117
Delco-Remy: 53; organizing, 73, 85; UAW, 113
Dell, Floyd, 32
Del Rio, James, 130
Delta Air Lines, 90: negotiations, 89
Democratic National Committee: "Colored Division" (1932-40), 66-67
Democratic Party: 33-34, 55, 57, 67, 70; National Convention (1964), 49
Demonstrations: anti-war, 125
Denise, Malcolm, 99
Dent, Mary, 26
Denver: ALPA, 89; UFW boycott, 118
Denver Federation of Teachers, 73
Dependent children: aid, 70

Deportation, 119
Depression: 54, 76; labor movement, 132
De Shetler, Irwin, 36-37, 48
Designing Engineers, Society of, 25
DeSilver, Margaret, 24
Dethmers, John, 41
Detroit: Amalgamated Clothing Workers, 53; AFL, 56; Archdiocese Labor Institute, 30; Archdiocese Social Action Department, 30; civil liberties, 65; civil rights, 65; civil rights in education, 72; community services, 77; economic conditions, 28; industrial development, 131; Labor Temple, 43; migration by southerners, 124; millage campaign (1959-63), 124; NAACP, 59; Pioneers Club, 76; police, 41; politics, 40-41, 65, 76; racial conditions, 28; recreation employees, 36; riot (1943), 50, 124, 130; riot (1967), 23, 46; TNG, 96; UAW, 104-5, 107-9, 112; UFW boycott, 118; United Public Workers, 80
Detroit Board of Education, 72
Detroit Citizens Housing and Planning Council, 32
Detroit Commission on Community Relations, 35, 123-24
Detroit Committee to End the War in Vietnam, 124
Detroit Common Council, 32, 41
Detroit Community Union, 131
Detroit Coordinating Council on Human Relations, 62
Detroit Council of Churches, 124
Detroit Education Association, 124-25: DFT, 124
Detroit Federation of Teachers (DFT), 42, 93: DEA, 124; relations with suburban locals, 48
Detroit *Free Press:* TNG, 96
Detroit Industrial Mission, 125
Detroit International Institute, 62
Detroit Housing Commission, 41
Detroit Public Bank: failure of, 36
Detroit Recorder's Court, 32
Detroit Society for the Study and Prevention of Tuberculosis, 131
Detroit Teachers Association (DTA): 124; Wayne State University, 125
Detroit *Times:* TNG, 96
Deverall, Richard, 120
Dewey, John, 22, 82
Dickinson, Lauren, 132
Dies Committee, 121
Digaetano, Nick, 37
Diggs, Charles, 22, 37, 72, 85, 123, 125-26, 132
DiGiorgio Corp., 117
DiGiorgio, Robert, 49
Dillard, Ernest, 134

175

Dillon, Francis, 29, 38, 45, 56, 61, 81, 105, 107
Dingell, John, 32-33, 41, 50, 55, 66 110, 125, 129, 130
Dingwell, Robert, 38
Dirksen, Everett, 37, 49, 123
Disabled veterans: UAW, 103
Disadvantaged: aid, 85
Discrimination: 34, 37, 103, 121; American Bowling Congress, 66; armed forces, 59; education, 130; employment, 126, 130; housing, 124-26, 130
Disputes: campus, 49
District of Columbia and Maryland: AFL-CIO, 114
District Council 26; UAW, 28
Ditzel, Joseph, 38
Doar, John, 49
Dodd, Thomas, 37, 40
Dodge, 73: organizing, 85
Dodge Revolutionary Union Movement (DRUM), 78
Doherty, Tom, 120
Dolgoff, Sam, 134
Doll, Tracy, 103, 108, 121
Donahue, Paul, 57
Dooley, Roy, 38
Dory, Edward, 39
Dos Passos, John, 82
Douglas, Helen Gahagan, 37
Douglas, Paul, 29, 37, 50, 77, 92, 115, 123, 129
Downey, Sheridan, 110
Downs, Tom, 127
Draft: abolition of, 43; peacetime, 128
Draft resisters: amnesty, 43
Drake, James, 134
Dreiser, Theodore, 32
Drob, Judah, 134
Dubinsky, David, 46, 57, 82, 105
Dufty, William, 39
Dukes, Ofield, 39
Dunayevskaya, Raya, 39-40
Dunn, Robert, 40
Dzendzel, Raymond, 127
Eagleton, Thomas, 130
Earhart, Amelia, 58
East Detroit: AFT, 94
Eastern Air Lines, 89
Eastman, Max, 32
Eaton Manufacturing Company: UAW, 106
Ebert, Robert A., 73
Eby, Kermit, 122
Economic conditions: Detroit, 28
Economics: discrimination, 133; UAW, 101; UAW in Canada, 75
Economic Opportunity, Office of, 120
Economic reform, 69
Ecorse, Michigan: AFT, 95
Eddy, Jonathan, 96
Edelman, John, 40, 55, 82, 103

Education: 57, 60, 82, 103, 128; adult, 99; AFL, 41; Communist Party, 78; consumers, 132; Detroit, 72; discrimination, 130; federal aid, 42, 50, 91-92; International Ladies Garment Workers, 79; legislation, 94, 119; Michigan State University overseas, 81; New York City, 74; public, 124; special, 129; state aid, 91; teachers, 68; UAW, 51, 61, 75, 98-99; UAW Local 80, 52; UAW Local 544, 52; UAW Region 3, 51; workers, 42, 66, 71, 92, 128. *See also* Labor education
Edwards, George, Sr., 40-41
Edwards, George, Jr., 41, 48, 85, 108, 112, 114, 130
Edwards, Hagburt, 134
Edwards, Leverett, 39, 74
Edwards, Neal, 41
Eisenhower, Dwight D., 58, 88, 128
Eisenhower, Milton, 64
Eklund, John, 26, 134
Elder, Arthur, 26, 41-42, 92-94, 103
Eldon, John, 42, 104
Elections: 103; flight attendants, 89; IAM, 60; Michigan gubernatorial (1970), 57; presidential (1964), 63; school boards, 119; 1940s, songs, 131; TNG, 96; UFW, 54; UMW (1969, 1972), 130
Electrical Workers, Brotherhood of, 120
Electrical workers' unions, 122
Ellickson, Katherine, 42-43
Ellis, E. K., 43
Ellman, Erwin, 43
Embree, A. S., 126
Employees Association: Guide Lamp, 51
Employers Association of Detroit, 134
Employment: blacks in government, 67; defense, 102; discrimination, 126, 130; Mexican nationals, 117; stabilization, 103; wartime, 101
Employment security: UAW, 102
Emrich, Richard, 46
Emspak, Julius, 116
Engle, Clair, 37, 120
Equal Employment Opportunity Commission, 39, 42
Equal rights: women, 40, 128
Erb, Mary, 71
Ervin, Charles, 22, 47
Espionage: industrial, 34
Ettor, Joseph, 79
Europe: labor unions, 99; postwar, 103; postwar (1918, 1945), 82; workers' education, 79
European recovery, 123
European refugees: aid, 52
European Relief Council, 131
Everett Massacre, 126
Evers, Charles, 49
Executive Order 10925, 27

176

Executive Reserve, 74
Eye Opener, 101
Factionalism: AFSCME, 77; AFT, 91; Communications Workers of America Local 400, 121; Flat Glass Workers Union, 37; IAM, 60; IAM Lodge 113, 77; UAW. *See also* UAW, factionalism; UAW Local 146, 50-51; United Public Workers, 48
Fafnir Bearing Company: UAW, 107
Fair employment practices, 27, 34, 62, 76, 99, 103, 112-13, 121; Michigan Coordinating Council, 44; UAW, 103, 105
Fair Employment Practices Commission, Michigan, 75
Fair Employment Practices Committee (FEPC), 44, 62, 77, 114, 128
Fair housing: 62; Birmingham, Mich., 125
Fair practices: UAW, 66, 73
Family: welfare, 129
Fantozy, Sam, 134
Farley, James, 67
Farm Bureau: Michigan, 128
Farm labor, 128, 130
Farm labor organizing: legislation, 54
Farm workers: collective bargaining, 49; health hazards, 117; importation, 54; IWW, 126; legislation, 120, 130; living conditions, 117; organizing, 120; Teamsters, 54; working conditions, 117. *See also* United Farm Workers (UFW); UFW boycott
Farm Worker Press, 117
Farm Worker Service Center, 29
Farmer, James, 124
Farmers' Holiday Association, 82
Farmers' unions, 128
Fascism, 121
Federal aid to education, 42, 50, 91-92
Federal Aviation Administration, 88
Federal courts: Ford Motor Company, 47
Federal Food and Drug Administration: UFW, 118
Federal government: airline regulations, 88
Federal Labor Unions; AFL, 107
Federal Mediation and Conciliation Service, 69
Federal Workers of America: State, County and Municipal Workers merger, 49
Federal works programs, 91
Federated Press, 27, 47, 65
Federation of Artists, Engineers, Chemists and Technicians, 25
Federation of Glass, Ceramic and Sand Workers, CIO, 37
Feinsinger, Nathan, 74
Ferency, Zoltan, 34, 55-56, 63

Ferguson, Homer, 36, 110, 112, 114, 129, 132
Field Foundation: legal services grant, UFW, 117
Finances: UAW, 102
Financial reports: UAW, 98
Financing: schools, 68
Finneran, Betty, 94
Firearms control, 34
Fiscal reform, 85
Fisher Body: NLRB, 113; UAW, 110, 113-14
Fisher Body Plant 1: sit-down, 78
Fisher Body Plant 2: sit-down, 66
Fishing: legislation, 82
Fishlow, David, 134
Fitzgerald, Frank, 132
Fitzsimmons, Frank, 110
Flanagan, Daniel, 37
Flat Glass Workers Union; AFL, 36; factionalism, 37; organizing, 37
Flesch, Fritz, 43
Flight attendants, 89: elections, 89; physical standards, 90
Flight crews: training, 90; working conditions, 90
Flight engineers, 74, 90
Flight Engineers Union: ALPA, 90
Flint: teacher dismissals (1937-49), 42; UAW, 112
Flint Civil Rights Commission, 23
Flint sit-down, 38, 46, 54, 66, 78. *See also* Automobile industry, Sit-downs, Strikes
Flores, Bishop Patricio, 117
Fluoridation, 124
Flying Tiger Air Lines, 89
Flynn, Elizabeth Gurley: 25, 32, 68, 82, 126; imprisonment, 25
Folksongs, 131
Food: shortages, 64
Forand Bill, 102
Ford, Gerald R., 55, 81, 110, 128
Ford, Henry II, 101, 120, 132
Ford Motor Company: 73; Atlanta, Ga., 27; blacks, 50; contract, 1941, 26; fair employment practices, 27; federal court hearings, 47; GM contract comparisons, 76; Iron Mountain Plant, sale of, 27; labor relations, 67; NLRB, 59, 83, 99, 101; negotiations, 99; organizing, 56, 59, 80, 83, 100-101, 110, 120; Richmond, Calif., 83; St. Louis, 59; strike (1941), 50, 53; strike (1949), 80, 84, 120, 128; strike (1958), 83; UAW, 99, 109, 112-13, 115. *See also* Strikes: War Labor Board
Ford of Canada: UAW, 110
Ford Hunger March, 56
Ford Service Department, 101
Foreign administrations: IWW, 126
Foreign aid, 123

177

Foreign policy: Canadian-American Conference (1951), 123; labor, 122
Foreign trade unions, 122
Foreman, Clark, 65
Forsen, Clemens, 134
Fort Smith: arrest and trial, 40
Fort Wayne: UAW, 107
Foster, William Z., 82
Francis, Everett, 43
Frankensteen, Richard: 43-44, 62, 69, 80-81, 85, 106, 110, 113, 120; Detroit mayoralty campaign (1945), 44
Frankfurter, Felix, 41
Free speech: IWW, 126
Free thought, 59
Freedom Democratic Party, Mississippi, 49
Freedom movements, 36
Freeman, Orville, 49, 76
Freud, Sigmund, 36
Fringe benefits: teachers, 93
Frontier Air Lines, 89
Fruehauf Trailer: UAW, 106
Fuller, Alex, 44
Fuller, Paul, 37
Fuller Homes, Inc., 84
Fund-raising: NAACP, 59
Furniture workers, 120
Gabriel Retirement Plan, 53
Gadsden, Alabama: rubber workers, organizing, 72
Galarza, Ernesto, 117, 120
Gallagher, Daniel, 44
Ganley, Nat, 44-45
Garbage workers, 31
Garland Fund, 31
Garman, Phillips, 45
Garmatz, Edward A., 114
Garst, Delmond, 45-46
Gastonia: strike (1929), 82
Gemmer Manufacturing Company: UAW, 107
General Motors (GM): Ford contract comparisons, 76; negotiations, 100; organizing, 100, 120; Oshawa strike, (1937), 77; strikes (1930s), 57; strike (1934), 43; strike (1937), 73, 81, 85; strike (1945-56), 45, 59, 73, 80, 100, 103, 110, 113, 120; UAW, 100, 106, 110, 112, 114. *See also* Flint sit-downs, Strikes
GM Diesel Division: UAW, 106
GM Ternstedt Division: job classification (1937), 33; wage rates (1937), 33
Genske, William, 46
Gentile, Charles, 134
George, Walter, 26
Gerber, Martin, 114
Germany: labor's role in occupation, 52
Germer, Adolph, 37, 44, 56, 75, 107
GI Underground Press, 125
Gibson, John, 75, 127

Gibson Refrigerator Company, 35
Gilmore, Horace, 46
Girardin, Ray, 130
Giumarra: boycott, 118; strike, 118
Glaberman, Jesse, 134
Glaberman, Martin, 134
Glass workers. *See* Federation of Glass, Ceramic and Sand Workers, CIO; Flat Glass Workers Union, AFL
Glicman, Henry, 134
Goldberg, Arthur, 35, 37, 40, 74, 110, 123, 132
Golden, Harry, 36, 65
Goldman, Emma, 32
Goldmann, William, 46-47
Goldwater, Barry, 24
Gompers, Samuel, 60, 71, 83
Goodell, Charles, 118
Goodman, Ernest, 121
Goodyear Tire and Rubber: unionization, 72
Gore, Albert, 81
Gorman, Patrick, 30
Gosser, Richard, 28, 30, 46-47, 62, 102
Gould, Jean, 47
Government: administration of coal mines (1946), 45; airlines policy, 88; IWW raids, 126; labor, 71; Michigan, 121
Government critics, justice for, 133
Grand Rapids: UAW, 108
Grand Rapids Education Association, 125
Grand Rapids Teachers Club, 126
Grapes: false labeling, 118; purchase by Defense Dept., 118
Grape boycott, 31, 34, 54, 117-18, 120
Grape growers, 117
Grape strike, 31, 117, 120
Greathouse, Pat, 30, 77, 98
Great Lakes: strike (1948), 132
Great Lakes Seaway, 132
Greece: 29; coup (1967), 30
Greek community: Chicago, 30
Green, Fred, 130
Green, William, 26, 29, 38, 43, 50, 56, 61, 72, 73, 88, 92-93, 105, 107, 130
Green Mountaineer, 67
Greenberg, Jacob, 52
Gribbs, Roman, 22
Grievances: ALPA, 88; AFT, 92; teachers, 94; TNG, 96
Griffin, Robert, 81, 124
Griffiths, Martha, 36, 55, 108, 125-28
Grosbeck, Alex, 132
Groves, Phyllis, 47
Guaranteed annual wage, 42, 44, 128
Guernsey, George, 92, 122
Guide Lamp Employees Association, 51
The Guggenheims, 65
Guggenheim, M., 65
Guthrie, Woody, 131

Haber, William, 57
Haessler, Carl, 47, 102
Haig, Robert M., 74
Halbeisen, Robert, 48
Hall, Covington, 22, 48
Hall, Ed, 38, 62
Hamilton, Henry, 48
Hammett, Dashiell, 121
Hamtramck: AFT, 95
Hanford, Calif.: community service organizations, 117
Hannah, John, 35, 48, 126
Hare, James, 34, 55-56, 78, 130
Harriman, Averell, 123
Harriman, J. W., 58
Harriman Lines: strike (1911-15), 68
Harris, Fred, 23
Hart, Philip, 27, 32-34, 37, 41, 55-57, 66, 68, 78, 81-82, 108, 112, 121, 124, 127, 132
Hartke, Vance, 53
Hartmire, Wayne C., 117-18
Harvard University: trade union program, 60
Harvest Workers Conference (1915), 57
Hatcher, Lillian, 129
Hatcher, Raymond, 134
Haughton, Ronald, 48-49
Haven Hill Conference, 93
Hawaii: UFW boycott, 118
Hayakawa, S. I., 52
Hayes, A. J., 24, 28, 60-61
Haywood, Allan, 37, 41, 75, 114
Haywood, William: 72, 126; departure for Russia, 79
Health: coal miners, 130
Health care: 128, 131: legislation, 102; UAW, 102
Health insurance, 40, 105
Health hazards: farm workers, 117
Health problems: 32; urban Russia, 32
Held, Adolph, 126
Helicon Home Colony, 32
Heller, Walter, 129
Henderson, Leon, 41, 123
Henderson, Lettisha, 134
Henderson, N. C.: strikes (1959), 82
Henney, Westray, 134
Henkelman, William, 134
Henrickson, Merle, 49
Henry, Aaron, 49
Henry, David, 121
Henson, Frank, 49-50, 127
Herrick, Mary, 50
Herrington, A. W., 111
Herstein, Lillian, 134
Hicks, Granville, 121
Higher education: 34; financial support by state, 68
Highways: federal acts, 60
Hijackings: airlines, 89
Hilberry, Clarence, 55, 71, 132

Hill, Charles, 50
Hill, Herbert, 126, 130
Hill, James, 134
Hill, Joe, 24, 126, 131
Hill, Lester, 26
Hillman, Sidney, 29, 37, 84, 103, 132
Hitler, Adolph, 82
Hobbs Corporation: organizing, 76
Hodges, Luther, 124
Hoffa, James R., 115
Hoffman, Bernard, 50
Hoffman, Clare, 121
Hoffman, Claude, 50-51
Hoffman, Paul, 123
Hoffman, S. L., 134
Hood, Nicholas, 32
Hood, Raymond, 134
Hood, William R., 50
Hook, Sidney, 32
Hoover, J. Edgar, 34
Hopkins, Barney, 48-49, 73, 127
Horner Woolen Mills: strike (1937), 48
Horton, Myles, 127
Hotel waiters: Buffalo (1917), 60
House, Kenneth, 36
House of Representatives: Michigan, 33, 38, 55, 68, 70, 78, 82
House Un-American Activities Committee: 45, 53, 119, 121; IAM Lodge 113, 67
Housing: 28, 32, 40-41, 75, 99, 103, 122-24, 128; cooperatives, 108; Detroit Commission, 41; discrimination, 124-26, 130; public, 110, 128; rural, 120; Schoolcraft Garden Cooperative, 48; Sojourner Truth Project, 50
Housing and urban development: federal task force, 75
Hudson Motors: Nash-Kelvinator merger, 108; strike (1951), 108; UAW, 108
Huerta, Delores, 34
Hughes, Arthur, 51
Hull, Cordell, 123
Hull House, 65
Human relations, 129
Humanism, 59
Humphrey, Hubert, 23, 34-37, 39, 41, 49, 56, 66, 76, 81, 85, 92-93, 99, 101, 123, 128-29, 132
Humphreys, William, 51
Hunger and Malnutrition in the United States, Citizens Board of Inquiry, 120
Hunger March, Ford, 56
Hunt, H. L., 76
Hunting: legislation, 82
Hutton, Carroll, 51, 77, 132
Hyshka, Nicholas, 51-52
I Break Strikes, 57
Ickes, Harold, 67
Ignasiak, Andrew, 52
Illinois: coal mining, 47: CIO, 45

179

Illinois Central Railroad: strike (1911-15), 68
Illinois Federation of Teachers, 83
Illinois Miner, 22
Immigrants: 129; licensing physicians, 129
Implied consent, 34
Importation: farm workers, 54
India: worker education, 66
Indiana: auto worker organizing, 70; CIO, 41; UAW, 41
Indianapolis: UAW, 111
Industrial Relations: U.S. Commission on, 68
Industrial safety: legislation, 38
Industrial Union Dept.: AFL-CIO, 29, 71
Industrial unionism: vs. craft unionism, 126
Industrial Workers of the World (IWW): 24, 32, 37, 48, 57, 66-67, 72, 79, 82, 126; Cleveland, 29; farm workers, 126; foreign administrations, 126; general administration dispute, 57; govt. raids, 126; Minneapolis, 134; strikes, 126; trials, 79, 126
Institute of Industrial Relations; Wayne State University, 35
Institute of World Studies, 26
Insurance: ALPA, 74; automobile, 85; health, 40; unemployment, 42; UAW, 102
Integration, 91
Interchanges: airlines, 87
Inter-Church World Movement: and steel strike (1919), 25
Inter-Professional Association, 81
International affairs: UAW, 100
International Association of Machinists (IAM), 27, 60, 68; aircraft industry, 60; elections, 60; factionalism, 24, 60; organizing, 60; UAW, 58, 60-61; and UAW no-raid agreement, 27
IAM Lodge 113: factionalism, 77; House Un-American Activities Committee, 67
IAM Lodge 1126, 27
IAM Lodge 1484, 27
International aviation, 74
International Civil Aviation Organizations (ICAO), 74, 87
International Confederation of Free Trade Unions (ICFTU): 29, 66, 100, 122; 3rd World Congress (1953), 70
International Education Association, 91
International Federation of Air Line Pilots Associations, 74, 87
International Harvester: labor relations, 77; Melrose Park, Ill., 85; NLRB, 107; UAW, 98, 105, 107, 116
International Institute, Detroit, 62
International labor bodies, 92
International Labor Organization, 35, 66
International Ladies Garment Workers: 57, 84; education, 79
International Metalworkers Federation, 100
International Press Correspondence, 69
International Review, 69
International Women's Suffrage Convention (1913), 82
Investigations: loyalty, 65, 74
Iron Molders Union, 39, 134
Irwin, Claude, 126
Israel, 36
Iverson, Lily R., 79
Ives, Irving, 115
Jablonower, Joseph, 52
Jackson, C. S., 109
Jacobs, Samuel, 52
Jansen, William, 74
Javits, Jacob, 118, 123, 129-30
Jeffrey, Mildred, 23, 46, 52, 57, 98, 103
Jeffrey, Newman, 52-53
Jeffries, Edward, 59, 121
Jenner, William, 111
Jensen, Erlen, 30
Jewish Labor Committee, 126
Jews: and South Africa racial policies, 43
J. I. Case Company: 30, 54; negotiations, 54; organizing, 34, 74; strikes (1938, 1945-47, 1960), 54
Job: transfers, 103; training programs, 103
Job classification: GM Ternstedt Division (1937), 33
John Deere Company: UAW, 98
Johnson, Arthur, 130
Johnson, Edgar, 53
Johnson, Hiram, 110
Johnson, Hugh, 43
Johnson, Lyndon, 37, 40, 58, 81, 88, 92-93, 123, 132
Johnson-Forest Tendency, 39
Johnstone, Thomas, 100
Jones, Brownie Lee, 122, 127
Jordan, David Starr, 26
Journalism: labor, 84
Jurisdictional raiding, 37
Justice: military, 125
Juvenile Court, Wayne County, 41
Juvenile correction, 129
Juvenile delinquency, 26, 41
Kadish, Jack, 53
Kahn, Mark, 134
Kaiser, Edgar, 74, 111
Kaiser Corporation: UAW, 111
Kaiser-Frazer Corporation: UAW, 108
Kansas: 26; politics, 26
Kanter, Irving, 134
Kanter, Robert, 53
Kavanagh, Thomas, 41
Keane, Jay, 134
Keast, William R., 55
Keating, Kenneth, 37

Kefauver, Estes, 25, 37, 40, 50, 121, 129
Kelly, Frank, 32, 38, 56, 72
Kelly, Harry, 23
Kelly, Harry F., 41, 132
Kelly, Matthew, 111
Kelsey-Hayes Corp.: NLRB election, 61
Kelvinator: UAW, 106
Kemnitz, Milton, 121
Kemsley, Bill, 30
Ken, 65
Kennedy, Edward, 49, 56
Kennedy, John F.: 32, 37, 40, 74, 81-82, 88, 92-93, 120, 123, 131; Midwest Democratic State Legislators for, 63; National Voters Registration Committee, 70
Kennedy, Robert, 32, 49, 117, 130
Kenny, Casper, 53
Kenosha, Wis.: American Motors, 127; State, County and Municipal Workers, 85
Kenosha Labor, 127
Kent-Montcalm-Ottawa Regional Recreation Area, 35
Kerr, Clark, 81
Kerr-Mills Bill, 102
"Key men", ALPA, 79
Khrushchev, Nikita: U.S. visit (1959), 42
Kierdorf Case, 63
Kincaid, Charles, 134
King, Martin Luther, 49, 92
King-Anderson Bill, 102
Kingery, Bruce, 53
Kingsford Chemical Company: strike (1953), 27
Kircher, William, 37, 49, 54, 117-18
Kirk, L. K., 54
Kitzman, Harvey, 54, 111
Klasey, Thomas, 54
Kleinert, Otto, 38
Kleinman, Rose, 134
Knight, O. A., 65
Knights of Labor, 42, 83
Knowland, William, 37, 110
Knox, Owen, 120-21
Knudsen, William, 105
Kobe, Matt, 55
Koch, Lucien: 55; federal security hearing, 55
Kohler, Walter J., Jr., 115
Kohler Company, 128: boycott, 115; McClellan Committee, 115; NLRB, 28, 115; negotiations, 28; organizing, 28; strike (1934-41), 115; strike (1954-60), 28, 84, 115; UAW, 115
Kohler Workers Association, 115
Kokomo, Indiana, 53
Korean War, 132
Kornbluh, Joyce, 126
Kowalski, Joseph, 55, 63, 122
Krane, Jay B., 30
Kraus, Henry, 56

Krebs, A. V., 29
Kuchel, Thomas, 37, 117, 120
Kuenzli, Irvin, 50, 92
Ku Klux Klan, 121
Kunstler, William, 36
Labeling: grapes, 118
La Bita, Frank, 56
Labor: Africa, 66; blacks, 132; California, 83; Canada, 42; church, 99, 125; Colorado, 73; communism, 119, 122; community involvement, 46; Depression, 132; Detroit Archdiocese, 30; education, 33, 40, 43, 52, 59, 64, 98-99, 122, 127, 132; foreign policy, 122; occupation of Germany, 52; government, 71; journalism, 84; legislation, 38, 42, 47, 99; library, 49; Louisiana, 48; management cooperation, 84; mediation, 62; New Orleans, 48; organizing, 46; organizing (1930s), 44; political action, 30, 68, 71, 79, 122, 128, 132; public libraries, 127; songs, 77, 79; Soviet Union, 132; Texas, 48; wartime, 102; World War II, 106, 122
Labor Action, 24
Labor and Automobiles, 40
Labor boards: under New Deal, 33
Labor Day: 55; Syracuse, N.Y. (1899), 34
Labor Defends America, 84
Labor Department, 35
Labor Education Week, 132
Labor Institute of Detroit Archdiocese, 30
Labor's League for Political Education, 128
Labor-Management Conference (1945), 45
Labor on the March, 57
Labor's Non-Partisan League, 102, 110, 127
Labor organizers: justice, 133
Labor and Public Welfare Committee, U.S. Senate, 60
Labor relations: Bendix, 69; Chrysler, 67; Ford, 67; International Harvester, 77
Labor Struggles in the Deep South, 48
Labor Temple, Detroit, 43
Labor unions: Europe, 99
Labor Views the News, 101
Labour College, Canada, 106
LaFollette, Robert, 25, 105, 121
LaFollette Committee, 25, 47, 51, 70
LaGuardia, Fiorello, 88, 123
Lamont, Thomas W., 65
Landis, James, 74
Lane, Garland, 56
Lane, Layle, 134
Lansing: UAW, 113
Latchem, E. W., 57
Latin America: CIO, 122

181

Lauck, W. Jett, 57
Law, John A., 126
Law profession: socialization of, 36
Lawrence, Frieda, 32
Lawrence, Mass.: strike (1912), 72, 82
Leab, Daniel, 134
League for Industrial Democracy, 41
League for Mutual Aid, 24
Ledbetter, "Leadbelly", 131
Lederle, Arthur, 134
Lefkowitz, Abraham, 26, 134
Legislation: air mail, 87; anti-labor, 128; anti-left, 45; education, 94, 119; farm labor organizing, 54; farm workers, 120, 130; fishing, 82; health care, 102; hunting, 82; industrial safety, 38; labor, 38, 42, 47, 99; offshore oil, 52; taxes, 103; textile industry, 40; unemployment, 70; UAW, 103; veterans, 37; wage and hours, 128; workmen's compensation, 38
Legislative apportionment, 128
Legislative redistricting, 128
Lehman, Herbert, 37, 123, 129
Leonard, Richard, 83, 102, 115
Lerner, Max, 83
Lesinski, John, 56, 121
Lettuce: boycott, 54, 118
Levin, Sander, 34, 57, 127
Levinson, Edward, 57-58, 84, 101, 104
Levitt, Arthur, 52, 74
Lewis, John L., 25, 29, 37, 46, 56-58, 69, 73, 78, 81-83, 85, 101, 105
Lewis, Sinclair, 32, 82
Lewis, T. L., 83
Liberal Party: New York City, 79
Library: labor, 49
Library Service to Labor Group, Joint Committee on, 127
Lincoln, James H., 55
Linden, N. J.: UAW, 112
Lindgren, Karl, 36
Lindsay, C. Z., 134
Lindsay, John, 24, 118
Linne, Henry, 94
Linville Award, 52
Linville, Henry, 26, 58
Lipton, Howard, 134
Liquor control, 55
Literature: indecent, 124; right-wing, 67
Livingston, E. M., 65
Livingston, John, 37, 58, 62, 77, 84, 100, 102, 109, 113-14
Livonia Education Association, 127
Llewellyn, Percy, 134
Lobbying: teachers, 93
Lockheed: negotiations, 61
Lockouts: TNG, 96
Lockwood, Charles, 119
Lohr, Frank, 58-59
Lomax, Alan, 131
London, England: UFW boycott, 118

London, Ont.: UAW, 106
Long, Huey, 132
Longshoremen, 24
LoPinto, Victor, 120
Los Angeles: 30; ALPA, 89; CIO, 72, 110; social work, 31; UAW, 110; UFW boycott, 118; welfare programs (1947-56), 37
Los Angeles Air Ways, 89
Louisiana: labor, 48
Lovestone, Jay, 26, 57
Lovett, Robert M., 83
Low, Solon, 109
Loyalty boards, 132
Loyalty investigations, 65, 74, 91
Loyalty oaths, 80
Lucas, George, 126
Luce, Clair Booth, 84
Luhan, Mabel Dodge, 32
Lutzai, George, 59
Lyons, George, 59
Maas, Melvin, 88
Machrowicz, Thaddeus M., 125
MacLean, Thomas, 104
MacLeish, Archibald, 123
MacMillan, Hugh, 60
Madar, Olga, 36, 52, 61
Magnuson, Warren, 123
Majerus, Ray, 134
Makarios, Archbishop, 30
Makris, Fotis, 30
Malay: workers' education, 66
Management: labor cooperation, 84
Manning, Michael, 38, 44, 61
Manning, Timothy, 29
Manpower, 123
Manpower development, 132
Mansfield, Mike, 81
Marcantonio, Vito, 121
Marine and Shipbuilders Union, 55
Marlatt, Ralph, 46
Marmon-Herrington: UAW, 111
Marquart, Frank, 61
Marrin, Blaine, 61
Marsh, Donald, 62
Marshall, Dorothy, 65
Marshall, Thurgood, 50, 123, 130
Marshall, Walter, 24
Martel, Frank, 32, 42-43, 55, 73, 132
Martin, Homer, 38, 42, 44, 53, 56, 62, 69, 71-72, 79, 80-81, 85, 98, 100-101, 105, 107, 110, 113-14, 121
Martin, Joyce, 74
Martin, Louis, 39
Martin, Paul J. J., 109
Marx, Karl, 40
Marxism, 81
Marxism and Freedom, 39
Marxist-Humanism, 39
Maryland and District of Columbia: AFL-CIO, 114
Mason, Gabriel, 134

Masters, Fred, 62
Masters, Mates and Pilots Local 88: factionalism (1958-61), 24
Materials: shortages, 103
Mathewson, Kent, 125
Matles, James, 116
Mattes, Albert A., 114
Matthews, Norman, 52, 62, 99-100, 108, 111-12
Mattson, Joseph, 30, 63
Maverick, Maury, 41
Mayors: U.S., 29
Mayor's Committee for Human Resources Development, 85
Mazey, Emil, 28, 30, 34, 49, 66, 83, 85, 98-104, 108-15
Mazey, Ernest, 36, 65, 119
McCarran-Walter Act, 123, 128-29
McCarthy, Eugene, 34, 132
McCarthyism, 76
McClellan, John, 123
McClellan Committee: Kohler, 115
McClendon, James, 59
McClure, Sandra, 28
McCormack, John, 40, 123
McCree, Wade, 130
McDermott, Dennis, 104
McDonald, David, 81
McDonald, Donald, 106
McGhee, Rosa, 59
McGough, Mary, 134
McGovern, George, 37, 92
McGraw, Ashby, 28, 59-60
McKay, Frank, 128
McKinnon Industries: strikes (1955-61), 109; UAW, 109
McLaughlin, Frederick C., 74
McNamara, Patrick, 40, 60, 68, 82, 113, 121, 124-25, 128-30
McNamara, Robert, 121
McNeely, James, 23, 57
McNeill, Bertha Cannon, 47
McNett, Thomas, 28, 60-61
Mead, James, 26, 88
Meany, George, 24, 26, 37, 39-40, 74, 80, 84, 88, 92, 110
Medeiros, Bishop Humberto, 117
Mediation: 30; labor, 62
Medical care, 71
Medicare, 42, 66, 102, 106
Meet the UAW, 101
Megel, Carl, 26, 73, 92, 94
Mellon's Millions, 65
Melrose Park, Ill.: UAW, 105
Memphis, Tenn.: UAW, 116
Mencken, H. L., 83
Mental health, 33, 78, 129
Mental retardation, 129
Mercouri, Melina, 30
Meredith, James, 49
Mergers: AFL-CIO. *See* AFL; AFL-CIO; CIO; Airlines

Merit pay: teachers, 93
Merit ratings: teachers, 94
Metal polishers Union: Local 52, 51
Mexican farm labor: importation, 128
Mexican nationals: employment, 117
Mezerik, A. G., 63, 121
Mezerik, Marie Hempel, 63
Miami: ALPA, 89
Michener, Lew, 83
Michigan: ACLU, 43; AFT, 93; AFSCME, 86; Attorney General's Office, 63; budgets, 128; Communist Party, 44-45; executive reorganization, 53; fair employment practices, 23; government, 121; government reorganization, 48; gubernatorial election (1970), 57; industrial development, 131; mining strikes (1916), 82; Plasterers Union, 80; politics, 41, 65, 100; prisoners of war in lumber industry, 128; supreme court, 41
Michigan AFL-CIO: 38, 75, 93, 127-28; Lansing office, 128
Michigan CIO, 49, 75, 120, 127
Michigan Catholic: TNG, 96
Michigan Civil Service Commission, 48
Michigan Commission on Displaced Persons, 129
Michigan Commission on Legislative Apportionment, 22
Michigan Commission on Migratory Labor, 53
Michigan Committee on Displaced Persons, 129
Michigan Committee on Immigration, 129
Michigan Commonwealth Federation, 24
Michigan CIO News, 128
Michigan Constitutional Convention, 22, 65, 78, 93, 121, 125, 128, 129
Michigan Education Association, 124, 126, 131
Michigan Fair Employment Practices Dept., 75
Michigan Farm Bureau, 128
Michigan Federation of Teachers: 42, 48, 64; convention (1963), 95
Michigan Fresh Air Society, 131
Michigan Institute of Local Government, 129
Michigan Labor Leader, 119
Michigan Labor Mediation Board, 107
Michigan Militant Newsletter, 124
Michigan Mobilization Committee, 124
Michigan, northern: UAW, 104
Michigan Osteopathic College, 33
Michigan State University: Board of Trustees, 81; overseas education, 81
Michigan Unemployment Compensation Commission, 35
Michigan, University of: Workers Education Service, 42

183

Michigan Welfare League, 41, 129
Michigan, western: UAW, 104
Michigan Worker, 44
Middle East, 36
Midland Steel: UAW, 112
Midwest Democratic State Legislators for Kennedy, 63
Migrant labor. *See* Migratory labor
Migration: south to Detroit, 124
Migratory labor: 32, 82, 128-29; Michigan Commission on, 53; Senate hearings, 117; Senate Subcommittee on, 118
Miles, Isadore, 63, 134
Militarism in Education: Committee on, 41
Military: boycotts, 125; use of civil aviation, 89
Military Affairs Committee: ALPA, 39
Military justice, 125
Millage elections: 95; Detroit (1959-63), 124
Miller, Jack, 134
Miller, Richard, 63
Milliken, William, 34-35, 78
Mills, Jewel, 64
Mills, Robert, 64
Milwaukee: CIO, 111; TNG, 97; UAW, 107; UFW boycott, 118
Mine, Mill and Smelter Workers, 120
Miners Bulletin, 55
Miners for Democracy, 129-30
Minimum wage: 40, 82; rubber industry, 131
Mining: accidents, 26; coal, 47; strikes, 26; strikes, Michigan (1916), 82; strikes, Minnesota (1916), 82; West Virginia, 42
Minneapolis: ALPA, 90; UAW, 115
Minneapolis-Moline: UAW, 115
Minneapolis Urban League, 75
Minnesota: mining strike (1916), 82
Minnesota Mining and Manufacturing: UAW, 106
Minow, Newton, 74
Minton, Sherman, 73, 105
Miriani, Louis, 36, 44, 112
Mishinkin, Vassily, 74
Mississippi: civil rights, 74; NAACP, 49; poverty programs, 49; voter registration, 49
Mississippi Child Development Group, 120
Mississippi Freedom Democratic Party, 49
Missouri: CIO, 45
Mitchell, Clarence, 130
Mitchell, H. L., 28
Mitchell, James P., 37, 123
Monmouth, N. J.: UFW boycott, 118
Monroe Auto Equipment: organizing, 76-77

Monroney, A. S., 73-74, 88
Montgomery, Donald, 64
Montgomery, George, 134
Moody, Blair, 46, 92, 110, 129
Mooney, Edward Cardinal, 120
Mooney, Tom, 110: defense, 32
Morgan, J. P., 65
Morgenthau, Henry, 84
Morris, Ken, 64, 108, 110, 112
Morrison, Frank, 61, 105
Morse, Wayne, 34, 37, 40, 46, 123
Mortimer, Wyndham, 30, 60, 62, 80, 107
Moscow trials, 81
Moses, Marion, 29
Mosher, A. R., 109
Murphy, Frank, 23, 42, 56, 80, 121, 132
Murphy, Judge George, 23
Murphy, George, 49, 120
Murray, James E., 115
Murray, Madalyn, 110
Murray, Milton, 48, 74
Murray, Philip, 37, 40, 42, 44, 46, 73, 75, 81, 85, 99, 107, 113
Murray Body: strike (1929), 56
Muste, A. J., 26, 43
Myerscough, Tom, 134
Nash-Kelvinator: 107; Hudson merger, 108
Nation, 65
National Advisory Committee on Agricultural Life and Labor, 130
National Advisory Council on Farm Labor, 130
National Air Lines, 89
National Association for the Advancement of Colored People (NAACP): 66-67, 123, 126; Detroit, 59; Detroit branch, 35, 130; fund-raising, 59; membership campaigns, 130; Mississippi, 49
National Association of County Officials, 32
National Campaign for Agricultural Democracy, 130
National Committee for Fair Play in Bowling, 101
National Council of Federal Labor Unions: automobile industry (1934-35), 38
National defense, 39, 74
National Defense Mediation Board, 72
National Education Association (NEA): 126; AFT, 64; conventions (1959-66), 124
National Educational Policies Committee, 91
National Farm Workers Association: 31, 117; AWOC merger (1966), 117; convention (1962), 117; service center, 117

184

National Industrial Conference Board, 61
National Labor Relations Act: UFW, 118
National Labor Relations Board (NLRB): 25, 30, 42, 47, 62, 111; Albion Malleable Iron Co., 51; automobile industry, 34; Fisher Body, 113; Ford, 59, 83, 99, 101; International Harvester, 107; Kelsey-Hayes, 61; Kohler, 28, 115; TNG, 96
National Lawyers Guild, 64
National Maritime Union: factionalism (1949-50), 24; strikebreaking, 58
National Negro Labor Council, 85
National Recovery Act, 43, 76, 83
National Security Resources Board, 123
National Sharecroppers Fund, 130
National Voters Registration Committee: John Kennedy campaign (1960), 70
National War Labor Board (NWLB), 27, 44, 51, 72
National Women's Trade Union League, 26
National Youth Administration: National Advisory Board, 26
Naturalized citizens, 129
Navy League, 26
Nearing, Scott, 32, 79
Nedzi, Lucien, 120
Negotiations: airlines, 73; ALPA, 39, 55, 89, 90; Boeing, 61; Chrysler, 51; Delta Air Lines, 89; Ford, 99; GM, 100; J. I. Case Company, 54; Lockheed, 61; teachers, 83, 119, 124, 126, 130-31; TNG, 96-97; UAW, 84; UFW, 54
Nelson, Gaylord, 81
Nettlau, Max, 24
New Britain, Conn.: UAW, 107
New Deal, 81
New Deal labor boards, 33
New Democratic Party, 106
New England: Communist Party, 78; TNG District Council, 96
New Jersey: UAW, 104
New Masses, 69
New Mexico: Socialist Party, 33
New Mexico Farm Holiday Association, 33
New Orleans: CIO (1939), 69; labor movement, 48; UFW boycott, 118
News and Letters, 39
Newspaper industry: organizing, 45. See also TNG
New Toronto, Ont.: UAW, 112
New York City: ALPA, 90; education, 74; Liberal Party, 79; teachers, 52, 74; teacher disputes, 42; UFW, 118
New York City Board of Examiners, 52
New York City Teachers Guild, 52, 74
New York City Teachers Union, 52

New York *Daily Call,* 47
New York State: UAW, 104; UFW boycott, 118
Night school: Dallas (1901), 40
Nixon, Richard, 123
Noise abatement: airlines, 87, 89-90
Noncommunist affidavit, 30
Non-Partisan League, 26, 67
Norris, Harold, 64-65
North American Aviation: strike (1941), 44; UAW, 115
Northridge, California: UFW boycott, 118
North Tarrytown, New York: UAW, 114
Northwest Airlines, 72, 90
No Strike Pledge, 44, 53
November Days, 124
Nowak, Stanley, 65, 121
Nunn, Guy, 77
Nyrop, Donald, W., 73
O'Brien, Lawrence, 130
Ochs, Phil, 131
O'Connor, Frank, 118
O'Connor, Harvey, 65
O'Donnell, James, 88
Office of Economic Opportunity, 120
Office of Education, U.S.: Wartime Commission, 26
Office of Price Administration (OPA), 77, 103
Office of Price Stabilization, 103
Offshore oil legislation, 52
Ogden, William, 65
O'Hare, Rolland, 119
O'Higgins, Pablo, 29
Ohio: right-to-work (1958), 70; UFW boycott, 118; United Organized Labor, 69
Ohio Federation of Teachers, 68
Oil industry, 65
Oklahoma Leader, 22
Oldenbrock, J. H., 30
Oliver, Robert, 40
Oliver, William, 27, 44, 65-66, 112, 126
Oneka, John, 66
Open housing, 34, 85
Orendain, Antonio, 117
Organization of Architectural and Engineering Employees: Detroit chapter, 134
Organizational Structure Study Committee: ALPA, 38
Organizing: aircraft industry, 59-60, 80; ALPA, 79; Allegheny-Ludlum Steel Corp., 56; Amalgamated Clothing Workers, 82; AFT, 92; Aurora-Caterpillar, 76; automobile industry, 40, 58, 82-83; automobile workers, Indiana, 70; Barber-Colman, 76; Chrysler, 85; coal mining, 83; CIO, 58; Delco-Remy, 73, 85; Dodge, 85; farm workers, 120; by Flat Glass Workers

185

Union, 37; Ford, 59; 80, 83, 100-101, 110, 120; GM, 100; Goodyear Tire and Rubber, 72; IAM, 60; John W. Hobbs Corp., 76; labor, 46; labor (1930s), 44; Monroe Auto Equipment, 76-77; newspaper industry, 45; pilots, 88; publishing industry, 45; rubber industry, 83, 131; rubber workers, Gadsen, Ala., 72; seamen, New York, 78; steel industry, 78, 82-83; textile industry, 72; textile workers, Michigan (1937), 48; TNG, 96; UAW, 42, 63, 81
O'Rourke, Francis, 66
Orr, Charles, 66
Oshawa, Ont.: strike,(1937), 81; UAW, 77
Osteopathic College, Michigan, 68
Owosso Education Association, 130-31
Overton, Carrie Burton, 66-67
Ovington, Mary White, 67, 134
Pacifica Foundation, 23
Pacifism: 131; World War I, 26; World War II, 126
Packard Company: UAW, 109
Packinghouse workers, 120
Pacoima, Calif.: UFW boycott, 118
Pagano, Joseph, 67
Palmer, C. F., 50
Palmer raids, 82
Pan American Airlines, 89-90
Panzner, John, 67
Papermaking unions: rank and file movements, 24
Parker, Frank, 67
Parker, Paul, 134
Parochial schools: aid to, 55
Paskal, Oscar, 67-68
Passaic, New Jersey: strike (1926), 82
Paterson, New Jersey: strike, 72
Patrick, William T., Jr., 126
Patterson, William, 121
Paulson, Harper, 121
Paxton, Tom, 131
Peace groups, 30, 65
Peacock, Hugh, 75
Pearson, Drew, 40
Peary, Robert E., 82
Peck, Raymond, 68
Pegler, Westbrook, 123
Pell, Claiborne, 130
Penal codes, 41
Pennsylvania: UAW, 104
Pensions: 62, 68, 105; airlines, 87; ALPA, 74; photo-engravers, 75; pilots, 39; UAW, 102, 107, 112
People's Artists, Inc., 131
Peoples Press, 65
People's Songs, Inc., 77
People's Song Library, 131
Perfect Circle: strike (1955), 114
Perkins, Francis, 29, 73, 123
Person, Carl, 68
Pesotta, Rose, 24, 56

Pesticides, 117-18
Peterson, Eric, 60
Peterson, Esther, 43
Petitpren, Vincent, 68
Petrides, N., 30
Philadelphia: UFW boycott, 118
Photo-Engravers Union: 75; pensions, 75
Physical health, 129
Physical standards: flight attendants, 90
Pickering, John, 38
Piconke, Joseph, 68-69
Pieper, Fred, 38, 69
Pilch, Alex, 135
Pilgrimage; UFW, 117
Pilots: collective bargaining, 88; organizing, 88; pensions, 39; professional standards, 87, 89; retirement, 39, 89-90; training, 39. *See also* ALPA
Pinchot, Mrs. Gifford, 40
Pioneers Club: Detroit, 76
Pissas, Michael, 30
Pittsburgh: AFT, 94; Communist Party, 78; politics (1930s), 65
Pittsburgh Labor College, 29
Plasterers Union: Michigan, 80
Plymouth: UAW, 106
Pokempner, Irving, 69
Poland, James, 69
Poland: invasion of, 82
Polar Ware Company: strike (1961), 107; UAW, 107
Police: 28; brutality, 121, 130; community relations, 85, 124; conduct, 119; Detroit, 41; training, 46
Political action: 44, 132; ALPA, 87; AFT, 92; labor, 71, 122, 128; UAW, 62, 77, 105-6, 110
Political Action Committee: 49, 107, 110, 114; UAW, 70
Political campaigns: 37; California (1953-68), 37
Political freedom, 121
Political prisoners, 126
Politics: 71; Chicago, 30; Connecticut, 84; Dallas, 40; Detroit, 40-41, 65, 76; labor, 68, 79, 131; Michigan, 41, 57, 65, 100; Oakland County, Mich., 57; Pittsburgh (1930s), 65; UAW, 103; U.S., 57
Poll tax, 121
Pollock, Sam, 69
Pollock, William, 40
Pollution, 33-34
Poor: training programs, 120
Portal-to-portal pay, 112
Post-war: seniority, veterans, 102; seniority, women, 102; reconversion, 44
Potofsky, Jacob, 37, 46, 48
Potter, Charles, 121
Poverty: 71, 120; rural, 120
Poverty programs: 28, 71, 132; Mississippi, 49
Powell, Adam Clayton, 37, 123, 130

Pragen, Otto, 135
Prashner, Albert, 126
Prayers: in schools, 126
Presidential election: (1964), 63; (1968), 57; role of blacks, (1968), 39
President's Commission on Equal Employment Opportunity, 39
Presidents, U.S., 28
Press: GI underground, 125
Pressman, Lee, 75
Price ceilings, 58
Price controls, 64, 84, 91, 102-3, 123
Price increases, 52
Prices: automobiles, 84
Priests: worker programs, 120
Prisoners: political, 126
Prisoners of war: use in Michigan lumber industry, 128
Prisons, 55
Probe, Ben, 120, 127
Production controls, 102
Professional standards: pilots, 87, 89; teachers, 83
Profiteering: World War I, 26
Progressive Party, 65, 100, 110, 128
Prophet Company: UAW, 114
Protest: students, 125
Provincetown Players, 82
Proxmire, William, 40, 115
Psychiatry, 36
Psychic phenomena, 32
Public assistance, 129
Public education, 124
Public employees: strikes, 49
Public housing, 128
Public Law 78, 120
Public libraries: labor, 127
Public power, 40
Public relations: AFT, 91; UAW, 39, 58, 84, 100; United Rubber Workers, 47
Public works, 60
Public Works Administration: Chicago, 32; Gary, Indiana, 32
Public Works Committee, U.S. Senate, 60
Publishing industry: organizing, 45
Pucinski, Roman, 30
Quadragesimo Anno, 31
Quesada, E. R., 74, 88
Rabaut, Louis, 61, 103, 110, 121
Racial conditions: Detroit, 27
Racial discrimination, 110, 133
Racketeering: unions, 34
Radicalism, 69
Radio: UAW, 101; UFWOC, Texas, 117
Rahoi, Philip, 70
Raiding: jurisdictional, 37
Rainey, Julian, 67
Ramesbottom, Gloria, 75
Ramsay, Thomas, 38
Rand, Donald, 28, 135
Randolph, A. Philip, 84, 92
Ratings: teachers, 92

Rationalism, 59
Rationing, 64, 103
Rauh, Joseph, 34
Ravitz, Mel, 32
Rayburn, Sam, 37, 41
Reapportionment, 55
Reaume, Arthur, 109
Reconversion, 44, 103
Recreation: 35-56, 129; UAW, 36, 61, 99, 101
Recreation employees: Detroit, 36
Red Caps' union, 132
Red Cross, 131
Redistricting: legislative, 128; schools, 124
Reform: economic, 69; social, 69
Refugees, 129
Regulations: prices, 123; wages, 123
Reisman, Mrs. Harry, 135
Religion, 124
Rent controls, 103, 123, 128
Reo Motors: strikes (1946, 1951), 113; UAW, 113
Rerum Novarum, 31
Research: UAW, 78
Retirement: Gabriel Plan, 53; pilots, 39, 89-90; teachers, 83; UAW, 108
Retraining and Reemployment Administration, 35
Reuss, Richard, 133
Reuther, George S., Jr., 74
Reuther, Roy, 32, 41, 52, 58, 61, 70-72, 114, 129-30
Reuther, Victor: 30, 34, 37, 46, 50, 58, 63, 70-71, 73, 80, 84, 99-100, 102-4, 106, 108, 112-13, 115, 122; shooting, 25, 34
Reuther, Walter: 23, 25, 30, 33-35, 37, 41, 55-56, 58-59, 62-64, 66, 69-71, 73-75, 80-82, 88, 92, 98-115, 117, 120, 122, 128; shooting, 25, 34
Revolution in Seattle, 65
Reynolds, Malvina, 131
Ribicoff, Abraham, 84
Richmond, Calif.: Ford, 83
Richardson, Herbert, 38
Riddle Air Lines, 89
Riesel, Victor, 37
Riffe, John, 37
Rigby, Charles, 133
Right-wing literature, 67
Right-to-work, 23: Ohio (1958), 70
Rinehart, Blanche, 71
Riordan, Mary Ellen, 64, 94
Riots: Detroit (1943), 50, 124, 130; Detroit (1967), 46
Robbins, Matilda, 24, 72
Roberts, George, 72
Robinson, Jackie, 39
Robinson, Ken, 104
Robinson, Remus, 72
Rockefeller, Nelson, 92
Rocker, Rudolph, 126

187

Rockford, Ill.: labor, 74
Rockwell, Robert, 72
Rodgers, W. J., 74
Roeder, Cecil, 73
Rogers, Mary Augusta, 125
Rogers, William, 123
Rogin, Lawrence, 122
Romanoff, Fred, 28
Romney, George, 34-35, 55-56, 68, 70, 78, 85, 103, 120, 124-25, 127, 132
Roosevelt, Dorothy, 32, 103
Roosevelt, Eleanor, 123, 128
Roosevelt, Franklin, 38, 58, 123, 128
Roosevelt, James, 37, 65, 120
Roosevelt, Theodore, 82-83
Roper, Elmo, 123
Rosenberg case, 76, 121
Rosenblum, Frank, 48
Ross, Harry, 73
Rossides, Z., 30
Roth, Herrick, 73
Rubber, Cork, Linoleum and Plastic Workers of America, 131
Rubber industry: collective bargaining, 131; minimum wage, 131; organizing, 83, 131
Ruby, Charles, 73, 88
Ruby, Jack: trial, 36
Rugh, Jack, 135
Ruppenthal, Karl, 74
Rural Americans for Johnson-Humphrey, 63
Rusk, Dean, 81
Russell Sage Foundation, 81, 83
Rustin, Bayard, 92
Rutledge, Philip, 130
Ruttenberg, Stanley, 122
Ryan Aeronautical Company: strike (1944), 44
Ryan, Harold, 94, 125
Ryan, William, 118, 135
Sacco and Vanzetti case, 32, 82
Safety: air, 73, 74; coal mines, 130
Sage Foundation. See Russell Sage Foundation
Saginaw Federation of Labor, 131
Saginaw, Mich.: Cigar Makers Union, 120
Sailors Union of the Pacific, 24
St. Catherines, Ont.: UAW, 109
St. Clair Shores, Michigan, 78
St. John, Vincent, 126
St. Louis, Missouri, 45: AFT, 94; Ford Motor Co., 59; TNG, 96; UAW, 78, 106
St. Marie, Paul, 120
St. Paul, Minnesota: AFT, 93
St. Paul Federation of Men Teachers, 93
St. Paul Federation of Women Teachers, 93
St. Paul Grade Teachers Federation, 93
Salandini, Father Victor, 135
Salaries: teachers, 50, 93-94, 126

Saltonstall, Leverett, 40, 123
Sandburg, Carl, 22, 115
Sands, Frank, 74
San Fernando, Calif.: UFW boycott, 118
San Francisco: ALPA, 90; AFT, 93; strike, AFT (1968, 1971), 93-94
Sanger, Margaret, 32
San Jose, Calif.: UFW boycott, 118
San Quentin Prison, 79
Saposs, David, 43
Sayen, Clarence, 39, 73-74, 88
Sayer, Albert, 74
Schactman, Max, 32
Schedules: airlines, 89
Schick, David, 135
Schnapper, M. B., 135
Schneid, H., 48
Schneider, Peter, 75
Schnitzler, William, 37
Scholle, August, 37-38, 49, 55, 73, 75, 80, 94, 103, 110, 113, 126, 127
Schools: financing, 93, 68; prayer, 126; redistricting, 124; taxation, 94
School boards: elections, 119
Schoolcraft Gardens Cooperative Housing, 48
Schrade, Paul, 117
Schroeder, Allen, 75
Schultz, A. G., 77
Schultz, Charles M., 111
Scottsboro case, 82, 121
Seabron, William, 75-76
Seafarers' International Union, 24
Seamen: organizing, New York, 78
Seattle: ALPA, 90; UFW boycott, 118
Secondary boycotts, 118
Secretary of State, Michigan, 22
Seeger, Peggy, 131
Seeger, Pete, 131
Segregation: AFT locals, 92
Selden, David, 73
Select Committee on Improper Activities in the Labor and Management Field, U.S. Senate, 28, 60. See also McClellan Committee
Select Subcommittee on Poverty, U.S. Senate, 60
Senate, Michigan, 56, 81, 85
Senate U.S.: 60; hearings on migratory labor, 117
Senate Subcommittee on Migratory Labor, 118
Senators, U.S., 29
Senior citizens, 59. See also Aged
Seniority: ALPA, 88; UAW, 103, 107; veterans, 102; women, postwar, 102
Service Dept., Ford, 101
Servicemen: Viet Nam War, attitudes, 125
Sexton, Brendon, 35, 52, 77, 98-99, 122
Shaffer, Leo, 76
Shanker, Al, 73
Sharecroppers, 130

188

Shear, Warren, 76
Sheboygan, Wis.: UAW, 107
Sheehan, Dilis, 75
Sheffield, Horace, 130
Sherwood, Lillian, 76
Shier, Carl, 76-77
Shiftbreak, 101
Shore, Ann, 121
Shortages: materials, 103
Shriver, Sargent, 49, 74, 120
Shultz, George, 130
Shy, Arthur, 98
Sifton, Paul, 40, 70, 77
Sigler, Kim, 132
Silber, Irwin, 77
Silicosis, 115
Silver, Paul, 77-78
Simons, Bud, 78
Sinarquistas, 82
Sinclair, Upton: 32, 132; gubernatorial campaigns (1934, 1936), 32
Single-Tax Colony, 32
Sing Out, Inc., 131
Siren, Paul, 104
Sit-Down, 80
Sit-downs: 27, 40, 56, 132; Anderson, Ind., 50, 85; automobile industry (1936-37), 24, 82; Fisher Body Plant 1, 78; Fisher Body Plant 2, 66; Flint, 38. *See also* Strikes
Skilled trades: 47; UAW, 50, 64, 68-69
Slinkard, Luther, 78
Smathers, George, 126
Smith Act, 44-45, 101, 121
Smith, Del, 36
Smith, Gerald L. K., 121
Smith, Hilda, 26, 55
Smith, Nancy, 135
Smith, Norman, 135
Smith, Otis, 130
Smith, Stanton, 135
Snyder, Joseph, 78
Sobell, Helen, 34
Social Action Department of Detroit Archdiocese, 30
Social Action School, Catholic University, 30
Social concerns, 71
Social Democracy of America: Local 3, 23
Socialism: 22-23, 45, 47, 69; Britain, 47
Socialist Labor Party, 23
Socialist Party: 26, 33, 58, 81, 84; conventions (1936, 1938), 40-41; Detroit, 33; New Mexico, 33; southeast Kansas, 26; Texas, 40
Socialized law, 36
Social Justice, 59
Social problems, 21
Social reform: 33, 47, 67, 69; songs, 77
Social Security: 40, 42, 106, 108, 123; legislation, 26; UAW, 102
Social work: Los Angeles, 31

Society of Designing Engineers, 25
Sojourner Truth housing, 50
Solidarity, 84
Songs: labor, 77, 79; social reform, 77
South Africa: racial policies, Jewish reaction, 43
South Bend: UAW, 105
Southeastern Michigan Community Research Corp., 32
Southern Airways: 89, 90; strike, 90
Southern Rural Action Program, 120
Southern United States: bombings, 126; textile industry, 42
South Gate, Calif.: UAW, 110
Soviet Union: and American labor, 132; anti-semitism, 126
Spanish Civil War, 25, 81
Spanish Republic, Committee to Aid, 63
Sparkman, John, 40
Sparks, Nemmy, 78-79
Special Committee on Aging, U.S. Senate, 60
Special education, 129
Spellman, Francis Cardinal, 123
Spencer, Fanny Bixbey, 79
Speth, Roy, 79
Spock, Benjamin, 37
Stabilization: employment, 103
Staebler, Neil, 34, 55, 57, 63, 68, 82, 126
Stark County, O.: UFW boycott, 118
Starr, Helen, 79
Starr, Mark, 42, 79
State aid to education, 91
State-Capitalism, 39
State, County and Municipal Employees: Kenosha, Wisconsin, 85
State, County and Municipal Workers: merger with Federal Workers of America, 49
Steel-Dictator, 65
Steel industry: organizing, 25, 78, 82-83; strikes (1919, 1936-37), 82; (1930s), 65
Steelink, Mrs. Fannia, 79
Steelink, Nicolaas, 24, 79, 126
Steelman, John, 123
Steel strike, 1919: Inter-Church World Movement, 25
Steel Workers Organizing Committee, 81
Steffens, Lincoln, 82
Stephan, Lionel, 79
Stettinius, Edward, 123
Stevens, Donald, 38, 135
Stevenson, Adlai, 81, 92
Stewards and stewardesses: United Air Lines, 90
Stimson, Henry L., 59
Stockholders: suits against Chrysler, 36; suits against Studebaker-Packard, 36
Stoddard, Lynn, 80
Story, Harold H., 79
Strachan, Stuart, 135

189

Strichartz, Richard, 28
Strikebreaking: 68; National Maritime Union, 58
Strikes: AWOC (1959-65), 117; airlines, 39, 74, 88-89; ALPA, 39, 88, 90; Allis-Chalmers, 112; Allis Chalmers (1939, 1941, 1946-47), 111; Allis-Chalmers (1947), 80; American Brake Company (1938), 100; AFT, 92; AFT San Francisco (1968, 1971), 93-94; Anderson sit-down, 50; Anderson, Ind. (1937), 70; automobile industry, 27; automobile industry (1930s), 40; automobile (March 1934), 56; Bendix, 105; Briggs (1933), 56, 61; Briggs (1939), 42, 109; Calumet copper mines, 55; Chrysler (1937), 85; Chrysler (1939), 42, 85; Chrysler (1950), 105-6; Chrysler-Los Angeles (1957), 47; Flint sit-downs, 46, 54, 66, 78; Ford (1941), 50, 53; Ford (1949), 80, 84, 120, 128; Ford (1958), 83; Gastonia (1929), 82; GM (1930s), 57; GM (1934), 43; GM (1937), 73, 81, 85; GM (1945-56), 45, 59, 73, 77, 80, 100, 103, 110, 113, 120; GM (Oshawa, 1937), 77; Giumarra, 118; grape, 117, 120; Great Lakes (1948), 132; Harriman Lines, (1911-15), 68; Henderson, N. C. (1959), 82; Horner Woolen Mills (1937), 48; Hudson Motors (1951), 108; IWW, 126; Illinois Central (1911-15), 68; J. I. Case (1938, 1945-47, 1960), 54; Kohler, 84; Kohler (1934-41), 115; Kohler (1954-60), 115; Lawrence, Mass., Mills (1912), 72, 82; McKinnon Industries (1955-61), 109; mining, Michigan (1916), 82; mining, Minnesota (1916), 82; Murray Body (1929), 56; North American Aviation, 44; Oshawa, Ont. (1937), 81; Passaic, N. J. (1926), 82; Paterson, N. J., 72; Perfect Circle (1955), 114; Polar Ware (1961), 107; public employees, 49; Reo Motors (1946, 1951), 113; Ryan Aeronautical (1944), 44; sit-downs, 56; sit-downs (1930s), 132; sit-downs (1936-37), 82; sit-downs (1937), 40; sit-down, Anderson, Ind., 73, 85; steel (1919, 1936-37), 82; steel (1930s), 65; Southern Airways, 90; teachers, 83, 92-94, 127; textile industry, 82; TNG, 96-97; Toledo Auto Lite (1934), 56; Toledo Chevrolet (1935), 56; UFWOC, Texas, 117; Yale-Towne (1937), 40-41
Stuart, Yale, 80
Studebaker: UAW, 105; UAW contract (1937), 65
Studebaker-Packard Corp.: stockholder suits, 36; UAW, 102
Students: protest, 125
Subsidies, 64

Suffrage: women, International Convention (1913), 82
Sugar, Maurice, 71, 80, 99, 101-3
Summer schools: UAW, 51, 99, 101, 113
Supersonic transport, 74, 87, 90
Supplemental unemployment benefits, 105
Supreme Court, Michigan, 41
Swainson, John, 34, 63, 78, 130
Swan, Joseph, 135
Sweet, Sam, 106, 114
Symington, Stuart, 58, 81, 123
Syracuse, N. Y., Central Trades and Labor Assembly, 34-35
Taft-Hartley Act: 40, 45, 77, 103, 122-23; noncommunist affidavit, provision of, 30
Taft, Philip, 135
Taft, Robert, 128
Tappes, Shelton, 80
Tassin, Algernon, 67
Taxes: 57, 60, 82, 128; schools, 94; legislation, 103
Teachers: anti-union activities, 73; certification, 68, 119; Chicago, 83; collective bargaining, 64; colleges, 91; Detroit Federation, 42; dismissals in Flint (1937-49), 42; education, 68; exchange programs, 26; fringe benefits, 93; grievances, 94; international organizations, 92; lobbying, 93; merit pay, 93; merit ratings, 94; Michigan Federation, 42; negotiations, 83, 94, 119, 124, 126, 133; New York City, 42, 52, 74; professional standards, 83; ratings, 92; retirement, 83; salaries, 50, 93-94, 126; strikes, 83, 92-94, 127; tenure, 42, 91-94; unions, 30; unionism vs. professionalism, 119, 127; university, 91; WPA, 91. See also AFT
Teachers Union of New York, 58
Teamsters: 132; organizing farm workers, 54
Technical workers: Wayne State University, 133
Telescope, 101
Television: UAW, 101
Tenant unions, 29
Tenure, 42, 91-94
Texas: child labor law, 40; labor movement, 48; Socialist Party, 40; UFWOC, 117
Texas State Industrial Union Council, 115
Textile industry: anti-union activity in the South, 40; conditions (1920s-1930s), 25; legislation, 40; organizing, 72; organizing, Michigan (1937), 48; South, 42; strikes, 82
Textile Workers Union of America: 40, 84; Washington office, 40
The Newspaper Guild (TNG): 96; arbi-

190

tration, 97; Associated Press, 96; Boston, 96; contracts, 96; conventions, 96-97; Detroit, 96; elections, 96; grievances, 96; lockouts, 96; *Michigan Catholic,* 96; Milwaukee, 97; NLRB, 96; negotiations, 96-97; New England District Council, 96; organizing, 96; St. Louis, 96; strikes, 96-97; United Press International, 96
TNG Local 22, 96
TNG Local 32, 96
TNG Local 47, 96
TNG Local 51, 97
Thirty-hour week, 33
Thoman, Tony, 135
Thomas, Norman, 22, 24, 29, 32, 41-42, 81, 84, 99
Thomas, R. J., 44, 56, 58-59, 62, 73, 80-81, 85, 99, 102-3, 105-7, 110-14
Thompson, Eugene C., 74
Thompson, Fred, 24, 79, 126
Thompson, Hugh, 81
Thompson, William, 59
Thurmond, Strom, 39
Tin: Bolivia mission (1951-52), 123; southeast Asia mission (1951-52), 123
Tindal, Robert, 130
Tobin, Maurice, 92, 128
Toledo: AFT, 94; UAW, 105-6
Toledo Auto-Lite: strike (1934), 56
Toledo Chevrolet: strike (1935), 56
Tool and die industry: UAW, 108
Toronto: UAW, 104
Tourism, 82
Townsend, Willard, 132
Trade unions: foreign, 122
Trade Union Unity League: 127; Automobile Workers Union, 56
Training: airlines, 87; flight crews, 90; pilots, 39; police, 46
Training programs: job, 103; to organize poor, 120
Trainor, James L., 28
Transportation: 32; national emergency planning, 74
Transport Workers Union: Airline Stewards and Stewardesses Association, 90
Trans World Airlines, 89
Treasury Department, U.S., 84
Tresca, Carlo, 68: Memorial Committee, 24
Trials: IWW, 79, 126
Trotsky, Leon, 81
Truman, Harry, 41, 78, 81, 123, 128, 132
Tuition grants, 33
Turner, Edward, 130
Tydings, Joseph, 110
Typographical Workers, 120
Udall, Stuart, 40
Uganda: AID mission, 53

Underdeveloped countries: assistance, 122
Unemployment: 40, 82; compensation, 128; compensation, UAW, 102-3; insurance, 42; legislation, 70; relief, 104
Unger, William, 126
Union Democracy, 31
Union Democracy in Action, 24
Unions: communism, 38; education, 106; farmers, 128; racketeer influence, 34; teachers, 30
United Air Lines: 89-90; stewards and stewardesses, 90
United Auto Worker, 47, 56
United Automobile, Aerospace, and Agricultural Implement Workers (UAW): 44, 67, 71, 120; Agricultural Implement Conference (1947), 63; agricultural implement industry, 76; aircraft industry, 39; Allis-Chalmers, 98, 111; AFL (1938-48), 119; American Motors, 106; American Seating Co., 108; Anaconda-American Brass, Ltd., 112; Anderson, Ind., 81, 113; appeal cases, 22, 102; apprenticeships, 103; AIWU-AFL, relations with, 30; Atlanta, Ga., 69; Baltimore, 110, 114; Bendix, 105; Bendix-Westinghouse, 106; Brantford Coach and Body, Ltd., 111; Briggs, 109, 114; Buick, 112; Canada, 28, 42, 75, 104, 109, 112; Canadian economics, 75; Caterpillar Tractor, 98; Chevrolet, 105-6, 114; Chicago, 33, 106; children, 101; Chrysler, 105, 109-10, 112, 115; collective bargaining, 64, 103; communism, 109; community services, 105; competitive shops, 47; CIO, 69; constitution, 67; Continental Aviation, 111; Continental Motors, 111; conventions, 64, 98; convention (1936), 56, 79; convention (1937), 28, 41; conventions (1946, 1953, 1957, 1959, 1961), 77; conventions (1947-53), 84; Dallas, 115; Delco-Remy, 113; Detroit, 104-5, 107-9, 112; Detroit, west, 108; disabled veterans, 103; District Council 26, 28; Eaton Manufacturing Co., 106; education, 24, 61, 75; electrical workers, 116; employment security, 102; factionalism, 22, 38, 42, 44, 46, 56-57, 59, 61, 63, 69, 70, 73, 80, 98, 105-7, 110, 112; Fafnir Bearing Co., 107; fair employment practices, 73, 103, 105; Federation of Artists, Engineers, Chemists, and Technicians, 25; finances, 102; financial reports, 98; Fisher Body, 110, 113-14; Flint, Mich., 112; Ford, 109, 112-13, 115; Ford of Canada, 110; Ford contract (1941), 26; formation, 38, 67, 69; Fort Wayne, 107; Fruehauf Trailer,

191

106; Gemmer Manufacturing Co., 107; GM, 106, 110, 112, 114; GM Diesel, 106; Grand Rapids, 108; health care, 102; Hudson Motors, 108; Indiana, 41; Indianapolis, 111; insurance, 102; IAM, 58, 60-61; International Harvester, 98, 105, 107, 116; John Deere Co., 98; Kaiser Corp., 111; Kaiser-Frazer Corp., 108; Kelvinator, 106; Kohler, 115; Linden, N. J., 112; legislation, 103; local union finances, 22; London, Ont., 106; Los Angeles, 110; Marmon-Herrington, 111; McKinnon Industries, 109; Melrose Park, Ill., 105; Memphis, Tenn., 116; Michigan, north, 104; Michigan, west, 104; Midland Steel, 112; Milwaukee, 107; Minneapolis, 115; Minneapolis-Moline, 115; Minnesota Mining and Manufacturing, 106; New Britain, Conn., 107; New Jersey, 104; New Toronto, Ont., 112; New York, 104; no-raid agreement with IAM, 27; North American Aviation, 115; North Tarrytown, N. Y., 114; organizing, 22, 42, 63, 81; Oshawa, Ont., 77; Packard Co., 109; Pennsylvania, 104; pensions, 102, 107, 112; Plymouth, 106; Polar Ware Company, 107; political action, 56, 62, 70, 103, 105-6, 110; Prophet Co., 114; public relations, 39, 58, 84; recreation, 36, 99; Reo Motor Co., 113; retirement, 108; St. Catherines, Ont., 109; St. Louis, Mo., 78, 106; seniority, 103, 107; Sheboygan, Wis., 107; skilled trades, 50, 64, 68-69; Society of Designing Engineers, 25; South Bend, 105; South Gate, Calif., 110; Studebaker, 105; Studebaker contract (1937), 65; summer schools, 51, 99, 101, 113; Toledo, O., 105-6; tool and die industry, 108; Toronto, 104; war effort, 107; war production, 80; West Allis, Wis., 111; white collar workers, 110, 115; Willow Run, Mich., 108; Windsor, Ont., 109-10, 112; Yale and Towne Manufacturing Co., 106

UAW Accounting Dept., 98
UAW-AFL, 56
UAW Agricultural Implement Dept., 54, 58, 63, 98
UAW Aircraft Dept., 58
UAW Bookstore, 135
UAW Borg-Warner Dept., 29
UAW Chrysler Dept., 51, 98
UAW Citizenship and Legislative Dept., 70
UAW Community Action Program, 135
UAW Community Relations Dept., 98
UAW Competitive Shops Dept., 135
UAW Die Casting Dept., 135
UAW Education Dept., 33, 42, 51, 98-99
UAW Fair Practices Dept., 34, 66
UAW Ford Dept., 27, 62, 99
UAW Foundry Wage and Hour Council, 51
UAW GM Dept., 62, 71, 100
UAW International Affairs Dept., 100
UAW International Executive Board, 21, 25, 45, 47, 61, 69, 71, 80, 100
UAW Library, 135
UAW Local 3, 44, 73, 85
UAW Local 5, 105
UAW Local 6, 85, 105
UAW Local 7, 33, 37, 105
UAW Local 9, 69, 105
UAW Local 14, 105-6
UAW Local 15, 22
UAW Local 25, 45, 78, 106
UAW Local 27, 106
UAW Local 34, 69
UAW Local 50, 62
UAW Local 51, 106
UAW Local 53, 106
UAW Local 57, 107
UAW Local 72, 127
UAW Local 75, 107
UAW Local 80, 52, 107
UAW Local 108, 107
UAW Local 133, 107
UAW Local 135, 108
UAW Local 137, 35
UAW Local 140, 51
UAW Local 142, 28, 108
UAW Local 146, 50-51, 85
UAW Local 154, 108
UAW Local 155, 44, 64
UAW Local 157, 61, 108
UAW Local 174, 44, 59, 71, 108
UAW Local 180, 30, 54
UAW Local 182, 113
UAW Local 190, 109
UAW Local 199, 109
UAW Local 200, 109
UAW Local 212, 64, 109
UAW Local 216, 30, 32, 110
UAW Local 222, 77
UAW Local 227, 67
UAW Local 230, 47, 110
UAW Local 235, 66
UAW Local 239, 110
UAW Local 240, 110
UAW Local 248, 111
UAW Local 280, 111
UAW Local 292, 53
UAW Local 309, 135
UAW Local 325, 59
UAW Local 341, 111
UAW Local 378, 74
UAW Local 397, 111
UAW Local 399, 111-12
UAW Local 400, 112
UAW Local 410, 112
UAW Local 444, 112
UAW Local 477, 30
UAW Local 506, 135

UAW Local 544, 52
UAW Local 560, 83
UAW Local 581, 46
UAW Local 595, 112
UAW Local 599, 112-13
UAW Local 600, 25, 33, 52, 73, 80, 113, 120
UAW Local 602, 113
UAW Local 650, 113
UAW Local 653, 135
UAW Local 662, 41, 73, 113-14
UAW Local 663, 50
UAW Local 664, 114
UAW Local 678, 114
UAW Local 742, 114
UAW Local 833, 114-15
UAW Local 870, 115
UAW Local 887, 115
UAW Local 889, 115
UAW Local 904, 133
UAW Local 932, 115-16
UAW Local 952, 27
UAW Local 988, 116
UAW Local 1088, 135
UAW Local 1139, 135
UAW Local 1444, 135
UAW Organizing Dept., 135
UAW Public Relations Dept., 100
UAW Public Review Board, 22, 101
UAW Radio Dept., 101
UAW Recreation Dept., 61, 101
UAW Region 1, 33, 56
UAW Region 1A, 135
UAW Region 1B, 64, 103, 135
UAW Region 1D, 104
UAW Region 1E, 104
UAW Region 3: 135; education, 51
UAW Region 4, 21
UAW Region 6: 47, 135; election of Director (1972), 32
UAW Region 7, 104
UAW Region 9, 104
UAW Region 10, 135
UAW Research Dept., 78, 101-2
UAW Saginaw, Mich., Sub-Region, 135
UAW Secretary-Treasurer, 102
UAW Skilled Trades Dept., 62, 135
UAW Social Security Dept., 62, 102
UAW Studebaker-Packard Dept., 102
UAW Unemployment Compensation Dept., 102-3
UAW Veterans Dept., 103
UAW War Policy Division, 103
UAW Washington Office, 52, 64, 103
UAW Welfare Dept., 41
UAW Women's Auxiliary, 113
UAW Women's Dept., 135
United Community Services, 131
United Electrical Workers: 33, 120; Canadian Congress of Labour suspension, 109; UAW, 116
United Electrical Workers Local 166, 107
United Electrical Workers Local 1146, 116
United Farm Workers (UFW): 37, 117; AFL-CIO, 54; coordination with AFL-CIO, 37; elections, 54; Federal Food and Drug Adm., 118; Field Foundation Legal Services Grant, 117; finances, 54; NLRA, 118; negotiations, 54; opposition, 54; pilgrimage, 117; strikes in Texas, 117; support, 54
UFW boycott: Arizona, 118; Boston office, 118; Chicago, 118; Chicago Heights, Ill., 118; Cleveland, 118; Columbus, O., 118; Denver, 118; Detroit, 118; Hawaii, 118; London, England, 118; Los Angeles, 118; Monmouth, N. J., 118; Milwaukee, 118; New York office, 118; New York State, 118; New Orleans, 118; Northridge, Calif., 118; Ohio, 118; Pacoima, Calif., 118; Philadelphia, 118; San Fernando, Calif., 118; San Jose, Calif., 118; Seattle, 118; Stark County, O., 118
United Farm Workers Organizing Committee (UFWOC): 29, 31, 117; strike, Texas, 117; Texas, 117; Texas radio, 117
United Federation of Teachers, 74
United Mine Workers: 58, 81, 129; elections (1969, 1972), 130
United Mine Workers District 50: Local 12229, 36
United Nations, 84, 123
UNESCO: adult education, 66
United Negro College Fund, 34
United Office and Professional Workers, 49
United Organized Labor of Ohio, 23, 69
United Press International: TNG, 96
United Public Workers: 49, 84; Detroit, 80; factionalism, 48
United Rubber Workers: 72, 84, 131; public relations, 47
United States: Canadian automobile trade agreement (1969, 1970), 75
United States-Canada relations, 104
United States government, 84
United Steel Workers, 84
United Transportation Service Employees Union, 123, 132
Universal Military training, 92
Universities: out-of-state fees, 68
University City II, 31
University of Michigan: worker education, 52
University teachers, 91
University of Wisconsin: summer school for workers, 29
Unruh, Jesse, 39, 117
Untermeyer, Louis, 32
Urban affairs, 21, 28, 75
Urban League: 100; Minneapolis, 75

193

Urban problems, 62
Urban renewal, 31, 85
Valeo, Tony, 30
Van Antwerp, Eugene, 36
Van Camp, Dorothy, 81
Van Camp, Lawrence, 81
Vandenberg, Arthur, 42-43, 59, 61, 108, 110, 112, 128-29, 132
Vander Laan, Robert, 38
Vanderploeg, Jan, 81
Van Kleeck, Mary, 81-82
Van Wagoner, Murray, 41, 75, 132
Vassilion, A., 30
Verri, Albert, 135
Veterans: legislation, 37; UAW, 103
Vice-presidents, United States, 28
Viet Nam War: 34, 43; servicemen's attitudes, 125
Villard, Oswald Garrison, 22, 83, 123
Vinitsky, A. Randall, 135
Vocational education: 26, 91; Missouri plan, 45
Vocirca, Vincenzo, 24
Voelker, John, 41
Voline, 24
Vorse, Mary Heaton, 71, 82
Voter: AFL-CIO registration (1962, 1964), 70
Voting: registration, Mississippi, 49; blacks, 67
Wadsworth, James, 130
Wage ceilings, 58
Wage controls, 84, 123
Wage Earner, 119
Wage and hour legislation, 128
Wage increases, 52
Wage rates, 62: aircraft industry, 58; GM Ternstedt Division (1937), 33
Wage stabilization: 44; World War II, 61
Wage Stabilization Board, 62
Wagner, Robert F., 38, 92
Waldron, Robert E., 55, 125
Wales, Gilbert, 82
Wallace, Henry, 22, 100, 128
War: 131; employment, 101; labor, 102
War bonds, 84
Ward, Lyman, 67
War effort: UAW, 107
War Labor Board: 45, 100, 107-08, 110-12, 115; Ford, 99; Region 5, 83
War Manpower Commission, 35
War policy: UAW, 103
War production: 58, 100-101, 110; UAW, 80
War Production Board, 72, 84
Washington, D.C.: AFT, 63
Waterfront, New York and New Jersey: crime, 82
Water resources, 33
Wayne County, 128
Wayne County AFL-CIO: 23, 132; Education Committee, 132; President's Office, 131
Wayne County Board of Auditors, 22
Wayne County Board of Supervisors, 22, 32
Wayne County CIO, 33, 44, 70, 84-85, 120
Wayne County Employees Local 771, 135
Wayne County Industrial Union Council, 49, 85
Wayne County Juvenile Court, 41
Wayne State University: 35, 125; AFT, 62, 95
Wayne State University Professional and Administrative Association, 135
Wayne State University Staff Association, 133
Weaver, George L. P., 40, 74, 123
Weaver, Robert, 121, 123, 129-30
Weber, Paul, 120
Weil, Truda, 135
Weinberg, Nat, 38, 102
Weiss, Henry, 73
Weitz, Leo, 74
Welfare: 34; children, 129; Child Welfare League, 41; family, 129; Los Angeles (1947-56), 37; Michigan Welfare League, 41; UAW Dept. of, 41; reform, 48
Welles, Sumner, 123
Wellman, Saul, 45
West Allis, Wis.: UAW, 111
West Central Organization, Detroit, 31
Western Air Lines, 89
Westman, Walt, 126
West Virginia: mining, 42
Wharton, A. O., 61
Wheeler, Doris, 135
Wheeler, Mary, 83
Whitaker, Claire, 126
White collar workers: 84; UAW, 110, 115
White House Conference on Children, 26
White House Conference on Children and Youth, 1960, 93
White, Josh, 131
White, Walter, 67, 123
Whitty, Michael, 135
Wreck, Edward, 81, 83
Wiley, Alexander, 115
Wilkins, Roy, 92, 123, 128, 130
Wilkinson, Frank, 65
Williams, G. Mennen, 23, 27, 32, 37-38, 41, 46, 55, 59, 63, 70, 76, 78, 82, 108, 110, 126, 128, 132
Williams, Harrison, 117, 120
Williams, John, 135
Williams, M. A., 83
Williams, Percy, 27
Willow Run Bomber Plant, 62

Willow Run, Michigan: UAW, 108
Wilse, Jack, 83
Wilson, Charles, 100
Wilson, Woodrow, 68
Windsor, Ont.: UAW, 109-10, 112
Winn, Frank, 83-84, 104
Wirtz, W. Willard, 68, 74, 117, 120
Wisconsin: Communist Party, 78; CIO, 111
Wisconsin Employment Relations Board, 127
Wishart, James, 102
Wohlforth, Robert, 34
Wolf, Herman, 84
Wolfgang, Myra, 38, 130
Wolfson, Louis, 36
Woll, Matthew, 26
Wolman, Leo, 45
Women: equal pay, 40; equal rights, 40, 128; socioeconomic conditions, 25
Women's auxiliaries: CIO, 76; UAW, 113
Women's rights, 42-43
Women's Work, Commission on, 81
Woodlawn Organization, 31
Woodcock, Leonard, 27-28, 30, 62, 77, 99, 103, 108-09, 111, 114, 128-30
Woods, Forrest, 38
Woodworkers, 120
Worker-priest programs, 120
Workers Defense League, 24, 32, 50, 133
Workers education: 26, 29, 32, 66, 71, 79, 92, 128; Africa, 79; Asia, 79; Europe, 79; India, 66; Malay, 66; University of Michigan, 52
Workers schools, 30
Workers Education Service, University of Michigan, 42
Work hours: airlines, 88
Working conditions: airlines, 88; coal mining, 65; flight crews, 90
Workmens compensation: 40, 44, 128; legislation, 38
Works Progress Administration (WPA): 25, 32, 67, 127; teachers, 91; workers education in Michigan, 24
World Crisis in Oil, 65
World Federation of Education Associations, 26
World Federation of Trade Unions, 122
World War I: pacifism, 126
World War II, 81: labor, 106; labor movement, 122
Wyoming, 67
Yale-Towne: strike, 40-41: UAW, 106
Young, Coleman, 84-85
Young, Holgate, 85
Young, Opel, 85
Young, Stephen, 94
Young, Whitney, 92, 120, 123
Youth Discussion Bulletin, 124
Youth Opportunity Program, 39
Youth problems, 129
Zaremba, John, 85
Zionism, 36
Zweibeck, Richard, 86
Zwerdling, A. L., 62, 102

Warner W. Pflug holds a B.A. degree (1959) and an M.A. degree (1965) from Wayne State University. He is an archivist in the Archives of Labor History and Urban Affairs, Wayne State University.

The manuscript was edited by Jean Spang. The book was designed by Richard Kinney. The typeface for both the text and display is Univers designed by Adrian Frutiger in 1957.

The text is printed on Sebago Antique Text paper and the book is bound in Columbia Mills' Chambray cloth over boards. Manufactured in the United States of America.

Ref ✓
Z
7164
T7
W34
1974